GW00992121

GYMNASTICS

Continental Sports
HUDDERSFIELD

GYMNASTICS

All the beauty and skills of this thrilling sport

General editor PETER TATLOW

Lyric

First published 1979 by Lyric Books Limited
66b The Broadway
London NW7

ISBN 0 7111 0004 7

Printed in Italy

CONTENTS

The Authors

Jenny Bott, Janet Mitchell, Pauline Prestidge, Wrio Russell, Peter Shilston, Christine Still, Colin Still, Peter Tatlow, Cliff Temple

FOREWORD

Gymnastics is not only a sport, it is a form of art and of self expression and there can be few more satisfying feelings than to be able to perform well. It takes a lot of hard work and dedication, but with the right amount of determination and guidance from the right source, anyone can improve their own level of gymnastics beyond recognition. In the USA right now we have some young men and women who have set their minds upon getting amongst the best in the world and on securing a permanent place alongside the Russians, Japanese and Rumanians at Olympic and world championships.

The proudest moment of my coaching career was to see Kathy Johnson win a medal at the 1978 World Championships in Strasbourg. While competing internationally is a marvellous experience, you can never forget the long road you have to travel to reach that moment.

Kathy started gymnastics at home in Louisiana at twelve years and her first really big competition was the US Olympic trials for the 1976 Olympic Games. Nervousness led her to a disappointing twelfth place, but instead of letting it get her down she resolved to work even harder to try to reach perfection, and it was that experience which helped her to make progress. Sometimes suffering a disappointment along the way can strengthen your resolve to do better.

Whatever your level of gymnastic ambition, this excellent book which covers our sport so comprehensively will help you. It not only explains how you can improve your performance, but gives you a deep insight into the organization and history of the sport which has now become one of the most popular in the world. I know you will enjoy reading it as much as I have, and remember, if not every gymnast can become an Olympic champion then at least each one of us can improve.

Vannie Edwards

Vannie Edwards
coach to
Kathy Johnson

Left: Kathy Johnson, the outstanding American gymnast, captured during her routine on the bars at the World Championships in 1978.

Page 1: Gillian Hodgson, British beam champion, practises her favourite pose at her local gym.

Pages 2/3: Olga Korbut, most famous of all Soviet gymnasts, performs a beautiful balance.

Pages 4/5: Alexander Detiatin, once thought too tall for gymnastics, is now world famous for his superb performances.

A WORLD SURVEY OF GYMNASTICS

Previous page: Nadia Comaneci of Rumania introduced a level of perfection to gymnastics never before known, and became the new goddess of a sport which has its roots in the nineteenth century. Here she is seen in 1978 competing on the asymmetric bars.

Above: Friedrich Jahn, the German father of gymnastics, who advocated the building of strength on the forerunners of modern gymnastics apparatus.

Below: This engraving shows the kind of apparatus used by German soldiers for fitness training, at the time of Jahn.

Early history

Although the origins of gymnastics are to be found with the Greeks, whose interest in physical recreation activities led to the staging of the original Olympic Games (held from 776BC to AD393), in modern terms two names stand out: Jahn and Ling. These two men, born in different European countries in the late eighteenth century, were the leaders of simultaneous, if fundamentally different, campaigns to promote their own visions of what gymnastics should be.

Friedrich Jahn was born at Lanz, near Wittenberg, Germany, in 1778 and served in the Prussian Army. In 1811 he established an open-air gymnastics centre on the outskirts of Berlin, the first of its type. He became known as the *Turnvater* (father of gymnastics), as he promoted the idea of building strength on apparatus such as parallel bars and the horizontal bar. In fact, he is generally credited with the creation of these and other gymnastics equipment.

Jahn favoured the club environment for encouraging such activities, and his inspiration gave rise nationally to the *Turnverein* (gymnastics club). He also included in his gymnastics programme such activities as hiking, swimming and wrestling. To him, gymnastics meant physical exercise in a more general way than perhaps we think of it today.

By contrast, Pehr Henrik Ling, a Swede born in 1776, saw gymnastics as an activity which should be developed through the schools, and he was more interested in the aesthetic side of human movement and the rhythm and fluency of exercise. He disapproved of Jahn's preoccupation with static apparatus such as the use of bars, which, he felt, could lead to injury.

These two opposite sides of the gymnastics coin were the subject of long and fierce debate, and even today still have supporters of both aspects, the physical and the artistic.

The sport of gymnastics itself was sufficiently established by the time of the birth of the Modern Olympics to be included in the programme for the first Games at Athens in 1896, as one of the nine original sports. Seventy-five gymnasts from five countries took part and there were competitions for men on the horizontal bar, parallel bars, rings, pommel horse and vault – five of the six elements of today's gymnastics programme for men – but instead of a floor exercise, there was a rope-climbing competition (won, appropriately, by a Greek, Nicolaos Andriakopulos). This rope climb was to be included intermittently in the Olympic Games programme until 1932, and in 1900 there had been a combined competition which also involved a high jump, pole vault, long jump and tug o'war!

The programme changed from Games to Games in those early days. In 1932, for instance, at the Los Angeles Olympics, tumbling and Indian club swinging were included, but these activities were dropped by the Germans at Berlin in 1936.

Women's events were included for the first time in the 1928 Olympics at Amsterdam but only as a team tournament. Netherlands were the first ever women's team gold medallists, with silver for Italy and bronze to Great Britain. Romania, now a leading country, were fourth, followed by France. Individual Olympic events for women started at the Helsinki Olympics in 1952.

The year of the Helsinki Olympics pointed to the future of the sport in other ways. The Soviet Union took part for the first time, as a total of over three hundred gymnasts from nearly thirty countries participated. Soviet gymnasts won the men's and women's team competitions, both individual combined championships (through Viktor Chukarin and Maria Gorokhovskaya), as well as three men's and two women's individual gold medals.

From that point the Soviet Union would continue to play a major role in the Games, and the Japanese also hinted at progression which was to become more apparent on the men's side a few years later.

Recent years

The post-war face of gymnastics was changing and developing, as great exponents like Larisa Latynina of the USSR, who won nine Olympic gold, five silver and four bronze medals (a record in any Olympic sport), Akinori Nakayama and Yukio Endo of Japan, and Vera Caslavska of Czechoslovakia were among those who dominated their sections of gymnastics. The sport which had begun in Western Europe now saw Eastern Europe and Asia taking over the leadership. Worldwide television coverage of the Olympics broadened to the accompaniment of universal admiration for the men and women who had developed their bodies to amazing degrees of strength, suppleness and agility. As the 1970s unfolded, the two biggest influences since Jahn and Ling were about to arrive.

It was at the Olympic Games that two girls, who were to provide perhaps the biggest recent contribution to the growth of gymnastics, made their mark. In Olga Korbut and Nadia Comaneci there were two young ladies so diminutive in stature that they would escape notice in a crowd. Yet they were to become so well known through the twin factors of Olympics and television that then, as now, no surname need be mentioned if you were talking about them, within the sport or outside.

Olga, at Munich in 1972, was first. Yet it was something she did not do which attracted the attention of the TV-watching millions. That something was to perform a good exercise on the asymmetric bars in the team competition, held early in the Games. Who on earth could have predicted that an unknown Soviet girl of seventeen, bungling a bars routine in the company of so many other gymnasts who performed better, could change the face of the entire sport? But bungle it she did, losing her rhythm several times, and her mark (previously in the Games no lower than 9.4 on other apparatus) was a mere 7.5. This tiny, devastated girl, just 1.47 metres (4ft 11ins) tall and weighing 38kg (six stone), crumpled on to a chair, and as the television camera moved in at that moment for a close-up of her reaction, the tears flowed down her cheeks and dripped off her chin, on to the floor.

Left: Larisa Latynina in a pose on the balance beam. Latynina was the most famous gymnast during the 1950s and early 1960s.

Above: Olga Korbut caught the imagination of the world with her performances at the 1972 Munich Olympics. She was, however, following in a strong Soviet tradition laid down by such stars as Larisa Latynina (left).

No one who saw the incident could fail to be moved by it, simply because it seemed so out of character with the normal stonewall expressions adopted by most top gymnasts, win or lose. And to see such a tiny, frail girl so bitterly upset at her misfortune brought out the mother and father instinct in every watching adult, and identification in every young girl, who knew exactly how she felt.

Olga came from Grodno, near Minsk, the fourth and youngest daughter of an engineer and a cook. She was the smallest child in her class at school, had desperately wanted to excel at something, and being good at gymnastics she was selected to attend a special school where she could be coached properly. Olga made progress quickly and here in Munich was the moment she had awaited for years, the Olympic Games. And now she felt she had disgraced herself.

In fact, had anything more potentially exciting than the women's team gymnastics competition been happening at that moment anywhere else in the Olympic Games, the chances are that Olga's heartbreak would never have been screened, as it was, throughout the world. Yet suddenly everyone was on the side of this miserable girl, urging and willing her to do better when she returned to the Sporthalle next time.

Olga had become an instant folk hero, with the crowd cheering her every move in the subsequent individual competition. They also howled their disapproval at the judges if they considered she had been undermarked, as they did when Olga performed (almost faultlessly this time) on the bars and received 'only' 9.8, to take the silver medal. Her performance, on the very apparatus which had been her downfall earlier in the week, was like the Phoenix rising from the Ashes, and the resulting din delayed the whole competition for ten minutes.

Right and opposite: The brilliant but temperamental Olga Korbut, whose appearance could guarantee a packed arena anywhere in the world. With her elfin charm and superb ability, she was the gymnast whom millions of young girls all over the globe most wanted to emulate. At her best, she was a sparkling performer, but injury dogged her career and with increasing frequency she had to drop out of major tournaments shedding tears of bitter frustration, as here in the 1975 World Cup at Wembley, where a weak ankle had given way.

Eventually Olga was to take back to Grodno Olympic gold medals for the team event, the floor exercise and the beam, as well as that silver for the bars, and her life would not be the same again. Nor would gymnastics. Technically, the outstanding performer of the Games had been her compatriot Ludmila Tourischeva, the overall champion, but the leading personality was undoubtedly Olga, whose range of visible emotions – from a cheeky grin of delight to utter, tearful desolation – had punctuated the atmosphere at the Games like vivid shafts of light.

Suddenly, young girls all over the world had someone of their size and around their age with whom they could identify. Olga could be their older sister, or even be *them*. She cried and she laughed, instead of being a rather straight-faced gymnast of the old school, deliberately suppressing emotion. There had been great gymnasts before, but suddenly Olga had broken down the invisible barrier between the star performer in action and the admiring audience. There was an identifying link. She had blood in her veins, not ice.

Gymnastics clubs all over the world did not know what had hit them. Suddenly there were long queues at their doors, with harassed mothers demanding that their daughters be turned into gymnastics stars 'like Olga'. (The girls usually had their hair already tied in bunches, the style Olga wore in Munich.) Waiting lists had to be established for club membership, for there were just not enough coaches available to deal with the rush. Auditions, every bit as tense as those for a theatre part, had to be staged so that the most promising gymnastic material could be chosen. And everywhere more and more girls were deciding: 'I want to be a gymnast – like Olga Korbut'. In Britain, fortunately, a badge scheme had been launched the previous year by the British Amateur Gymnastics Association and the *Sunday Times*, and this helped to quench the thirst of thousands of embryo-gymnasts.

The sport of gymnastics had not changed at all, but Olga's appearance in Munich had directed interest to an activity which already existed yet normally received little attention. The boys had always had sports like soccer, rugby and cricket in Britain, or baseball and football in the USA, but now the girls suddenly realized that they had their own little niche, which combined the opportunity for fame and glory at a young age with total femininity and artistic qualities. It was an ideal sport for them; why hadn't someone told them before? The flood-gates were open.

Olga's appearances at competitions and exhibitions after the Olympics were met with rapturous acclaim and intense public interest. Stories of how temperamental she could be, and her proneness to injury, merely combined with the daring brilliance of her routines at their best, and her instant crowd rapport, to make her the most fascinating and famous personality in the long history of the sport.

Right: Rumania began to give the Russian women gymnasts some stiff competition in the form of young Nadia Comaneci, seen here during a routine on the balance beam.

Below: A new queen mounted the throne at the Montreal Olympics, and Olga Korbut had to acknowledge not only the superiority of Nadia Comaneci, but also the increasing threat of the Rumanian gymnasts to the Soviet girls. Here runner-up Olga congratulates bronze-medallist Teodora Ungureanu at the presentation ceremony for the beam, as Nadia looks on.

The impact made four years later by Nadia Comaneci of Rumania was somewhat different. Unlike 1972, everyone was already looking towards the Olympic gymnastics arena at the Montreal Forum anyway, anxious not to miss anything. Nadia, as a thirteen-year-old, had been the sensation of the European Championships a year earlier, winning four of the five gold medals, and it was she who captured the Olympic stage from Olga this time in what was their first meeting in an international arena.

Olga, suffering from persistent injury in recent competitions, was still a popular figure, but Nadia's 'perfect' form, with which she scored the first ever 10.0 mark in Olympic history and then went on to repeat it six more times, was unsurpassable. At only fourteen, she seemed already to be the Perfect Gymnast, and although her approach was less emotional and more clinical than Olga's, she did at least make a definite attempt in Montreal to establish a rapport with the crowd. She waved vigorously at the end of her exercises to dispel the rather stony-faced image she had already earned before the Games.

If Olga could not be at her best in Montreal, then the youngsters now had an even more youthful champion to be their heroine in Nadia (and among the many thousands of gymnastics-orientated young girls there were naturally a fair proportion who did not remember Olga from four years earlier, which can seem an eternity if you are nine or ten!).

So Nadia took over as the new leader of the gymnastics multitude, elected by public demand, and even if the Rumanians could not depose the Soviet Union from their long tenure as women's Olympic team champions, they had at least taken away one crown.

International competitions

The Olympic Games, held every four years, is obviously the pinnacle of the competitive calendar, the moment when the eyes and ears of the entire world are on sports like gymnastics, track and field athletics and swimming. But interwoven around the Games is a network of other championship events of only marginally less importance (and some would say equal importance).

The World Championships, which from 1979 are being held on alternate years, are the closest in standard to the Olympics, with all the top gymnasts taking part. The European Championships are almost equal in stature, being short of only the Japanese and Americans on the men's side, and Americans on the women's side. At the 1976 Montreal Olympics, for instance, the top twenty-three women in the combined individual exercise all came from Europe (as did thirty-seven of the leading forty).

The selection of the nations for future Olympics is being based on results at the previous year's World Championships, and the top twelve men's and women's teams will compete. The countries finishing in thirteenth to fifteenth place are entitled to send three individual gymnasts each to the Olympics, and the next three teams (sixteenth to eighteenth place) can enter two individuals each.

Nine other individuals in both the men's and women's sections will be selected by the International Gymnastics Federation's Technical Committees, based on outstanding performances during the previous year, but the gymnasts chosen must come from nations outside the first eighteen in the World Championships.

This attempt to spread gymnastics further and to increase world-wide participation, has its critics, who say that if, for example, twenty Soviet gymnasts are of good enough standard for the Olympics, then they should all take part. But that would obviously result in a very insular competition for the largest sporting festival in the world, and perhaps not be in the best interests of the development of the sport.

The World Cup competition, now an annual event, was started at Wembley in 1975, and caters for only the élite gymnasts of the world, but much larger gatherings at the multi-sports games, like the Pan-American Games and the Mediterranean Games, include gymnastics as part of their programme. In 1978 gymnastics also made its début at the British Commonwealth Games in Edmonton, Canada (after a demonstration of the sport at the previous Games in 1974), but although it was one of the most popular spectator attractions there, the Games Federation voted to drop it from the 1982 Games in favour of archery, which was a great disappointment to those who had for so long campaigned to get it into the programme.

Apart from major championships and games, most countries hold their own invitation international tournaments, like the American Cup in New York, the Chunichi Cup in Tokyo, and the Champions All tournament in London. Additionally, straight international matches between two countries take place all year round, at senior and junior level, to help with the constant development of new talent through international experience. At the lower levels of the international competitive pyramid come national tournaments, which often have a regional and very local starting point.

Thus it is possible for the outstanding gymnast to climb the ladder step by step from his or her local club, through regional, national and international competition, to the highlight of any gymnast's career – the Olympic Games. There, a single performance can inspire a boy or girl, watching on TV anywhere in the world, to try and emulate the champions, and thus perpetuate the sport.

Above: The increasing number of tournaments and championships all over the world meant no shortage of competition for leading gymnasts like Alexander Detiatin of the Soviet Union, performing here on the rings.

Above and below: Without the financial support of commercial sponsors like Coca-Cola and the Daily Mirror, few national gymnastics federations would be able to cope with all the demands being made of them by the sport's boom. In the picture above, Elena Gurina tests her skills on the bars at the Coca-Cola International Gymnastics Tournament at Wembley, 1978. In the photograph below, a member of the Russian display team performs on the beam at the Daily Mirror event in 1976.

Sponsorship

The cost of running any amateur sport is high, and when that sport is a booming one, like gymnastics, with millions of active participants all over the world and the general public hungry to see the world's top stars in action again and again, the financial support of commercial sponsorship is vital. In return for having their name connected with a particular competition, training scheme or tour, a sponsor will underwrite the costs of putting it on. Without such help, most, if not all, national federations would be unable to cope with all the demands made of them.

In one of the biggest sponsorship-links to date, the United States Gymnastics Federation signed a contract in August 1977 with the makers of Dial Soap for an initial three-year build-up to the Moscow Olympics, which could be worth more than a million dollars to the sport in the USA. The money will go towards paying for training schemes, gymnasts' competition expenses in national élite championships, foreign tours, and the staging of major international events. In March 1978 the American Cup tournament at Madison Square Garden in New York was renamed the 'Dial-American Cup', and was able to assemble its biggest and best-ever field.

Dial executives admitted that when thinking about which sport to sponsor as part of their advertising campaign they decided on one which was 'amateur, with male and female participants, had family spectator appeal, was "clean", with no partisan rooting or violence, could get on television by itself and do well in the ratings'. After going through the list of possibilities, they said, gymnastics was the only sport which met all these requirements, and that has been a similar conclusion among sponsors the world over.

Dial has by no means been the only gymnastics

sponsor, even in the USA. The Nissen Corporation, makers of gymnastics apparatus, were involved long before the current boom in the sport, and other national sponsors have included AMF, Coca-Cola, Burger King and Danskin, the leotard manufacturers.

Newspapers are also keen to sponsor such a flourishing sport. The *Moscow News* stages a tournament in the Soviet Union in April, the *Chunichi* newspaper sponsors one in Japan each November, and in Britain the Champions All tournament (at which, in 1975, Nadia Comaneci made her first competitive appearance in the West) was sponsored originally by the *Sunday Times* and now by the *Daily Mirror*. The *Mirror* also sponsors display teams from overseas and awards an annual scholarship for a boy and girl to train in the Soviet Union for a month. The *Sunday Times* no longer sponsors events but its badge award scheme, started in conjunction with the British Amateur Gymnastics Association in 1971, is flourishing and has distributed around three million badges since then.

The sport, with its great interest for mother and daughter alike, also attracts sponsors like Lilia-White feminine hygiene products, Gold Top Milk, and Speedo, the sports clothing manufacturers. Additionally, Coca-Cola, with popular annual events in the athletics and swimming calendar already established, sponsored a new international gymnastics tournament from 1977.

By understanding each other's needs and limitations, both federation and sponsor can mutually benefit from such joint ventures, but the chief recipient must always be the sport of gymnastics itself.

Left: One of Britain's most exciting young gymnasts, Kathy Williams, who was able to spend a month training in the Soviet Union with her coach in 1978, as a result of winning a scholarship awarded annually by the Daily Mirror newspaper. She earned rave reports from the Soviet coaches, who said she was the best British girl they had seen, but without the sponsorship Kathy's training would have been limited to England.

Above: The current President of the International Gymnastics Federation (FIG), Yuri Titov of the Soviet Union, during the competitive days in which he won medals at three Olympic Games (1956–1964). He is seen here performing an exciting exercise on the high bar.

The International Gymnastics Federation

The world-wide governing body for the sport is the International Gymnastics Federation (usually called the FIG, after the French translation of its name) which now has seventy-four constituent nations drawn from all five continents and representing some fourteen million gymnasts.

The FIG has grown with the sport from small beginnings. It was founded in 1881 at Liège, Belgium, by Nicolas Cuperus, who was President for the first forty-three years of its existence, and who brought together as the original constituent members Belgium, Holland and France. The early days had their share of problems but progress was made as the sport moved into the twentieth century and the Federation grew. By 1903 the FIG was organizing an international tournament in Antwerp, but in those days the sport overlapped to some extent with field athletics in its endeavours to discover all-round ability, and pole vaulting, shot putting, high and long jumping were included.

By the 1930s, the ever-increasing membership of the FIG and the wider acceptance of artistic gymnastics brought about a change, and the inaugural World Championships were staged in Hungary in 1934. The Second World War halted development in all but the neutral countries, and the next surge forward did not come until the post-war years, when the Soviet Union entered the international arena at the 1952 Helsinki Olympics with resounding success. The Japanese began to make their presence felt too, and in recent years the men have dominated the world scene.

There have been seven presidents of the FIG. The current occupant of the office, Yuri Titov of the Soviet Union, was elected at the age of forty in 1976. Titov was one of his country's most successful international gymnasts in a ten-year competitive career which yielded a host of medals from World, European and Olympic appearances.

FIG Presidents

1881–1924	Nicolas Cuperus	BELGIUM
1924–1933	Charles Cazalet	FRANCE
1933–1939	Adam Zamoyski	FRANCE
1946–1956	Goblet d'Alviella	BELGIUM
1956–1966	Charles Thoeni	SWITZERLAND
1966–1976	Arthur Gander	SWITZERLAND
1976–	Yuri Titov	USSR

The honorary Secretary-General of the FIG is Max Bangerter of Switzerland, a former insurance company executive, who now devotes most of his time in retirement to the FIG. He was an active gymnast himself fifty years ago with the Aarburg and other Swiss clubs. He rose through the ranks, having been elected secretary of his local club, then of his district federation, and then of the state, before becoming secretary of his national federation. Strangely, for such a large and comprehensive sports body, there is no headquarters for the FIG, and most of Bangerter's work is carried out in his home town of Lyss.

The vast membership of the FIG is reflected in the very composition of its executive committee. Apart from a Soviet President and a Swiss Secretary-General, the committee currently comprises three Vice-Presidents, from Japan, the USA and France; a Treasurer from Yugoslavia; and members from Spain, West Germany, Rumania, East Germany, Italy, Bulgaria and Czechoslovakia.

There is no doubt that the sport is still rapidly growing. In the Soviet Union, for instance, there are now nearly 700,000 gymnasts and 18,000 qualified coaches, and gymnastics is the fifth biggest sport in the country. The governing body in America, the US Gymnastics Federation, has bloomed into a flourishing and active organization from its beginnings in a room off the kitchen in the Arizona home of its current director, Frank Bare, less than twenty years ago. Bare is now a Vice-President of the FIG.

In West Germany the Deutscher Turner-Bund follows the tradition established by Friedrich Jahn in 1811, and has seen its own membership grow from 913,983 in 1951 to 2,802,895 in 1977.

Of that figure around 100,000 are involved in artistic gymnastics and, although not wealthy, the DTB owns the German Gymnastics School in a beautiful part of Frankfurt, with a hotel and competitive centre.

Holland, one of the original FIG members in 1881, has a longer history than the Federation itself. Its own Royal Dutch Gymnastics Federation was founded on 15 March 1868 in Amsterdam, and now has a membership of 285,000. Of those, 15,000 joined during the post-Montreal Olympic 'Nadia' era alone. Now the Dutch, after one or two stagnant spells in their long history, have a girls' training scheme in operation under former Olympic gymnast Albert Azarian, based at a national centre in Papendal, near Arnhem, where a dozen specially selected girls train for three hours a day, living with foster families during the week, and returning to their own families at weekends. The Dutch hope that this may lead to an improvement on their ninth team place at Munich in 1972 and eleventh at Montreal in 1976.

However, not every country is thriving gymnastically. Almost inevitably, one or two are suffering lean spells. In Sweden, ironically, there have been no Olympic medal winners for the land of Pehr Henrik Ling since William Thoresson won the floor exercise at the Helsinki Games in 1952, and at Montreal the country did not even have a team. Despite Ling's teaching that the sport could develop through schools, virtually all of gymnastics in the country is now carried out at private clubs, and the national emphasis is on keeping fit rather than developing élite gymnasts.

The most interesting recent international development is the decision by the FIG to admit China, a country with almost 900 million people, as a member. Their gymnasts, of undoubted ability, had performed very successfully in tours of Europe and Canada prior to the decision to admit them (in place of Taiwan) which was taken during the 1978 World Championships at Strasbourg.

The Chinese staged a big international invitation tournament in Shanghai in June 1978, and observers were particularly impressed by a fourteen-year-old Chinese girl, Yen-Hung Ma, who was awarded a 9.95 mark for the asymmetric bars.

It could be that in the already long history of world gymnastics, another chapter is about to be written.

Below: World gymnastics is governed by the International Gymnastics Federation, which was founded in 1881 and now has 74 constituent nations drawn from all five continents and representing 14,000,000 gymnasts. Here the flags of several competing member countries are displayed, as is customary during any big international tournament.

PREPARATION AND TRAINING

Above: These 'callisthenic exercises for lady muscular Christians' were an attempt to teach women freedom and grace of movement in the days when clothes were heavy and restricting.

Previous page: Gillian Hodgson, British beam champion, rehearses a move in her gym at Loughton.

CLOTHING AND SAFETY

Costume for competition
Men's costume has changed little over the years. The Code of Points lays down the clothing for competitions: a shirt or vest, long trousers, which are white in colour and fasten under the instep with an elastic strap, and footwear, either socks and slippers or socks only. For the vault and floor exercise shorts may be worn, with or without footwear.

Women's costume has come a long way since the British team appeared for the 1928 Olympics in gymslips, long knickers, thick socks, shirts and ties! Nowadays women wear the leotard, a close-fitting single-piece garment that usually covers the arms to the wrist but leaves the legs free. It is named after its inventor, Jean Leotard, a nineteenth-century French acrobat. The Code of Points stipulates that the leotard shall be 'correct' and made of non-transparent material, and there are warnings against 'immodesty' in dress. Women usually wear slippers without socks, though many nowadays perform in bare feet, especially on beam and floor. For team competitions, both men and women should have a

uniform costume, displaying the same colours.

Failure to abide by the regulations on dress can lead to a deduction of 0.3 points, or 0.5 points if an entire team is involved. Gymnasts in competition should always have clean and neat costumes in well-chosen colours, otherwise much of the aesthetic appeal of the exercises may be lost.

Safety in gymnastics
Gymnastics is not a dangerous sport as long as care is taken to follow the rules set out in the safety manuals. (The official manual of the United States Gymnastics Safety Association is particularly useful.) Because so many gymnasts are very young children, most of the responsibility for safety will fall upon the coach. Points which may be borne in mind can be grouped under a number of headings.

The apparatus The apparatus should meet with the proper specifications, with frequent checks to make sure it has not become worn or damaged. Care must be taken in planning the layout of a gymnasium, so that a gymnast at work is not hampered or endangered by being too close to walls, doors, tables and other sharp edges, and the other pieces of apparatus. There should be sufficient space between the apparatus for gymnasts to work without interfering with each other, for instance by crossing each other's path on run-ups. Also, gymnasts coming off the apparatus may run several paces and then fall. If a competition is being held, spectators must be placed where they will not distract the gymnasts.

All apparatus should be correctly erected, stable, secure and upright, with guyropes properly secured. The asymmetric bars will need to have its guyropes constantly adjusted to the correct tension; we all remember the near-disaster of Tourischeva on the bars at Wembley in 1975! All areas around the apparatus where the gymnast may dismount or fall should be covered with mats of sufficient thickness, and these should fit closely together without gaps or lumps. There must be crashpads if a gymnast is learning a skill and is liable to fall.

Training sessions Chalk, or more correctly magnesium carbonate, is used by gymnasts, and care should be taken with its application, since clouds of dust in the atmosphere can greatly irritate the eyes and throat. So much time is spent swinging from the hands that all gymnasts should also have handguards. These are usually made of lampwick or suede. For young gymnasts, they must be checked to make sure they are worn correctly and fastened tightly enough. Many gymnasts prefer padding around their wrists under the guard straps. Boys occasionally wear gloves for training on the horizontal bar.

Girls practising wraparound and bounce movements on the asymmetric bars can wear foam rubber padding across the lower abdomen to guard against bruising.

At the start of a training session, all gymnasts should be properly 'warmed up', exercising and stretching their entire bodies by easy stages. Pulled muscles or similar injuries may result if

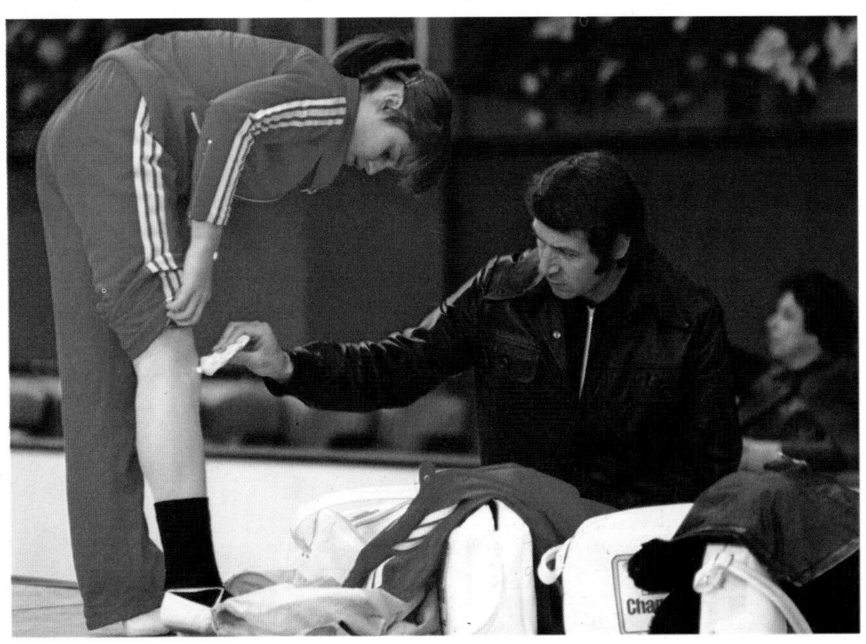

Below: Here Nadia Comaneci has her knee tended to by her coach Bela Karoly. Every gym needs a properly equipped medical kit in case of minor accidents.

Above: Members of the audience held their breath when the asymmetric bars collapsed during Tourischeva's routine at the World Cup in 1975. Fortunately she was unhurt, but this is a reminder that equipment must be constantly checked for safety.

this is neglected. A gymnast who arrives late at a training session must therefore be made to go through a proper warm-up routine before moving on to the apparatus.

Coaches should be familiar with the techniques of *spotting*, supporting or assisting of a gymnast when working a move. Usually this is done by hand, but many gyms now have special equipment for this. For instance, a somersault may be assisted by means of a belt round the waist supported by a coach on either side, and for work on the higher apparatus the belt may be supported on ropes mounted on overhead pulleys. In an advanced gymnasium, the danger from falls is greatly reduced by having pits full of foam rubber beneath the apparatus.

The gymnast A coach will have to take great care over the safety of the young gymnasts. Discipline and control will be necessary, because any horseplay, unauthorized experiments on the apparatus or general fooling about can easily lead to accidents. A coach must make sure his gymnasts are correctly dressed for their work, with clothing that allows free movement without being so loose that it can catch on the apparatus. Tracksuits or similar outer clothing can be useful for warm-up work.

Jewellery and watches are always taken off before training, and any spectacles worn should be properly secured, and preferably made of safety glass or plastic. Long hair is tied back, well away from the eyes, so as not to obscure vision. Long nails will only get painfully torn.

Most of these rules also apply to the coaches themselves!

Generally speaking, a coach when spotting will need to be quick and alert, reasonably strong, thoroughly familiar with the routines, and able to think one move ahead and anticipate any difficulties which may arise. He will also have to be able to explain to the gymnast exactly what is required, and what has been done wrong if a move has not succeeded. All this will not only greatly reduce the risk of injury, but will also enable the gymnast to work with much greater confidence.

General and medical It is always essential to have a suitably qualified person in charge at a gym, who can take full responsibility for whatever occurs. This person must be completely familiar with the health and physical condition of all the gymnasts, especially with any recent injuries they may have suffered, and must not let them work if there is any danger.

There is bound to be a number of small injuries as in any sport: bruises, abrasions, sprains and muscle damage; occasionally there may be more serious mishaps, such as fractures, dislocations or concussion. Every gym should therefore have a properly equipped medical kit, and at least one person present should have a good knowledge of first aid, and of what should be done while waiting for proper medical help to arrive. Needless to say, there should be the means of summoning a doctor and/or an ambulance quickly in emergency.

Although to a layman gymnastics may look an innately hazardous occupation, there is no reason why it should be more dangerous than any other sport, provided sensible precautions are taken.

BASIC SUPPLING

If a club wished to produce top flight gymnasts, it would follow the tradition of the very best ballet schools and select young children according to a complex system of physical criteria. Assessments would be made of physical proportions, co-ordination, range of movement and strength, and sense of spatial awareness (the gymnast must have a keen sense of his whereabouts when in the air).

Ideally the club would also assess qualities of mind and character; the ability to learn and concentrate, the degree of courage, and so on. However, it is rarely possible to do this to any great extent, although many clubs can and do apply more random means of selection for their Olympic gymnastics classes. It is important for these clubs to make some assessment of candidates' co-ordination, range of movement, running ability, strength and mental application.

The young gymnast who wishes to pursue the sport seriously must have an innate, reasonable suppleness and range of movement. Exercises to improve this suppleness are an essential part of daily training, and ideally should be combined with specific ballet training suitable to the development of the gymnast. Before the gymnast performs these exercises, he should first warm up for up to five minutes to increase his rate of circulation. This can be done in a number of different ways, by running, skipping, jumping, hopping, arm-circling, or by playing a variety of different games in which the body is constantly on the move. He should then spend at least another 15 minutes on working on his range of movement. The exercises detailed below are a sample selection that will be of use to the gymnast, but it is important first to learn to stand correctly.

Exercise 1, photos 1–2: Palms must remain on the floor, and the legs must be fully straightened.

Exercise 2, photos 3–4: Arms and legs must be kept straight.

Standing position The heels must be together with the feet slightly turned out, the legs straight, the hip girdle turned under so that the lower back is not hollowed, the back straight, the shoulders relaxed but not drooped forward, the arms straight down by the sides, the neck long and the head high with the eyes looking ahead.

Exercise 2

3

4

Exercise 1

1

2

Exercise 1 The gymnast starts in a crouch position with the palms of his hands on the floor in front of his feet. He does a double bounce in crouch, and on the third beat he straightens the legs, pushing the knees back and stretching the hamstrings, with the palms of the hands remaining on the floor. This must be repeated several times, with a smooth three-beat rhythm.

Exercise 2 The gymnast must stand correctly with his hands clasped above his head, with arms straight. He moves the arms back and forth with a double bounce, stretching in the shoulders, and then bends forwards with legs straight to double bounce his hands on the floor. A four-beat exercise.

Exercise 3 The gymnast stands with his legs straddled. Bending forward from the hips, he reaches forward and places his hands on the ground in front of him, then drives his chest and arms between his legs to place his hands on the ground behind him, and swings his chest and arms forwards and up, and then repeats the exercise. A three-beat exercise.

Exercise 4 The gymnast starts in kneeling position with his arms straight and back flat, and swings one leg up, to the side, back, and down, and repeats with the other leg. A four-beat exercise.

Exercise 5 The gymnast sits with his legs out together and straight, knees pressed against the floor, ankles stretched, back straight. He reaches forward from the hips with his hands stretching beyond his feet, bouncing forwards three times,

Exercise 3

5

6

7

Exercise 4

8

9

10

Exercise 5

11

12

13

Exercise 6

14

15

Exercise 3, photos 5–7: The gymnast must reach right forward (5), right back (6), and then stretch through the shoulders (7).

Exercise 4, photos 8–10: The arms and swinging leg must be kept straight.

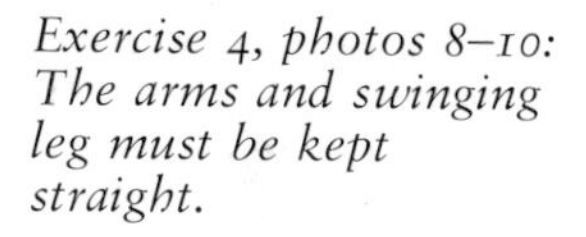

Exercise 5, photos 11–13: The gymnast must start with the back straight, and keep the knees pressed against the floor.

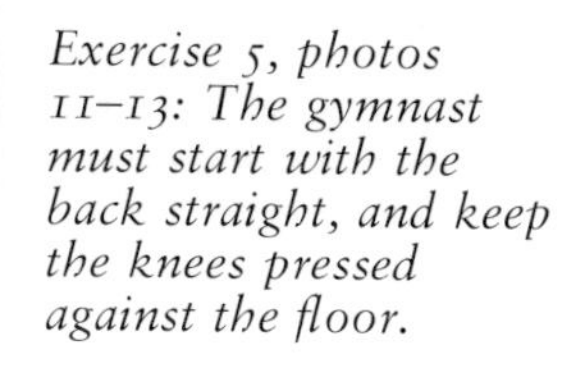

Exercise 6, photos 14–15: The gymnast must pull the chest towards the feet and keep the knees pressed against the floor.

and returning to straight-backed sit with his hands on the floor out to the side. A four-beat exercise.

Exercise 6 The gymnast begins as in Exercise 5, except that his ankles are not stretched. He then reaches forwards, and grasps under his heels with his hands, pressing the backs of the legs against the floor and holding the piked position for a good five seconds, with his chest on his thighs, before releasing.

Exercise 7 The gymnast reaches his arms over his head to the opposite foot, stretches his chest on to the floor, reaches his other arm over his head, and then returns to a straight-backed sitting position. A four-beat exercise, or six-beat exercise if he does a double sideways stretch.

Exercise 8 (ankle exercises) a) The gymnast kneels with his feet together, and rocks tightly back on to his heels to stretch his insteps with his hands on the floor by his feet. b) The gymnast sits with legs out straight and feet pushed back. He stretches first his ankles, then his toes, and pushes his toes back, followed by his ankles. A four-beat exercise.

Exercise 9 (wrist exercises) a) The gymnast kneels with his hands turned in flat on the floor and the arms straight. He then proceeds to walk his hands out away from each other until his arms start to bend or the heel of the hands lift off the floor, and then he walks them back in again. b) The gymnast clasps the hands together and rolls the wrists around.

Exercise 10 The gymnast must push up from the floor and rock the shoulders back and forth

Exercise 7, photos 1–4: The gymnast must sit in wide straddle position, knees pressed against the floor, and swing the arm right over the top of the head to the opposite foot.

Exercise 8b, photos 5–6: The feet must stretch from the ankles.

Exercise 9a, photos 7–8: The gymnast must keep his arms straight.

Exercise 10, photo 9: The knees must be pushed back towards the hands.

Exercise 7

1

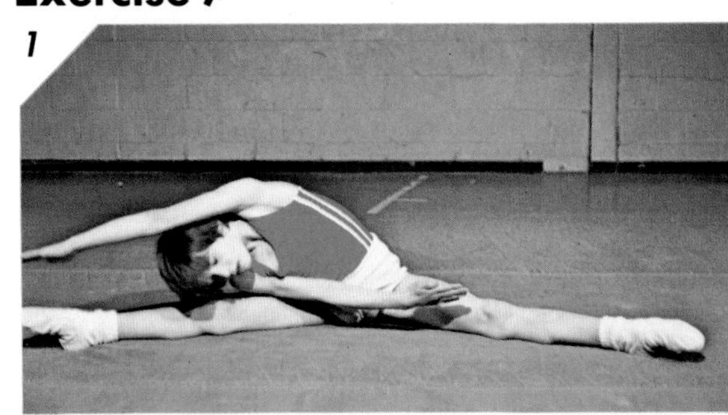

2

3

4

5

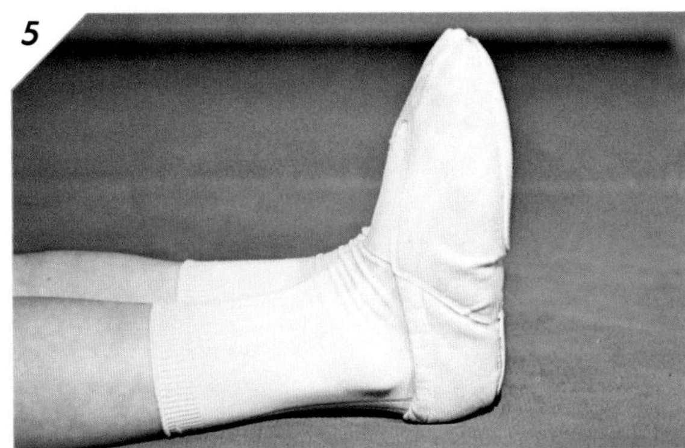

6

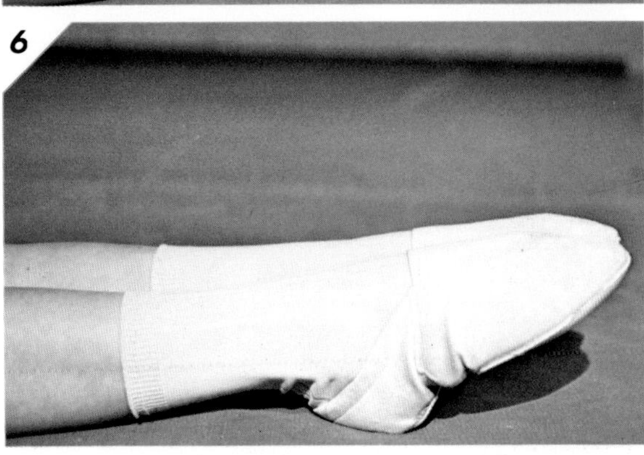

Exercise 8 (above)

Exercise 9

7

8

Exercise 10

9

over the hands, four or five times, straightening his knees as he pushes back.

Exercise 11 The gymnast must stand up straight with one foot slightly turned out, and swing the free leg up to the side with the knee facing upwards, and the hips facing forwards. Repeat the swing ten times with each leg.

Exercise 12 The gymnast must stand correctly and swing the leg up forwards from the hips, accelerating the swing upward.

Exercise 13 The gymnast faces the wall bars, holding on with arms straight and the chest as upright as possible and hips and shoulders facing forwards. He then swings one leg up to the back and down again, repeating the exercise ten times with each leg.

Exercise 14 The gymnast must lower into side splits without bending forwards, and use his hands for support until he is down all the way, with legs remaining straight.

Exercise 15 The gymnast must use his hands for support and keep the legs straight, with the back knee and foot facing downwards and the hips and shoulders square.

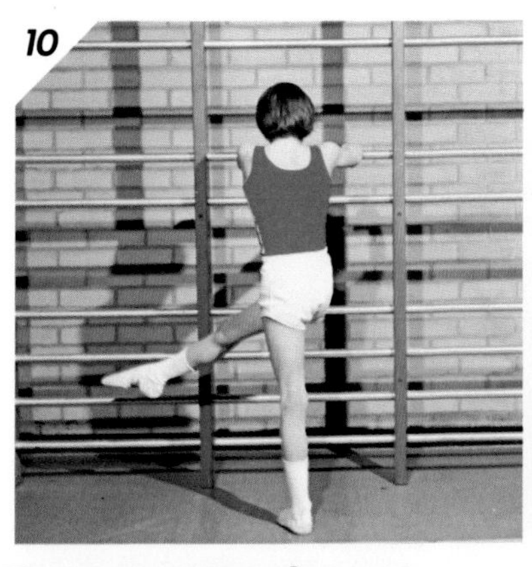

11

Exercise 11 (above)

Exercise 12 (below)

Exercise 13

Exercise 14

Exercise 15

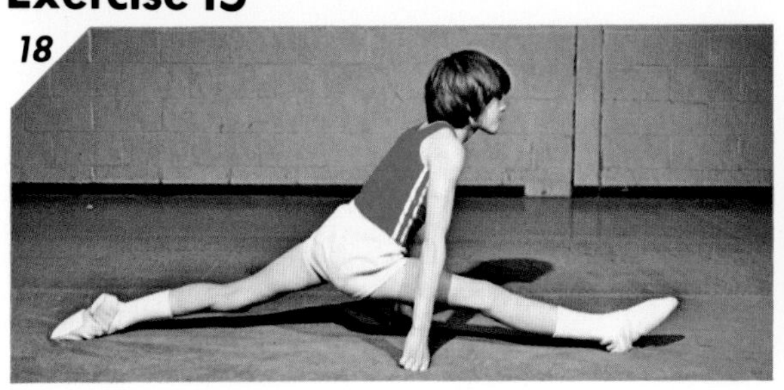

Exercise 11, photos 10–11: The gymnast must swing with straight leg, knee facing upwards.

Exercise 12, photos 12–13: The body must remain upright, with the leg swinging through straight.

Exercise 13, photos 14–15: There must be no turn of the body during the swing.

Exercise 14, photos 16–17: The hips and feet must be in a straight line.

Exercise 15, photos 18–19: The back foot must be turned under, the shoulders relaxed and arms out to the side.

CONDITIONING AND STRENGTH

Before a gymnast can proceed beyond the most elementary moves, he must, under the guidance of his coach, pursue a thorough programme of exercises for preparing his body to correctly learn and perform gymnastics. Although many of the basic skills are part of the conditioning process, there must be a period during every training session when the gymnast can concentrate on exercises to improve his strength so that he can handle his body weight in all circumstances; he needs also to condition his body to remain tight for given periods, for example, when he is performing a sidehorse exercise in which the legs must be constantly stretched and for most of the time tight together. This conditioning programme is best done at the end of the skill training session; a session-minded gymnast will also work on conditioning training at home, if he is unable to get to the gym twice a day.

For the young gymnast, the combination of range of movement training, conditioning and strength training, postural and style training, are of prime importance in preparing him for acquiring the many skills in this complex sport. All good coaches realize that a correctly conditioned body must be developed before the skills can be taught; a gymnast cannot learn a double leg circle if he is unable to support his own body weight. The gymnast himself has to realize that the quest for amplitude and virtuosity requires a methodical programme of range of movement and conditioning exercises, and that training cannot be solely concerned with the acquisition of skills.

In general, the gymnast should spend between 20 and 30 minutes on his conditioning programme at the end of his training session. There are many different ways of training for strength and these include the use of such aids as elastic strands, weights, pulleys, and the gymnastics apparatus itself. The exercises given here require nothing more than the basic apparatus.

Press-up

Press-up, 1–2: The gymnast must keep the chest in, body tight, and the elbows in by the body.

Parallel bar dip, 3–4: The shoulders and arms do the work while the body remains tight.

Handstand dip, 5–6: The gymnast must lower down to headstand and press up again with body tight and elbows in.

1

2

Parallel bar dip

3

4

Handstand dip

5

6

Exercises in repetition

1 **Press-up** This must be performed with the body tight and the upper back rounded, the elbows in, bending towards the hips. The object is to use the upper arms to raise and lower the whole body. The exercise can be done on the floor or the feet can be raised on a bench or a wall bar to incline the body. High repetitions are recommended.
The gymnast must keep the body tight, and bend the elbows in by the hips.

2 **Pull-up** It is better to do this exercise on a high bar. The gymnast must keep tight and lift the chin above the bar. For an advanced form of the exercise, the gymnast can pull up in overgrasp and when the shoulders are above the bar, turn the wrists and press up to front support.
The gymnast starts from straight-arm hang, and pulls up until his chin is above the bar.

3 **Handstand dip** For the younger gymnast it is better to do this with support. With hands shoulder-width apart, he lowers from handstand to headstand, keeping his elbows in and lowering his head forwards of his hands. He must keep his body tight and his legs together. An advanced form of the exercise requires the gymnast to kick to handstand on a bench and lower his head on to the floor.

4 **Parallel bar dip** The gymnast must perform this exercise with body straight and no swing. He must bend with the elbows in by the chest, until the angle at the elbows is no more than 90°, and he must perform the exercise smoothly. Two sets of at least 10 repetitions should be done.
The gymnast must keep the elbows in, and bend the arms with the body tight and without a swing.

5 **Hang and pike** It is better to do this exercise on a high bar. The gymnast hangs in overgrasp and pikes the feet to the bar without bending the legs. The pike must come from the hips without setting up a swing. A partner can steady the back.
The gymnast keeps the legs straight and pikes the feet to the bar.

6 **V-sit** The exercise starts with gymnast lying on his back and his arms above his head. He then pikes his hands to his feet with as tight a pike as possible, and his back to extended back lying. He must not bend his legs and should do at least 2 sets of 15 repetitions.
The gymnast keeps his arms up and pikes tight with legs straight.

7 **Back arching** The gymnast can either lie on his front with his feet under a wall bar or, better still, lie on a box-top bending forwards over the end, his feet held down by a partner. With his hands on his head or his arms above his head, he arches his back as high as possible, and then lowers. At least 2 sets of 12 repetitions.
The gymnast raises as high as possible and then lowers, with legs together.

8 **Hop jump** The gymnast hops along the length of the gym, lifting the knees to the chest and keeping the back upright. He must use both the knees and the feet and ankles to lift to the jump, and the feet should be stretched in the air. As a variation, he can hop forwards from side to side over a bench or, as below, over a chair.
The gymnast must lift his knees to his chest and use both knees and ankles for the jump.

V-sit

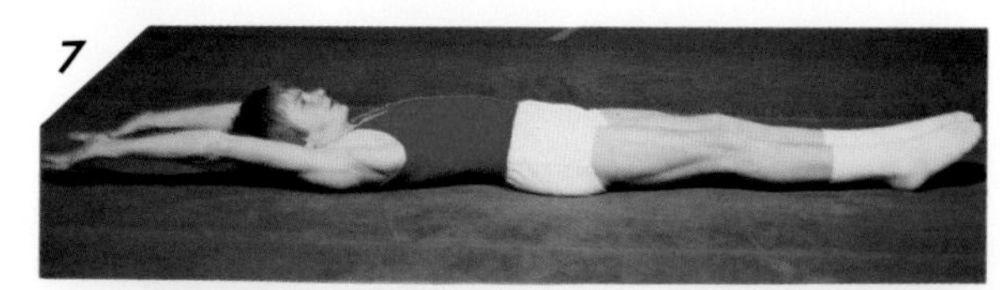

7

8

Back arching

9

10

Hop jump

11

12

13

V-sit, 7–8: The hands reach for the feet and the legs keep together.

Back arching, 9–10: The gymnast must lift as high as possible.

Hop jump, 11–13: The gymnast must use his arms to aid the jump, lifting his knees to his chest.

Pike and lift, 1–3: The gymnast must suck in his stomach as he lifts his hips, and not move his hands too far in front of his feet.

Half-lever (L-balance), 4: The legs must be tight, the hips between the arms, and the shoulders pressing down.

Front arching hold, 5: The legs must be pressed tight together, feet just off the floor.

Back arching hold, 6: The body must remain as tight as possible, particularly the legs.

Wide push-up hold, 7: The gymnast must push hard against the floor, chest in.

Pike and lift

1

2

3

Half-lever (L-balance)

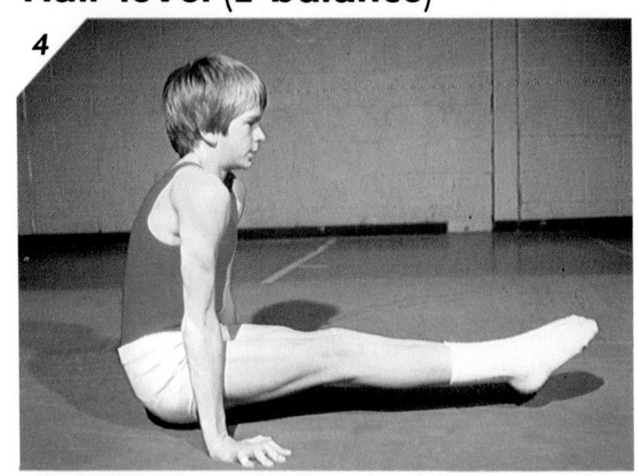
4

Front arching hold

5

Back arching hold

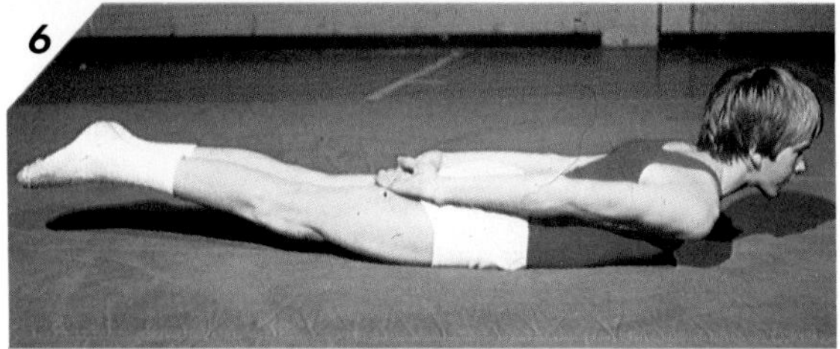
6

Wide push-up hold

7

9 **Pike and lift** The gymnast must keep his legs straight and, with hands on the floor, lift his hips to bring his feet close to his hands, move his hands forward, and repeat. His feet should never be more than 18 inches (45cms) behind his hands. The gymnast must lift his hips to bring his feet to his hands, and move the hands 12 inches (30cms) forward with each step.

Exercises for tension

1 **Half-lever (L-balance)** This must be practised frequently by the gymnast, not only on the floor but also on the parallel bars and the rings. The legs must be tight together and parallel to the floor, the hips between the arms, the shoulders pressing down (not hunched) and the head high. The gymnast should also practise the straddle half-lever, with the legs outside the arms, the knees up by the elbows but not balancing on them, shoulders pressed down, head up, and a good pike at the hips. Each balance should be held for 5 seconds.
The gymnast must have the legs tight together, head high, shoulders pressing down, and hold for 5 seconds.

2 **Front arching hold** The gymnast must lie on his back with his upper back and legs off the floor, head forward, stomach tight. The hands should be reaching to the knees. The position should be held from 20 to 30 seconds.

3 **Back arching hold** The gymnast must lie on his front with his chest and legs off the ground, body tight and hands behind the head. He must not be too arched. The position should be held from 20 to 30 seconds.

4 **Wide push-up hold** The gymnast must lie on his front with his arms out to the side, and push up off the floor pressing down with the palms of his hands. His upper back must be rounded, his whole body tight. Each repetition should be held for 5 seconds.
The gymnast must have his body tight, chest in, and press against the floor for 5 seconds.

BALLET FOR GYMNASTS

The Soviet Union women's gymnastics team have held every Olympic title since their first participation in 1952. They lost the world title only once to Vera Caslavska's Czech team in Dortmund in 1966! During that same span of years they have won no less than twenty gold medals for individual floor exercises alone! Why are the Russians so successful?

Many believe it is because they have one of the finest training systems in the world, and a system which includes a long and thorough training for both boys and girls in the techniques of classical ballet. It is one of the best ways to develop correct alignment and placement of the body, legs, arms and head. In addition, the basic exercises taken at the barré, strengthen and mobilize the feet, legs and back. Furthermore the dance steps are an integral part of the floor and beam exercises for the girl gymnast and to some extent also in boys' and men's floor exercises.

Reports say that young girl gymnasts in the Soviet Union can spend fifty per cent of their early training in the ballet class! This is quite evident from their superb performances; their foot extension is quite exquisite and their presentation throughout their entire gymnastics programme is elegantly beautiful.

There are many first class ballet schools in other countries today and some very excellent teachers. Take lessons if you can from one of these. Failing that, then the exercises set out in this chapter will help to provide the qualities mentioned above. Try to follow the exercises carefully and practice every day. The terminology is in simple French, but will not be too difficult to understand. Many of the names will be familiar to you as they are used quite frequently in the gymnastics scene today.

If you are taking your lessons in a recognized ballet school or class you will perform your first exercises at the barré: this is a round pole fixed horizontally around the room or hall at approximately waist height. If in the gymnasium, use a wall bar or the beam. If at home, practice is possible with an ordinary kitchen chair. It is important that this support is used only for balance and not for leaning upon. Its purpose is in helping to maintain an upright and correct stance as well as giving confidence and assistance in balance.

Stand comfortably and firmly on your own two feet, heels touching with toes apart. This is called the first position. In dancing there are five basic positions of the feet and all are essentially relevant, but for the purpose of this series of exercises it is sufficient to use only the first two. In second position the legs are apart, not too wide. The width can be measured by the width and a half of one's foot.

All positions in classical ballet require 'turnout'. This turnout of the legs and feet is important as it encourages a greater range of movement in the hip joint. Care must be taken not to allow the feet to roll forwards with all the weight over the big toes. Spread the toes evenly, stretch the legs and tighten the seat muscles. Straighten the spine by tilting the pelvic bone towards the back. The shoulders should be relaxed, the neck extended and the chin lifted.

Above: The ballet dancer demonstrates battement tendu. Her right foot has been pushed away from first position and is extended to the front with toes pointed. Note the turnout of the feet. Her arms are in fifth position.

The stance described with the feet in first position is the correct posture for beginning every exercise. Take this position at the barré with one hand resting, but not gripping, and follow the exercises carefully.

The battement tendu

Tendu means 'tight'. Applied to this exercise the muscles in the legs contract as the foot pushes against the floor and slides away from the supporting leg to a stretched position on the big toe. Slide and pull back again to the starting position.

The weight must be entirely upon the supporting leg. The battement tendu may be taken forwards, sideways and backwards. Allow the heel to push forwards and upwards when taking the leg to the front, forwards when to the side and underneath when to the back.

Repeat the exercise with each leg by turning around and holding the barré with the other hand.

The plié

Plié means to bend. The bend occurs only in the leg, at the knee, which creates a secondary angle in the ankle and hip joint. The angles increase according to the depth of the bend.

A demi plié and a full plié may be performed in all five positions of the feet, but we will only concern ourselves with the first and second positions.

Right: A full plié in second position. The arms are also in second.

Far right: The 'attitude' is a classical position. Here the leg has been partly unfolded and is held at this point. If the leg were to be extended completely, then a full développé would have been performed. The arms are in fourth.

Below: This is an arabesque. The right leg shows the extended position of the grand battement.

Opposite page, below: A relevé on to the toes of one foot. Arms are in third.

Opposite page, right: A sauté from second position, with arms 'bras bas'. Note how the shoulders are kept down, even though the ballet dancer is jumping upwards.

The demi plié (demi means half) is a small bend at the knees, keeping the heels on the floor. This exercise is essential for all jumps. Keep the head, shoulders and hips in line with the feet – perpendicular. Do not collapse into the bend, but press against the bending action throughout, as though trying to keep 'tall'.

When performing the full plié in first position, keep the heels down until the half bend is reached then allow them to lift as the bend increases, until the thighs are horizontal. In second position, the heels remain on the ground.

Keep a slow rhythm when performing the pliés. Repetitions of these movements will strengthen the thighs, calves and back muscles.

Grand battement

Battement means beating or thrashing. The grand battement is a development of the battement tendu. As the foot reaches the extended position on the toe the action continues, lifting the leg until horizontal with the hip joint, returning again to the closed first position. The leg should be perfectly straight during the lift and the action powerful. The pattern may follow that of the battement tendu, forwards, sideways and backwards, remembering the position of the heel throughout. The supporting leg must of course be straight, with the heel firmly on the ground. When the leg is lifted to the back the body may lean forwards, but in the sideways and forward lift the body must be upright.

Développé

This exercise follows the same pattern as before, but the leg action is one of unfolding. It is particularly beneficial for strengthening and enables the leg to be held in the lifted position as in the arabesque.

The working leg is first bent at the knee with the knee pointing sideways and the ankle bone resting just below the knee of the supporting leg. The leg continues to lift first bent then slowly unfolding to an extended position as in the grand battement. When fully extended and horizontal, hold there for three seconds. Return the leg to the starting position. Repeat to the side and to the back. When lifting to the back the body may lean forwards.

Relevé

The relevé is a rise up on to the toes. The exercise should be dynamic and begins with a very slight bend at the knees followed by a snatching of the feet together upon the toes. The emphasis of the action is through the instep. The quick repetitions of the rise and return of the heel will increase muscle strength in the foot. The relevé may be taken from two feet or from one.

During the exercise keep the body upright with the weight slightly poised forwards and well centred over the supporting leg. The shoulders should be completely relaxed and kept down and the stomach muscles held well up.

Sauté
This is a spring from two feet. Stand in first position. Begin with a small bend of the knees, thrust downwards through the feet and spring upwards extending ankles and knees. The insteps must stretch in full and the toes pointed when in the air. The heels must be lowered to the floor on alighting, but the lowering of the heels must be with resistance and should be soundless. It is very important to keep the shoulders down.

Port de bras
This means carriage of the arms. Remember when using the arms in conjunction with dance steps in floor exercises or on the beam, that they should be used with expression. Try to obtain feeling in the hand and arm movements and carry the feeling through to the upper body and head. Follow the line of the hands with the eyes. When moving the arms in and out of the five basic positions do not lose sight of them: keep them within your peripheral vision and move both arms through a position in front of the body, holding them loosely and slightly rounded.

The arm movements used in gymnastics are many and varied. Not all are strictly classical, but if one remembers that the arms are an extension of the body and therefore should move as from the body then any position will be acceptable. However, it is helpful if the classical positions are fully understood.

Dancing has much in common with gymnastics: both have a long and noble tradition, both demand discipline and both are expressions of physical art. Because ballet is so essentially an art form many young men and boys are shy of becoming involved. I would say to them that if they can meet the physical challenge and the hard work of ballet training the quality of their gymnastics will be greatly enhanced. Especially do I recommend that they include in all their training sessions the exercises concerning the legs which are given here.

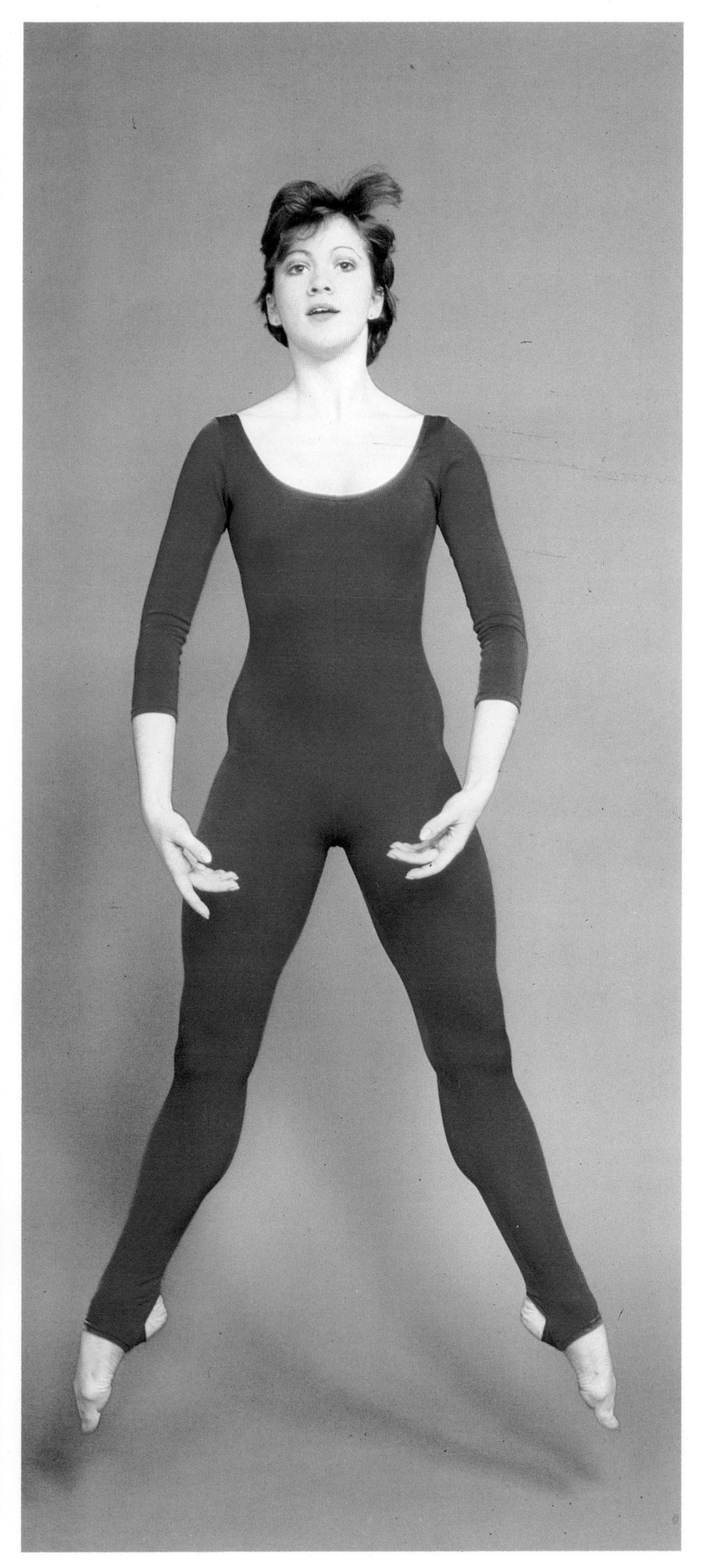

TUMBLING

Although men's and women's floor exercises are very different in their overall composition, they have one aspect in common – tumbling elements. Tumbling, therefore, plays a big part in the training of both boys and girls, and indeed it provides a basis for the training of many moves on the apparatus. Tumbling refers to those elements that are acrobatic in nature, as opposed to balances, linking elements, or dance steps. It starts with forward and backward rolls and moves through the progressions to full twisting double back somersaults, arabian one and a half front somersaults, and so on.

Backward roll through to handstand

This move is not only used in floor and beam exercises, but is also a preparation exercise for the short clear circle to handstand on horizontal bar or asymmetric bars, for the undersomersault to handstand or streuli on parallel bars, and for the upward circle to handstand on rings. It is therefore a very important element for the young gymnast to learn.

First of all, it can be learned from back lying, with legs straight. The gymnast places the hands by the shoulders to push up into the handstand, and then rolls the legs back and up, with the coach taking the feet to direct the body into handstand.

The gymnast can then start from standing, piking forward as he sits back into the roll, once again with legs straight, and once again with the coach taking the feet.

When the gymnast can perform the move to handstand with bent arms, he can proceed to work it with straight arms.

Handspring practises

The handspring is one of the essential forward tumbles, and must be perfected if the gymnast wishes to progress to such moves as the hand spring front somersault or the handspring full - twisting flying roll. It should also be used as a progression towards the handspring or long-arm vault. The gymnast must break down the move and learn it in its four parts – first flight (reach on to hands), strike, second flight, and landing.

For the first flight, the gymnast must extend the body and arms, and reach forward on to the hands with the shoulders behind the hands at the moment of strike. He can practise this with kick to handstand and forward roll, with straight arms throughout.

Backward roll through to handstand, 1–4: The gymnast must start stretched, keep the legs tight, and push hard through the arms to come to an extended handstand.

Handspring practices, 5–7: The coach places his hand behind the shoulder blades of the gymnast, to aid the upward lift of the handspring.

Backward roll through to handstand

1

2

3

4

Handspring practices

5

6

7

Roundoff practices

8

9

10

11

Back somersault practices

12

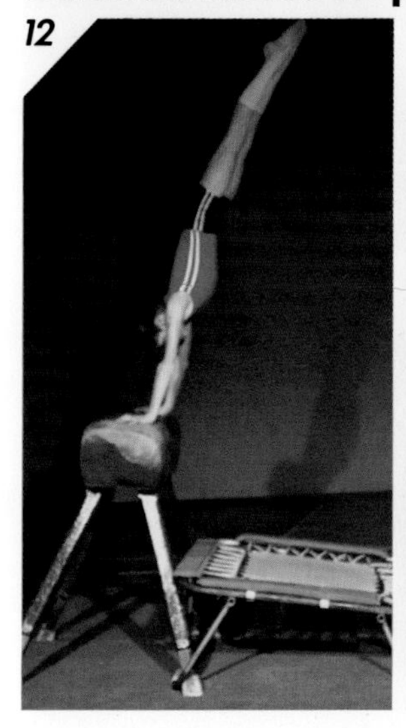

13

14

15

16

The strike is a 'blocking' process, where the shoulders stop their forward momentum and are driven upwards through the 'punch' off the floor. The gymnast can practise this by kicking to handstand and bouncing off the hands many times; he must learn to get off the hands, 'punching' through the shoulders and arms.

For the normal handspring, the gymnast must tighten the back in the second flight, with the head between the arms, and land the move firmly with slight knee-bend to absorb the landing, feet together. The gymnast can practise this by performing the handspring off some type of low platform to land on a crash mat, with the coach supporting with one hand on the shoulder to help 'block' the strike and the other on the back to aid the lift.

The gymnast can also practise the move by performing a handspring from hop-step off a springboard to land on a crash mat, particularly to develop strike and the straight back. This practice is also useful for the handspring vault.

Roundoff practices

This 'change-of-direction' move precedes backflips, back and side somersaults and is used for the first flight into a tsukahara vault.

First, the gymnast must be able to cartwheel correctly, reaching forward into the move, the second hand facing the first.

The gymnast can then practise cartwheel with quarter turn to face the direction from which he has come; then the same thing, but bringing the feet together for the landing, then, adding the hop-step into the cartwheel; and finally, with push through the arms and chest, performing a roundoff and upward jump.

Back somersault practices

Rotations in the air such as somersaults require what is known as 'spacial awareness' (awareness of where you are in the air). Back somersaults are, of course, used not only on floor, but as dismounts in many different forms off the apparatus.

The trampette, and thick crash mats, can be usefully used for somersault practice. First the gymnast must learn to jump up and slightly back from the trampette into the crash mat with the arms lifted and the body stretched, without rotating. Then he can practise tucked somersaults, with head in – extending, rotating by lifting the hips over the head, extending again, and landing with arms out to the side.

Roundoff practices, 8–11: The gymnast must reach into the cartwheel and turn the second hand towards the first. He finishes first with his feet apart and then with his feet together.

Back somersault practices, 12–16: The gymnast must lift the arms into the jump and then drive the hips and knees over the top for fast rotation.

Walk around sidehorse

1

2

3

Front support swing

4

5

Back support swing

6

7

Walk around the sidehorse, 1–3: The gymnast must press down strongly through the arms, with chest in.

Front support swing, 4–5: The gymnast must transfer his support from one arm to the other.

Back support swing, 6–7: The hands must be forward on the handles, and the gymnast must swing from the shoulders.

Straddle support swing, 8–9: The gymnast must transfer the weight from arm to arm, and lift the opposite hand off the pommel for a high swing.

PREPARATION FOR SIDEHORSE

Also known as the pommel horse, this is a vaulting horse used at the same height as for women's vaulting in competitions, standing at 110cm (3ft 7in), with the two pommels running crossways and bolted through the body. The pommels can be adjusted from 41 to 44cm ($15\frac{3}{4}$ to $17\frac{3}{4}$in) apart, and the legs can be shortened for younger gymnasts during training.

The gymnast's early preparation for sidehorse is mainly concerned with developing support strength and learning to swing in the vertical plane (single leg swinging, shears or scissors) and in the horizontal plane (double leg circles). There are many ways of achieving this.

Walk around the sidehorse

The gymnast must start in a good front support position, with chest in, upper back rounded and shoulders pressing down, and with the body tight. The gymnast then moves one hand on to the other handle in front of the other hand, and travels the other hand out on to the end of the horse, maintaining a strong support position.

He then travels around the end of the horse, back on to the handles facing the other way, and continues around the horse until he is back where he started from.

Front support swing

The gymnast must start in front support, with the hands slightly forward of centre on the handles, and then develop a pendulum swing through a wide arc, with the legs apart all the time. The swing must come from the shoulders, not just the hips, and as the gymnast swings he transfers his weight from one arm to the other; when he swings up to the right the weight is transferred on to the left arm so that the right hand can release as the hips lift above the horse, and vice versa.

The gymnast should be able to swing so that the bottom leg lifts at least level with the top of the horse.

Back support swing

The gymnast must start in back support position with the hands grasping on the forward edge of the flat part of the handles, and with the hips extended so that when he swings he will not hit the handles.

Once again, the legs must be kept apart during the pendulum swing, and the gymnast must transfer his weight from one arm to the other with the swing.

Straddle support swing
As with the other pendulum swings the gymnast must transfer his weight from one arm to the other, releasing the hand on the side to which he is swinging so that the swing of the hips can lift above the level of the handles. The shoulders must be kept square during this swing, and the gymnast must practise the exercise with each leg forward in turn.

Single leg swinging on rings
The gymnast starts in hang, and aims to swing with as big an arc of the legs as possible, with the legs wide apart. The shoulders must be kept square.

Doubles swing on parallel bars
The double leg circle is the main fundamental of sidehorse work, and it can be practised in a number of different situations. The gymnast can learn the correct shape of the circle without having to be in support by working it in this way.

The hips and legs must describe as wide a circle as possible, without the hips turning in the direction of the circle. The legs must be kept tight together, and the hips must not drop at the back of the circle.

Doubles on the buck or 'mushroom'
The gymnast can learn to double on the buck without having to worry about the pommel handles.

He must learn to circle with legs tight, with legs and hips extended, and with no turn of the hips.

When he can double correctly, he can practise doubling with a slight turn in each double in the opposite direction from the circle of the legs. He must move his hands very quickly off and on again for good support.

10

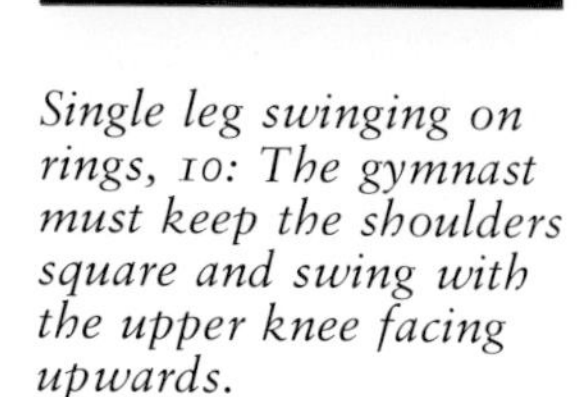

Single leg swinging on rings, 10: The gymnast must keep the shoulders square and swing with the upper knee facing upwards.

Doubles swing on parallel bars, 11–13: The gymnast must make a big circle with the legs, and not turn the hips.

Doubles on the buck, 14–16: The gymnast must keep the body tight and extended, and aim to cover the hands with the hips when he doubles.

Straddle support swing

8

9

Doubles swing on parallel bars

11

12

13

Doubles on the buck

14

15

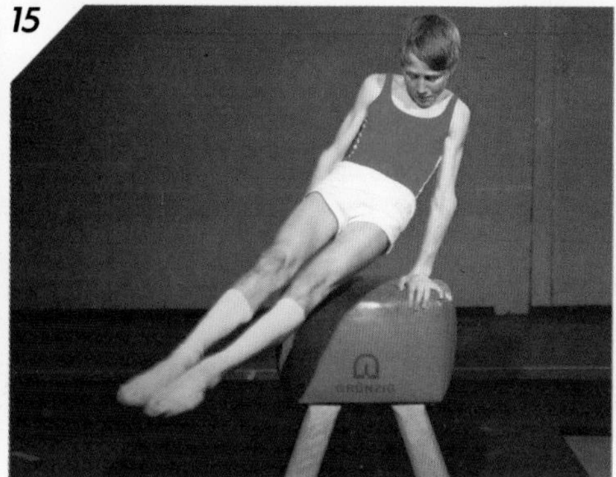

16

PREPARATION FOR PARALLEL BARS

The two wooden bars, supported on uprights mounted on a single steel base, are 350cm (11ft 6in) long and 175cm (5ft 6in) high for competitions. The bars can be adjusted from 42 to 48cm ($16\frac{1}{2}$ to 19in) apart.

Parallel bars require good support strength, as much of the work is done above the bars, and the ability to swing dynamically, both above the bars and in hang. The gymnast must therefore follow a training programme to develop support strength and swinging ability.

Walk or hop along bars

1

2

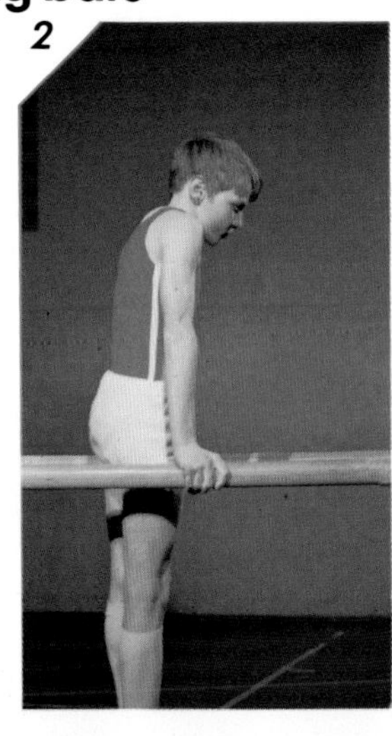

Walk or hop along bars, 1–2: The gymnast must keep the body extended and not bend the arms.

Swing in support, 3–6: The gymnast must keep the body tight and swing from the shoulders.

Swing on upper arms, 7–10: The gymnast must not have the shoulders too close to the hands, nor must he allow the shoulders to sink through the bars.

Walk or hop along bars

The gymnast must keep the body tight and not bend the arms as he walks along the bars. The same thing applies when he hops along the bars, using the arms and shoulders to thrust off the bars with each hop. He must walk or hop along the bars at least twice.

Swing in support

The bars must be shoulder-width apart, no more. The gymnast must swing from the shoulders with the body straight and tight. He accelerates the forward swing with the feet, and on the backward swing he must not hollow the back.

Eventually, the upper back leads the swing to handstand, but first of all the gymnast must learn to swing tight and straight no higher than horizontal, and not to extend his head as he swings up the back.

Swing on upper arms

The gymnast must first of all adopt the correct position on the bars, with the angle at the elbows at about 90° so that the shoulders are not too close to the hands, and with the elbows pressing down so that the shoulders do not sink below the bars. The swing comes from shoulders, with acceleration on the forward swing from the feet.

The forward swing eventually leads the body above the level of the bars, and the backward swing takes the body and arms above and off the bars.

Swing in support

3

4

5

6

Swing on upper arms

7

8

9

10

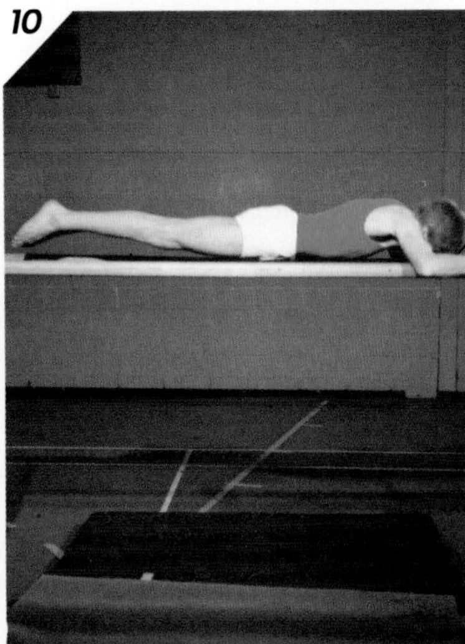

Underswing from box top

11

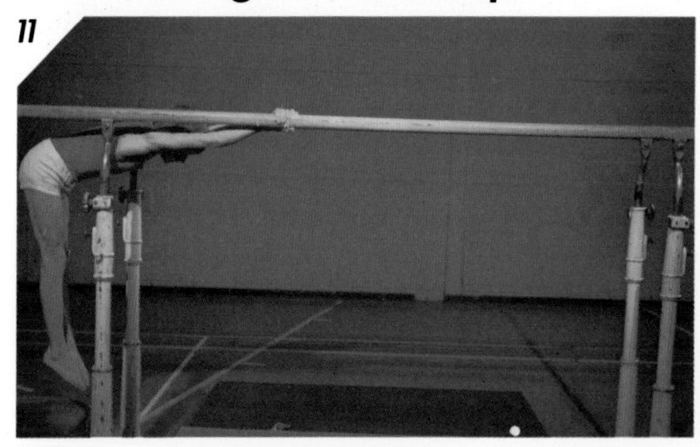

12

Underswing from box top, 11–12: The hips must start as far back as possible (11). The gymnast must not hollow in the extended position (12).

Practices on benches, 13–15: The gymnast must move the arms first into the support position.

Handstand practices, 19: The handstand must be done with the body tight.

Press to handstand practice, 16–18: First the gymnast must lift the hips over the hands before circling the legs to handstand.

Practices on benches

13

14

15

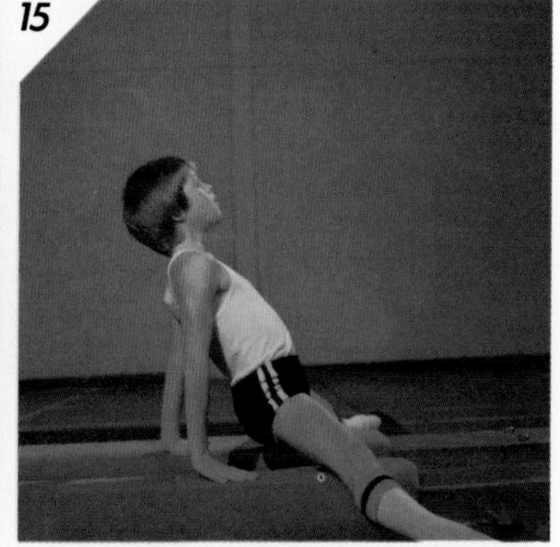

Press to handstand practice

16

17

18

Handstand practices

19

Underswing from box top
This is the preparation glide swing for the long upstart (or underswing kip).

The gymnast reaches forward to grasp the bars, with the body and arms extended apart from the angle at the hips. He then jumps the hips back and up as high as possible and glides the body under the bars, extending as he goes. At the end of the forward swing the body must not be hollowed, but kept slightly dished, ready for the upstart pike. In this exercise, the gymnast then swings back to place his feet on the box top.

Practices on benches
The young gymnast can use mat-covered benches to learn a number of basic parallel bar skills. For example, he can practise the shoulder-stand and forward roll to straddle sit.

In the shoulder-stand the elbows must press down on the benches, and as the gymnast moves into the forward roll he must transfer his arms fast to gain his new position of support at an early stage in the move.

Handstand practices
The gymnast must practise handstands as often as possible, as many of the big moves on parallel bars start and finish in handstand. He can practise handstands both on the floor and on mini-bars and parallets. The handstand must be straight-bodied and extended in the shoulders.

Press to handstand practice
This is another essential element that the gymnast must perfect, and he can work on it between turns on the apparatus. He can first practise lifting from half-lever to place his feet on the bars, and then press from there. Also, he can practise with the aid of a partner who will assist the lift of the hips.

PREPARATION FOR RINGS

Basic swing, 1–2: The gymnast must accelerate the forward swing with the feet, pushing the rings away from the feet at the front and back of the swing.

Lay-out from inverted hang, 3–5: The gymnast must push the hips up and out with the swing.

Underswing dismount, 6–8: The gymnast must kick through and then throw the rings away behind him.

Muscle-up, 9–11: The gymnast must have a good grip over the rings, and then turn the rings under the shoulders.

Half-lever (L-balance), 12: The gymnast must press down on the rings, hips between the arms.

Shoulder balance, 13–14: The gymnast must lift the hips into the shoulderstand, with the elbows in.

Basic swing

1

2

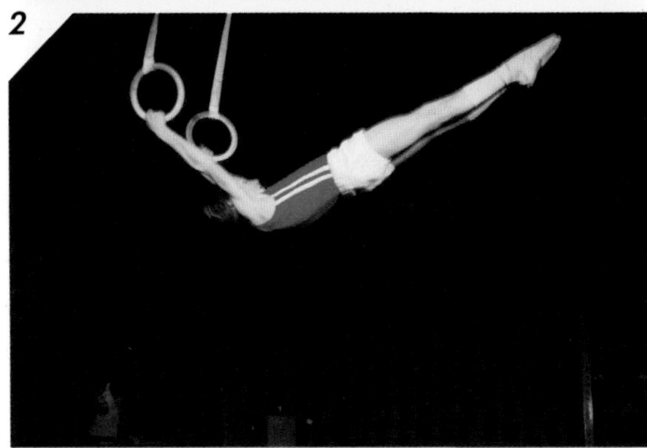

Lay-out from inverted hang

3

4

5

The rings are completely circular, made from laminated wood, and suspended by straps and plastic-covered cable from a steel frame 550cm (17ft 6in) high, which is supported by four guyropes. When hanging freely the rings are approximately 50cm (1ft $7\frac{1}{2}$in) apart and are 255cm (8ft 3in) above the ground at their lowest point. During training for this apparatus, the prime factor is learning to swing correctly, displacing the rings in the opposite direction from the swing of the feet.

Basic swing
The gymnast must grasp with the thumbs around the rings. He initiates the swing by kicking with the feet, and as he swings forward he must press the rings behind him at shoulder-width apart, head looking forwards, and without lifting the hips or chest at the top of the swing and causing the body to hollow.

On the back swing, he must keep the back tight and press the rings out in front of him, aiming to lift the shoulders and chest by pressing down on the rings.

Lay-out from inverted hang
From piked inverted hang, as the gymnast extends the hips and legs up and out he must pull up on the rings and extend them behind him smoothly to move with as big a swing as possible.

This should be first learned on low rings, and with support on the high rings.

Underswing dismount
The gymnast kicks hard through the bottom and up the front, and then extends through the chest and shoulders throwing the rings away behind him, for the dismount.

Muscle-up
The gymnast adopts a grip with the hands right over the top of the rings. He pulls up until the hands are below the shoulders, then he turns the rings, brings the shoulders forwards and presses up into half-lever (L-balance).

Half-lever (L-balance)
This must be practised regularly by the young gymnast. The shoulders must be pressed down, head up, and wrists pressing down on the rings with the straps clear of the arms.

Shoulder balance
This is a first step to learning the handstand and the gymnast must regularly practise the press with this balance, on the small rings. He must keep the rings and elbows in, and lift with body tight and a reasonably open angle at the elbows. Later, he can open the elbow-angle further until he is half-way to handstand.

These last three exercises are essential strength and balance preparations for the young gymnast.

Underswing dismount

6

7

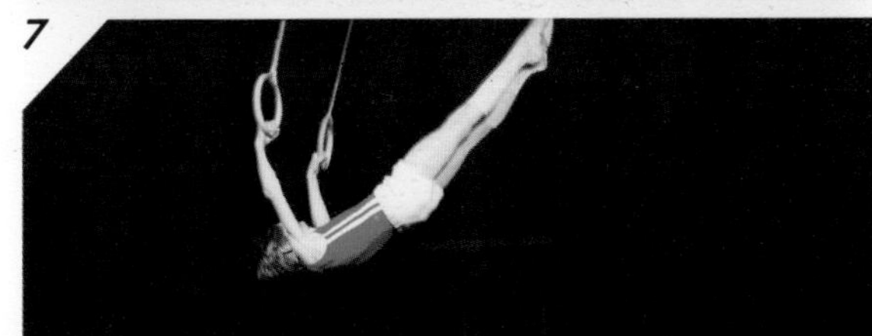

8

Half-lever (L-balance)

12

Shoulder balance

13

14

Muscle-up

9

10

11

Back hip circle

1

2

3

4

Back hip circle, 1–4: Note position of hands and hips as the gymnast circles around the bar.

Underswing dismount, 5–6: The gymnast keeps the chest in, and drops the shoulders back into the circle.

Run through upstart, 7–11: The gymnast must pike his legs to the bar, and press the bar up to the hips.

Run through upstart (run through kip)

7

8

9

Undergrasp beat-up

12

13

PREPARATION FOR HORIZONTAL BAR

The horizontal bar is made of steel, round in cross-section, with a diameter of 2.8cm ($1\frac{1}{4}$in). It is 240cm (7ft 11in) long and its ends are slotted into two steel uprights 225cm (8ft 3in) high. These are supported on four guyropes.

For the young gymnast, much of the basic preparation is on a low bar, but at the same time he must also learn to swing on the high bar. The first four are some useful exercises on the low bar:

Back hip circle
This is a short back circle from support to support, which prepares the gymnast for circling round the bar and also for building up the short clear circle to handstand.

The gymnast beats the bar in overgrasp, then circles back into the bar with body tight and chest in, and pushes the shoulders back with the circle round the bar. He must turn his wrists round the bar to come back to support.

Underswing dismount
This is another preparation exercise for the short clear circle to handstand.

He begins as for the back hip circle, but as the shoulders begin to circle up the front he opens up the shoulder-angle pulling the bar away from the hips, with the legs shooting up and out. The gymnast then releases the bar, and straightens the body for the flight and landing.

Underswing dismount

5

6

10

11

Lay-out into swing

14

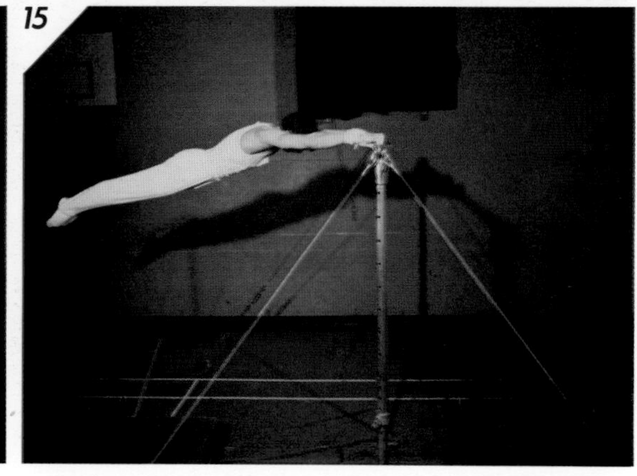
15

Undergrasp beat-up, 12–13: Photo 12 shows the start position for the beat-up, which will react with the swing up and lift of the legs and hips, and extending of the arms.

Lay-out into swing, 14–15: This is a swing on the high bar.

Run through upstart (or run through kip)
The upstart is one of the essential moves for taking the gymnast from below to above the bar.

It can be practised by the young gymnast, running through under the bar, opening the shoulder-angle, and then beating the feet off the ground, taking the shins to the bar and pressing the bar up the front of the legs to the hips, thereby closing the shoulder-angle and bringing the body above the bar to support.

Undergrasp beat-up
The gymnast must be sufficiently conditioned to beat-up off the bar, both in overgrasp and in undergrasp to handstand, in order to attain a position from which to move into longswings.

In undergrasp, the gymnast must pike slightly with slight arm-bend, and then beat strongly off the bar, extending the arms, into handstand. When in handstand, he must tighten the body, bring the head between the arms, and swing down into a crash mat.

Lay-out into swing
The gymnast pikes, hollows and pikes his legs up to the bar and out into the swing. The swing must be tight, with acceleration on the forward swing coming from the feet, with no hollow at the front and with the head between the arms.

At the top of the back swing, which must not be hollowed, the gymnast presses down on the bar, loosens his grip, and regrasps for the downward swing. He can also practise swinging with half-turn, leading his legs with the path of the following swing, and regrasping in overgrasp with the hands close together.

1: The gymnast uses a trampette to aid the spring into first flight.

2–3: The vaulting horse can be lowered to suit even the smallest gymnast.

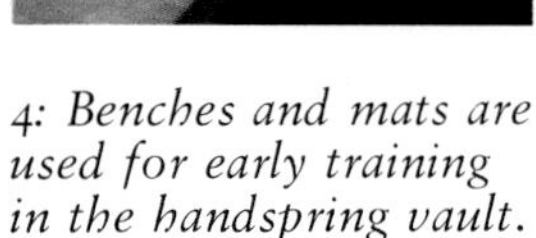

4: Benches and mats are used for early training in the handspring vault.

5: A trampoline saves the gymnast a great deal of energy when training many times over to perfect a vault.

6: Gymnasts can help each other in training. Here the older girl pushes against the shoulders of the younger gymnast, to give her the feel of the correct forward lean for the run up to the vault.

PREPARATION FOR VAULT

A vault is a unique routine in the sport of gymnastics because it is all over and done with in a matter of four to five seconds. The brevity of the movement may suggest to a spectator that it is an easy technique to master but any coach or gymnast will tell you a different story.

Vaulting is a fast run up and a jump from a springboard, two flights – one on to the horse (first flight) followed by a thrust off into second flight and a landing on the other side. All competition vaults these days are in the inverted position (that is, handstand or near to it) for the fraction of a second the gymnast is actually touching the apparatus. The journey on the other side includes either a somersault or a twist or both and the landing is frequently facing the direction the gymnast has come which means he/she is travelling backwards for the landing.

It is understandable that the trainee gymnasts might feel apprehensive, but there is no need for fear because they prepare in gradual stages and their coach does not sanction the full vault or even major elements of it, until the gymnast is ready.

The coach will first consider the run up and upward jump and push for the first flight to the horse. For this the trampette (or mini tramp) is most useful together with four benches placed longways in twos and side by side to provide an elevated run up.

The trampette is a mini trampoline complete with frame and canvas square held by elastic supports. It is placed alongside the benches and the trainee gymnast runs the length, jumps on to the trampette and then to the horse.

Another aid to stimulate courage at the jumping stage is the use of two springboards, one on top of the other. Because the jumping off spot is higher, it seems the horse is lower. The advantages of this method for the trainee gymnast are that the first flight is reduced and more spring is available.

Second flight and landing are frightening to most trainees. A full sized trampoline can be used to help them by placing it on the far side of the horse. A crash mat is placed on top of the trampoline to alleviate landing anxieties whilst twisting and somersault techniques on the far side are being developed.

A trampoline may also be used to assist training. It eliminates constant repetition of the run up so that the trainee can concentrate on the flight from the horse. The trampoline is slightly slanted downward towards the horse. When it is realized that thirty to forty vaults can be obtained with this set-up, it is realized what a saving of energy this method allows the gymnast.

Two benches with a crash mat on the other side are often used instead of a horse in the early stages of handspring vaulting.

Gymnasts must be like sprinters on the athletic track. That is to say, they must lean forward during the run up. A training aid for this is to wear a belt with a rope running through it. The coach will pull the ends of the rope in his two hands to encourage the gymnast into the right position.

The greatest aid of all for gymnastics training is a foam pit. There are only too few in the whole world when you consider the vast number of gymnasts. Many more are needed for they provide a high degree of safety. Foam pits give complete protection even for head landings.

In competitions the men's vaulting horse is 135cm (4ft 5in) high and is placed lengthways. For women it stands 110cm (3ft 7in) high and is placed crossways. During training, the horse can be lowered to suit younger gymnasts. Both men and women use a springboard for performance of their vaults, but the men have a restricted run-up of 20 metres (65ft) for competition work.

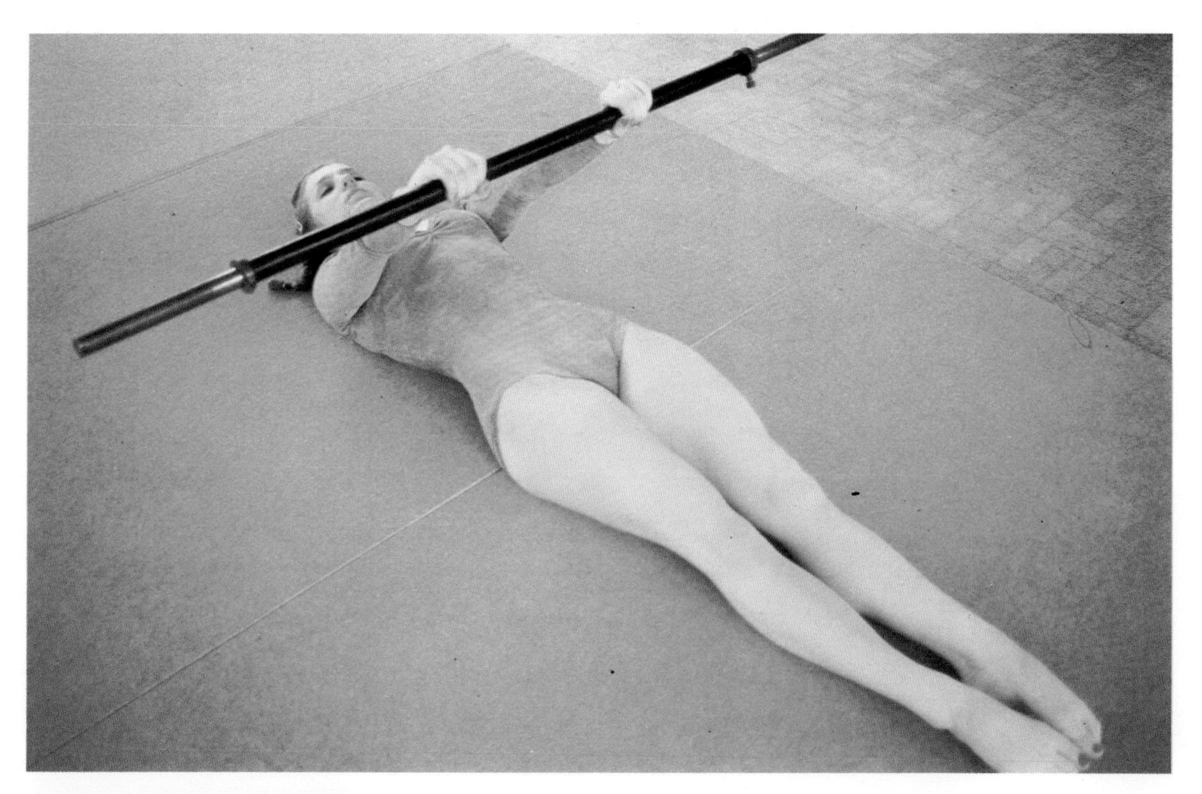

PREPARATION FOR ASYMMETRIC BARS

The asymmetric bars consists of two bars of laminated wood surrounding a steel core. They are slotted into two sets of steel uprights, 230cm and 150cm high respectively (7ft 6ins and 4ft 11ins), and have the same length as the men's horizontal bar. When vertical, the uprights are 70cm (2ft 3½ins) apart, but they are hinged to a steel base and the distance between them can be adjusted by means of a screw-thread. Thus the actual distance between the bars can vary from approximately 90 to 120cm (2ft 11½ins to 3ft 11ins). The apparatus is supported on four double guyropes.

Bars are the hardest of the four women's apparatus and they call for a lot of strength exercises.

Among the many training aids is a low bar about four inches from the floor which is particularly useful for handstand coaching. The handstand is a vital element in bars work.

More than half the elements at this apparatus can be done on a single bar. So often in training the top bar is removed and the low bar is placed at its normal height. The advantage for the trainee gymnast is that whilst practising certain elements, there is no danger of hitting the top bar with the head or body.

Many coaches recommend elastic from upright to upright in place of the high bar. Again it saves dangerous contact above through misjudgments and, at the same time, provides assimiliation as to the position of the top bar. This is very helpful for front somersaults (radochla) between the bars because slight deviation in the flight path during training can result in an accident.

A trampoline is frequently used for twisting training and is helpful for spatial awareness. Knowledge of the position in air in relationship to the bars is vital to a gymnast.

As for all other apparatus, a foam pit is top priority. The bars can be set up above the pit and somersaults and dismounts may be worked in complete safety.

For strength exercises a six-foot weight-lifting bar can be used. The gymnast lies flat on her back on the floor and, holding the bar at shoulder width, lifts it above the head and down to the thighs and back again. This method is useful for upstarts and free hip circles to handstand.

Above left: A gymnast conditions her muscles by lifting a weighted bar.

Below: Here a mini-bar is used for handstand training.

Above: Complicated moves on the beam can be practised in complete safety by piling up crash mats on either side of the apparatus.

Above right: Lines painted on the floor can assist the gymnast in perfecting the vital alignment of the body, and in finding the exact positions required for hands and feet.

Right: An up-turned bench is ideal for practising the perfect balance and control needed for a pose like this.

PREPARATION FOR BEAM

Beam training is greatly helped by basic ballet exercises for good posture and correct leg alignment with the body when walking.

Most of the beam elements are first practised on the floor progressing to a low beam four inches to a foot from the floor.

Junior gymnasts work the beam 110cms (3ft 7ins) from the ground; in full competitions it is 120cms (3ft 11ins). When first attempting difficult moves on the high beam, mats are often piled up to the level of the beam. They can be removed one by one as the confidence of the gymnast increases.

The beam is the least complex of the apparatus but frequently it is the decider in competitions. It needs a cool head and any nervousness shows up straight away. Distractions and nerves lead to falls and loss of rhythm. Total concentration by shutting out everybody and everything around is absolutely vital.

Only a few years ago, when Olga Korbut initiated her daring backward somersault, the beam was solid hard wood, but now it is constructed to provide a small amount of give and is covered with suede. It is 500cm (16ft 5in) long, and is mounted on two steel legs standing altogether 120cm (3ft 11in) high.

Left: A young trainee fills in her notebook faithfully. Work plans and comments can help a gymnast to progress systematically and to understand his or her own good points or limitations.

TRAINING NOTEBOOKS

A very useful guide to a gymnast's progress is the keeping of a training guide. In fact, most top gymnasts regard it as essential to record everything they do. Really it is like keeping a personal diary for it calls for scrupulous honesty and precise detail.

To a gymnast the training book is an indication of progress of routines and the single elements within them, and it is of particular value in the run-up to a competition when a gymnast is constantly turning over in his mind which elements of difficulty he ought to retain or leave out.

A rough exercise book is quite sufficient for it is a personal document which is not going to be kept and bound for the benefit of posterity. Just as with a diary, it is very personal to the gymnast and to his coach.

No gymnast has the exclusive attention of a coach. The one gymnast to one coach situation is a pipe dream that could be of little lasting benefit to either party. In Eastern Europe, coaches are able to give more attention to their protégés but it is unlikely that any gymnast has the exclusive individual attention of his coach for every minute in the gymnasium. It would be restricting to the ideas of the coach and mentally overpowering to the gymnast.

So the coach must know precisely what the gymnast is doing in his absence and to that end, he will either set a target for the session or he will ask the gymnast to write down exactly what he has done. In both cases, the absolute integrity of the gymnast is essential and his future success will rely entirely on it.

Many gymnasts who have been lucky enough to train in other countries have returned with the training book idea high on their list.

Former British national champion Avril Lennox (1973–8) started one up when she came back from Rumania in 1974. She regards it as essential for the progress of new moves, which a gymnast does not normally risk trying out in competition unless reasonably sure of success.

Miss Lennox programmed herself with her coaches Harold Davies and Bill McLoughlin to a given number of elements per session. As every move was completed, she logged it in her own brand of gymnastics shorthand with different marks for excellent, good, indifferent or bad. As Miss Lennox says, no one can recall from memory even a few hours afterwards all the twists and turns for good or bad that occurred in a session, but reading the training book at leisure later, tells a gymnast just how things are going overall.

Avril Lennox coaches young girls at Charles Keene College, Leicester, where her over-elevens starting out on the more advanced moves, all have training books.

The reigning British champion Ian Neale regards his training book as a vital predictor provided he is honest with it. On bad days there is a temptation to record a failure as a success or, at least, to minimize it. By so doing, the gymnast may be released from the immediate wrath of his coach but he will not be fooled for long, if at all. The truth of the matter is that if an element is showing around a sixty per cent failure, then it is better to have it out of the routine for the time being at least.

Ian Neale regards his training book as essential in a pre-competition build-up because after every session he can go back over what he has been doing. A gymnast must do a lot of thinking outside the gymnasium. The sport is not a thing just to be forgotten about in off hours.

The training book ensures a gymnast is fully aware of the total movement pattern; it forces a gymnast to do another routine when he least feels like it and compels him to concentrate on weaknesses. A gymnast might think he is doing better than he is until reading over the notes.

To Neale the notebook is a predictor, a target maker, a disciplinarian and, above all, a character builder.

Above: *Even top gymnasts have to go through rigorous conditioning and suppling exercises, and here Olga Korbut warms up with her team mates before a big performance at Wembley in London.*

Right: *The ballet training, which contributes to the outstanding success of Soviet gymnasts, is here evident in the graceful pose on the balance beam performed by the beautiful Grozdova.*

Overleaf: *Typical layout of a gymnastics arena for a big competition.*

TRAINING IN RUSSIA

The system and structure of gymnastics in the Soviet Union is well established and is part of the curriculum in all schools. This provides a very broad base on which to make selection for more specialized training.

Selection is made scientifically, and children must be of a certain body type and must successfully complete various tests. Selection will also take into consideration the history and statistics of the child's parents and family. In simple terms coaches choose the right material, perhaps as few as six children from around two thousand, and then begin to work on it.

Once selected, the children attend a specialized school where gymnastics is their main subject. The number of hours they spend training will be relative to their age and ability.

Generally selection is made at six years of age for a trial period of eight months, to see how responsive the children are to the training. During this trial period they train for two hours, six days a week, with thirty minutes of choreography each day. They are in groups of eight, under one coach, and are given training clothes or anything else they need for their gymnastics. If the gymnasts prove to be successful, at the end of eight months a long term programme will be worked out for them, which begins with an increase in training time.

The most any of the gymnasts train would be six hours a day, six days a week; this is split into two three-hour sessions, and would only be for the advanced gymnasts. The academic subjects are then fitted in between their training times.

All gymnasts in the Soviet Union, whether girls or boys, spend time each day doing some form of dance training. In the early stages it is mainly ballet exercises to create muscle strength in the legs, but will be developed so that the gymnasts have complete muscular control throughout their bodies, and will therefore be able to apply it to their gymnastics. The majority of the schools are mixed and have students studying other forms of gymnastics, for example *moderne*, but each school will specialize in one area, for which they will provide more facilities and have the most pupils. For example in one specialist school there are 840 gymnasts, 300 of which are girls, and 70 of these do modern rhythmic gymnastics. For the 500 boys there are 32 coaches and 18 coaches for the girls. On top of this there are five dance teachers all of whom have their own pianists.

All of the coaches must be qualified by specializing in gymnastics at an institute where they spend a minimum of two years. It is also preferable that they will have been a gymnast and hold a Master of Sports.

All coaches must start at the bottom by preparing young gymnasts. They are continually under the supervision of the director of the school, who will discuss and advise during the preparation of programmes. The actual coaching of the gymnasts is the responsibility of the appointed individuals. If for some reason the gymnast does not improve and the coach does not know what to do he must go to the director. If the director decides it is the fault of the coach, he will transfer the gymnast to another group of the same ability, but if it is the fault of the gymnast then he/she will be moved down to a lower group. The coach must always have reasons and explanations for the things he does and the results he gets. The authorities are now trying to bring in a new system whereby all coaches must be able to teach the children another subject as well as gymnastics, which makes it much more difficult to become a successful coach.

As the gymnasts become older they are moved into smaller groups of three or four if they are exceptional cases, which means they would be very talented if they had their own coach. By this time they train for six hours a day, six days a week, each day beginning with forty-five minutes of choreography. All gymnasts have a holiday during the summer for two weeks, although they are expected to keep in good shape by doing simple exercises.

The Soviet competition structure is very similar to the European. Each region or republic has its own competitions, and depending on how well the gymnasts do at this level, they may be able to take part in further competitions, for example at national level. From the national competitions, squads are selected from which the teams will be picked. The Soviet Union has three such squads, one senior and two junior. The senior squad is limited to girls over fourteen years of age, in which there are twelve gymnasts; the teams are mainly selected from this group. The next in line are the second junior squad, in which there are eighteen gymnasts between the ages of twelve and fourteen. The top six of these girls may be called on at any time to take the place of any one of the seniors. Then there is the first junior squad, which is the largest of the three squads, with twenty-four gymnasts, all under twelve; this is where the coaches will begin to prepare all the future champions.

Gymnasts in the Soviet Union are looked after very well indeed. Once selected for a national squad, they are given all their training kit and receive a food allowance. Their health is continually checked and a doctor and masseur are always present during training sessions.

Maybe now it can be understood why the Soviet system produces the very best gymnasts, and whilst they continue to improve their system the gap between them and the rest of the world will continue to increase.

GER 2 USA 1 JPN 3
45,65
46,20
45,75
45,30
46,55
45,15
91,85 91,85

OLYMPIC MOVEMENTS

Forward walkover

FLOORWORK

The women's floor exercise is the most expressive piece of the four disciplines, differing from the men's exercise by virtue of the fact that it is choreographed to music. The music can be played on any instrument (but just one) and it is generally the piano.

The exercise has a time limit of one minute to one minute thirty seconds.

It is recognized that a floor routine must contain balletic movements, turns, jumps and good interpretation of the music. Routines can vary from Elvira Saadi's classical style to the offbeat of Maria Filatova. But the routines must have at least three tumble runs, the first near the beginning, the second somewhere around the middle and the third close to the end.

The tumbles are done across the diagonals and it is advisable for the gymnast not to use the same diagonal twice from the same direction. The rest of the floor routine must cover the floor area equally, the area of which is twelve square metres. It is slightly sprung and carpeted.

Rhythm is an important factor and there must not be any interruptions likely to disturb the rhythmic flow of the exercise.

Forward walkover

A forward walkover goes from a standing position through handstand and back to the standing position. With good posture in the upright position and hips pulled under, back straight, shoulders down, stomach muscles tight and legs straight, the gymnast lifts her arms above the head, ensuring there is no angle between the body and arms.

One leg moves forward into a deep lunge taking all the weight of the body while the back remains straight with arms still above the head. The fingers reach towards the floor and when they make contact, the back leg leaves the ground. It must be very straight with the ankles and toes extending and as the back leg swings

Backward walkover

5

6

7

8

overhead, the underneath (lunging) leg straightens and eventually leaves the floor, but not before there is an angle of at least 180° between the two legs.

As soon as the fingers touch the floor, the shoulder girdle should be fully extended with the head in line and the arms touching the ears. The fingers will be slightly bent with the tips pressing into the ground to help keep balance.

As the legs move over the head, the body will move into a handstand position with the legs split to show an angle of 180° or more. At this point, the shoulders are still extended, the arms straight, the stomach and back muscles are contracted to keep the back straight and the body upright. The legs are of course straight and the ankles, feet and toes fully extended.

The first movement towards the forward bend is made by pressing the shoulders backwards over the hands in the direction from which the feet have come. The back remains relatively straight and the body is still in an on-balance position over the hands. Maintaining the on-balance position, the first leg is lowered slowly to the ground with the toes making first contact followed by the whole foot. The first leg will have to bend slightly on contact with the floor but the angle of 180° between the two legs is maintained and the second leg points vertically upwards.

The momentum is continued as the hands leave the floor and the stomach muscles contract to pull the head and shoulders up from the floor. Arms remain in line with head, the underneath leg straightens and hips remain static over the supporting leg. The second leg moves slightly forward and upward.

The forward walkover finishes with the underneath leg straight and turned out, back straight, hips tight and the second leg held straight well above horizontal rotated outwards. Arms are held up in line with the head, shoulders are pressed down and the head is slightly upward.

Backward walkover

The backward walkover is the reverse of the forward walkover. Start in an upright position with good posture. The arms are lifted vertically upward and stay straight as they are pressed back as far as shoulder mobility allows, while one leg extends forward so that the foot is pointed and just off the floor with the muscles taut and the leg rotated outwards. Hips are kept square, the back straight with the head in a natural position.

Arms start to move backwards as the front leg lifts off the ground. The supporting leg remains straight for as long as possible and the body bends backwards as the other leg lifts.

As the hands reach the ground the leading leg should have at least reached a vertical position and then continues towards the horizontal. The shoulder girdle is fully extended and the back and stomach muscles contract to straighten the body.

The supporting leg straightens and leaves the floor, maintaining an angle of at least 180° between the two legs. Body weight is then completely on the hands with control through the fingers as in a handstand. The head is still in line with the arms without an angle between body and arms.

The leading leg continues to move, keeping a complete splits between the two legs until it reaches the ground. The toe makes first contact and as the foot lowers, the shoulders press slightly backwards with both legs remaining straight. The second leg stops in a vertically upward position. Then, as the upper body lifts off the ground, raising the head and keeping the arms in line with it, the second leg lowers as necessary according to the mobility of the gymnast.

The move finishes with the supporting leg straight and rotated outwards, the body upright, the second leg extended horizontally behind, the arms vertically upward pressed back to show maximum shoulder mobility, the head slightly lifted and the shoulders pressed down.

Roundoff

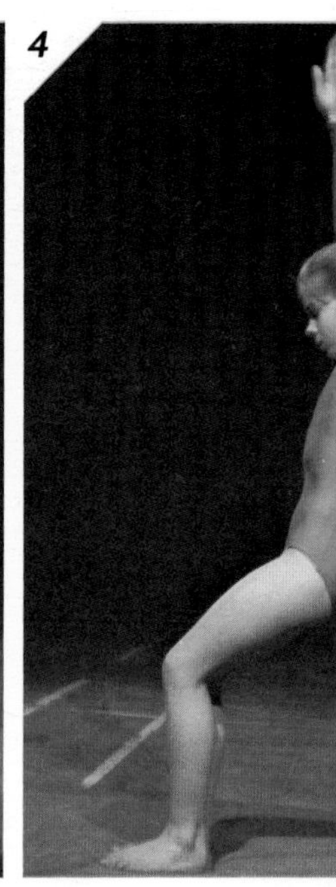

Roundoff

A roundoff is a method of changing direction on the move and consists of a brisk run to a cartwheel, a momentary handstand followed by a quarter turn and the gymnast is then facing the way she came, in readiness for the next move.

The huddle (hop) step for the roundoff should be done leaning forward, arms a shoulder width apart and stretched above the head. As the back leg starts straightening, the trunk of the body comes close to the leading thigh and, as the leading leg starts straightening, the hands move towards the floor. It is stressed at this point that the arms must not drop from the position they are in.

Just before the hands make contact with the floor, a turn is made to complete the first half of the roundoff. Assuming the turn is made with a left hand lead, the left hand is placed very slightly to the right of the leading leg. The turn is made by the right shoulder rotating behind the left.

The head must stay between the arms throughout the whole move and especially through this part of it. The second hand is turned in so that when it is placed on the floor, it can thrust in the direction of the move. When the hands are on the floor, they will end up diagonally across the line of the move.

As the hands contact the ground, the arms should be allowed to bend very slightly in order to help the second half of the roundoff. If everything is done correctly to this point, the gymnast should be in a support position before the handstand is reached. She should now be in the right position for the second half of the roundoff, the 'snap down'.

At this point the back will be slightly arched and this can be used effectively as a spring. Once both hands are on the floor, thus completing the first half of the roundoff, the arms and shoulders extend while the back snaps through to a concave position.

If everything has happened correctly, the whole body should have rotated to the finishing position which will depend on the move to follow. Assuming it to be a flip, the feet should land flat with shins angled backwards and thigh parallel to the floor. Hips should be tilted under the body, shoulders should be behind the hips with the chest pulled in to give the body a concave effect. Arms should still be shoulder width apart and above the head.

The back flip

The back flip is rarely used as an isolated move. It increases linear speed and is ideal for setting up the gymnast for more complex tumbles such as the somersault.

The starting position is the same as the end of the roundoff and the gymnast starts by straightening the legs as quickly as possible. At the same time the arms must be driven backwards towards the floor. At this point it is stressed that the chest must be held fixed and the head kept forwards. If this is done the effect will be a very straight back and a fast first half to the back flip together with a sound position to complete the move.

The arms should be moved as fast as possible towards the floor because they are the main rotating force of the move. The hands should be turned in slightly so that the little fingers touch the ground first and arms should be allowed to bend slightly to facilitate a good thrust from the floor.

If the first half of the back flip is done correctly, the hands should touch the floor with the body not yet at the vertical position. From there, arms and shoulders straighten very quickly to maximize thrust and at the same time,

Whip over

Previous page, below: Nelli Kim, the Russian gymnast, is particularly renowned for her beauty of movement on the floor.

Roundoff, 1–4: The object of this move is to change direction, and in the fourth picture (4) this is accomplished. Note the arms in line with the body in the second photo (2). The arms never cross the face. Photo 4 shows the classical ending of the roundoff.

Back flip

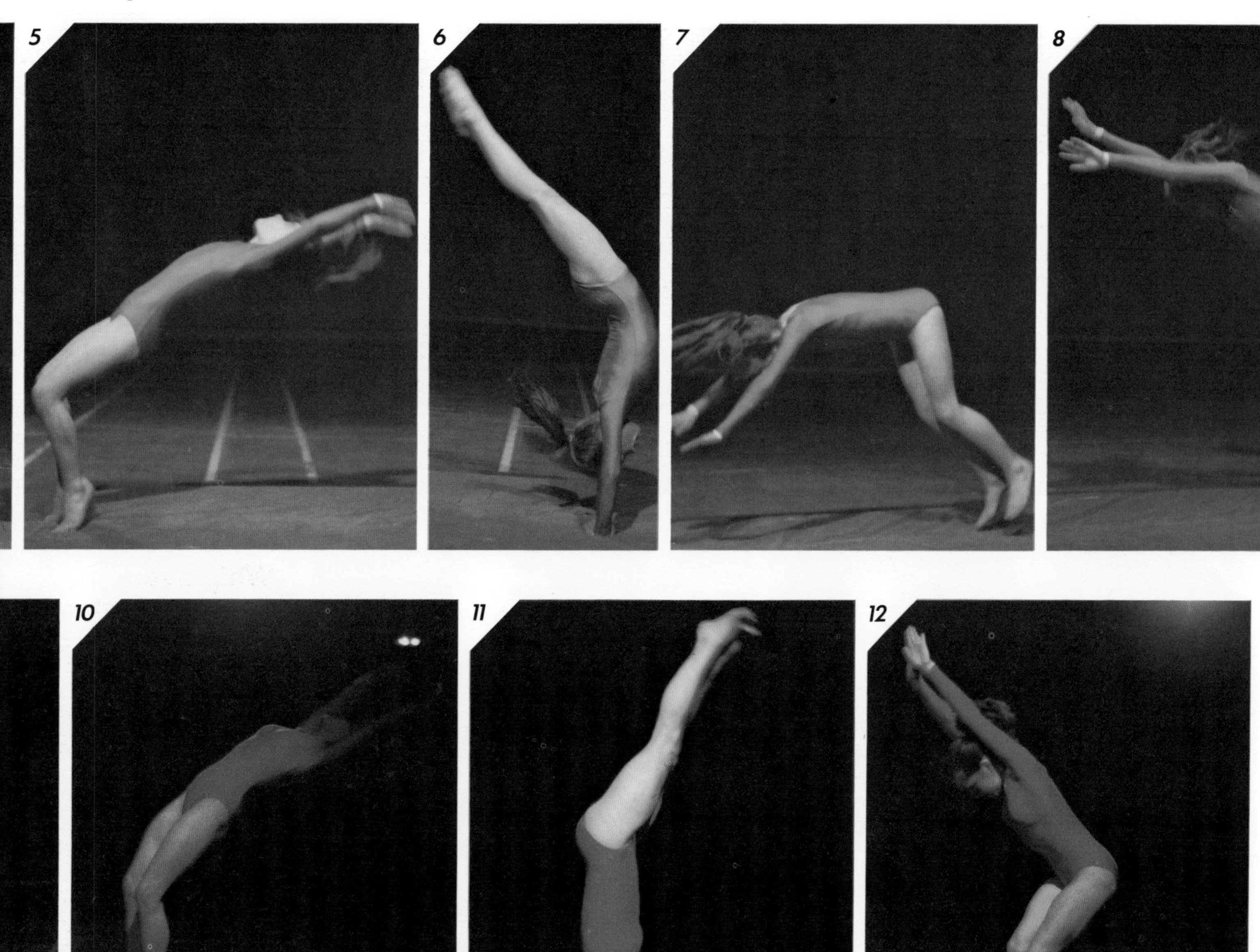

the lower back snaps down to rotate the body to its finishing position.

The actual finishing position will vary according to the move next to be attempted. If it is another back flip, then the body must be rotated back to the original starting position. If it is to be a somersault, the body must finish in a vertical position, hips in, chest in and tight and arms raised above the head to the point where they stop.

Whip over

This move resembles a back flip, but as it is done without the use of hands it must be classified as a somersault.

The most common entry to the whip over is a back flip. When the gymnast finishes the back flip she will be almost in the same position as for another back flip, i.e. head between the arms, chest in, hips kept under the body and the shins pointing backwards in the direction of the move.

One main difference from a flip is that the weight is kept over the balls of the feet. From this position the knee and hip angle extend and the body is driven into a slight arch position. The arms will stop very suddenly while the feet are still in contact with the floor. This will have a transfer of momentum effect from the top half of the body to the bottom half.

From this position, the legs stay straight and pike over the top to land back on the floor. The landing position is very important. The positioning of the body will depend on what the next move will be.

The most common exit is another backflip. To execute this properly, the gymnast must land

Back flip, 5–8: This back flip starts from the final position of the roundoff. The move goes backwards to handstand and then to the starting position again usually ready for a more complex tumble. Note the head stays forward (5) and hands touch the floor before the rest of the body hits vertical (6).

Whip over, 9–12: The whip over usually comes after a back flip and is similar but classed as a somersault.

Tuck back somersault

1

2

3

Full twisting back somersault

4

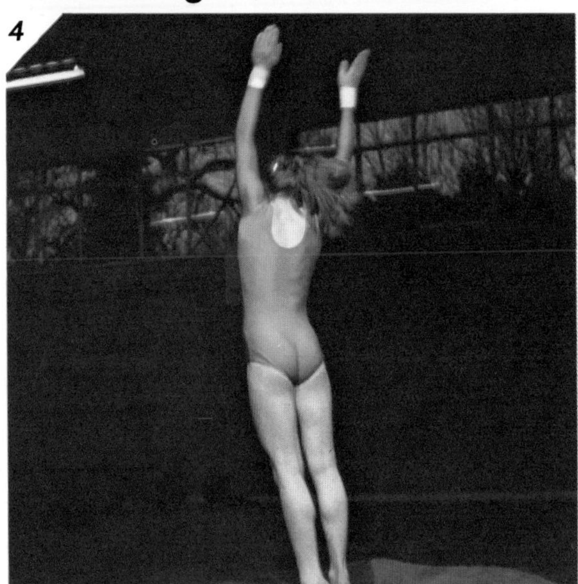

5

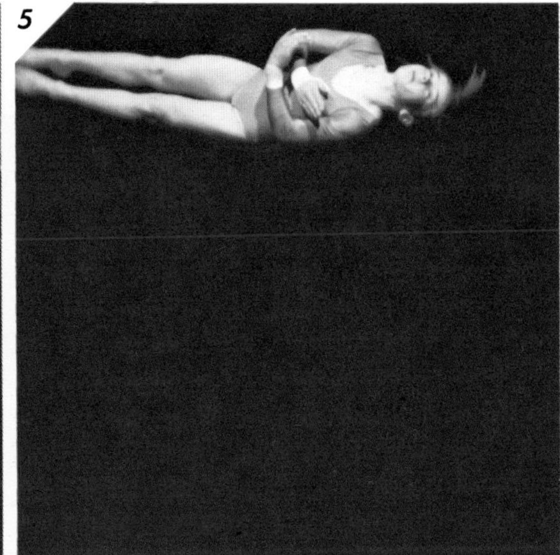

6

The arabian somersault

8

9

10

Tuck back somersault, 1–3: Usually following the roundoff or flip, the tuck back somersault is in full flight by the second picture (2). As the gymnast turns over, her knees are tucked towards her chest. On take off the chest is in, arms vertical.

in an off-balance position going backwards. Feet should be flat on the floor, the shins angled backwards, and thighs no less than parallel to the floor with hips under the body, chest pulled in and arms over the head. From this position, a fast efficient flip is possible.

The height of the move will depend on the efficiency of the stopping action of the top half of the body at the start of the move. It is possible to do more than one whip over at a time but the landing position of the first must be the starting position of the second as already described.

Tuck back somersault

The tuck back somersault is the most basic one of all. It is the first to be mastered before moving on to the more difficult somersaults.

The tuck back generally comes from the roundoff, the back flip or just from standing, but the technique should not change for any entry into the somersault. At the point of take off the arms should be above the head pressed back to their natural stopping position. That will only be accomplished if the chest is held in as tight as possible. The head should be held forward throughout the somersault without a tendency to look for the floor behind. The body should be as upright as possible; slight compensations may have to be made forwards but there should never be any backwards, behind the line of the upright.

Good height and rotation will be attained by good leg extension through the knee and ankle (generally a stabbing action) coupled with the natural stopping action of the arms. The arms must stop while the feet are still in contact with the floor so that the transfer of momentum can happen and the whole body will rotate.

The tuck back somersault has a three phase movement. There is a stretch position on take off followed by the tuck and then to a stretched position again. In this sequence the body will be taking off as a half-lever; it is then shortened by the tucking action which accelerates the rotation; and the final stretched position slows the somersault down for landing. If the take off is not efficient enough, then the somersault becomes a two phase movement with no stretch at the end.

7

Full twisting back somersault, 4–7: The first picture (4) shows a good take off with arms above the head, right shoulder pulled back very late. By the next photo (5) she is half way through the turn, and by the third (6) it is complete, just before landing.

Arabian somersault, 8–10: In this arabian the gymnast tucks, but it can be done straight or with a pike.

Full twisting back somersault

The full twisting back somersault must come from either a roundoff or from a roundoff back flip. The idea is to complete a very high, very straight somersault and to put in it a 360° twist.

The body needs to be as straight and as upright as possible on take off. The twist itself is taken off the floor and it is left as late as possible so that the somersault itself is not distorted.

If the twist is to the left, then as both arms are taken above the head, the left shoulder is pulled back slightly. Care must be taken not to drop the shoulder. Just a turn is needed.

As soon as the body is in the air and the turn has started, the arms can be drawn into the body. As long as they are as close as possible to the axis of twist, the necessary amount of turn will result.

Younger gymnasts have problems trying to remember mechanics in this way, and it helps if they think of something more positive: they should think of lifting a large beach ball above their heads and, as it gets there, they should turn it to the side wall and squeeze it very hard to press all the air out of it. The head throughout the twist should stay in a neutral position and not turn sideways. This will help the gymnast when she starts multiple twisting.

The arabian somersault

The arabian somersault is backward with a half turn and it can be done in a tuck, pike or straight position. It is generally used as a middle tumble and can either come from a roundoff or from a back flip.

The take-off position is exactly the same as for the tuck back somersault with the body upright, head in and arms lifted. At the last moment the left shoulder should be pulled back to set a left twist in action.

The arabian should be done in three definite stages. First, there is the lift and turn, then comes the tuck or pike and the third is the opening stage. For a 180° only turn there should be no need to wrap the arms in as for the full twisting somersault (360°). The body should be opened to a straight line before landing and the legs land one after the other, ready for the next move. Both legs must land in a slightly flexed position, firstly, so that there is no damage to the knee joint should it be pushed backwards and secondly, so that the muscles of the leg can be used to drive the body into the next move.

Ideally, the body should land in an off balance position going forwards. This will produce more stability and a stronger faster action can be employed into the following move.

Handspring front somersault

Handspring
The handspring can almost be described as a running handstand which finally ends up back on the feet. It can be used as an introduction to a front somersault or it can be walked out into another handspring, an aerial (movement through the air without hands touching the ground) or simply into a cartwheel.

The best handspring is usually done from a small run. At the end of the run, there is a huddle (hop) step. In this huddle the body must stay in an off balance position, i.e. leaning forwards. The head should stay between the arms and the arms must be in line with the rest of the body. The chest should be held in as tightly as possible.

When the gymnast makes contact with the floor, both legs should bend and the chest must be close to the leading thigh. At this point the back leg straightens very quickly while the arms and the rest of the body move towards the floor. At this point, there should be little angle at the shoulder and the head must stay between the arms.

By the time the hands hit the floor, the first leg should have fully straightened and be moving over the head and the second leg will be straightening. When the first leg is in the air and the second has finished its drive, the first leg must be deliberately stopped by the gymnast. This action has a transfer of momentum effect, that is to say, if one part of the body is stopped quickly, the momentum that has been created will transfer to another part of the body. This action is the main factor that gives the body rotation.

The second leg must catch up to the first as quickly as possible and at the same time, the shoulders will extend to thrust the body into second flight. In second flight the body should stay as straight as possible, the arms staying above the head.

Even though the arms in this position will have an adverse effect on the rotation, it is necessary for any move such as a somersault which may follow the handspring.

If the handspring is to be followed by a somersault, the feet should land from the handspring with the body just short of vertical and the weight of the body should come on to the feet at the vertical position.

If the handspring is to be followed by a roundoff or another handspring, then the second flight and landing change slightly. As the second leg catches up to the first in the second flight of the handspring, the first leg is driven down to the floor and the leg should land with the body just short of vertical and in a slightly bent position. As weight comes on to the leg, the body can be propelled quickly into the next move with no loss of time. The second leg should be stretched well forward and land in a bent position ready for driving the body forward. Throughout the whole of this landing phase, the hips should be kept in line with the body, the chest should be kept in and the arms stretched above the head.

Handspring front somersault
The handspring part of this move has already been described. The idea is to get as much rotation as possible in the handspring so that it may be converted into height and rotation for the tucked somersault. The body should be leaning very slightly forward on take off for the somersault. The gymnast should think of the hips in relation to the shoulders because the height of the somersault is determined largely by the position of the shoulders at take off.

If the shoulders are low, the hips will rotate around them very easily and cause fast rotation but it will be at the expense of height. The ideal position is to have the shoulders as high as possible and make the hips do a lot of work in getting around them. This is why the speed and rotation of the handspring is very important.

If the body leaves the floor in a slight forward concave position, then a long lever (the length of the body) has started the rotation. By tucking the body up as tight as possible, a long lever in rotation will be shortened and the rotation accelerates and performs the somersault.

As soon as the body has left the floor there is no mechanical reason to delay the tuck because, for better or worse, the centre of gravity has already been set on its course. But note the shape of the body will not affect its height.

If the rotation and height is sufficient, then the somersault can be clearly defined in three phases: the take off; the tuck; and finally an opening phase.

The take off and action for the piked front somersault is the same as for the tucked described above – except, of course, that the body is piked. But note that because a pike is not as tight as a tuck, the handspring and take off for

Handspring rudolf

Handspring front somersault, 1–5: There is a good drive of the leading leg in picture 1 and by 3 the gymnast is landing from the handspring just short of vertical, to prepare for the take off just past vertical for the front somersault.

Handspring rudolf, 6–9: The gymnast does a one and half twist through the straight front somersault. There is a good heel drive at the beginning of the move (6 to 7), with the left arm initiating the twist.

the somersault has to be even more efficient.

The layout front needs even greater efficiency than the tuck or pike although the take off is the same. The gymnast goes into a slight pike in the air, then drives the heels very hard over the top while the arms are driven downwards very quickly to the side of the body.

The biggest problem with the move is rotating the long lever, i.e. the body. This is why the arms drive downwards to the side of the body to shorten the lever as much as possible.

Handspring rudolf

The handspring rudi is a handspring layout front somersault with one and a half twists with the handspring performed in exactly the same way as for the other front somersaults.

On take-off the body goes into a slight pike position in order to create a quick and fast rotation. As the pike action comes in, one arm is swung across the body very quickly down and across the knees to finish up on the opposite hip. The second arm must stay above the head because when a body is in rotation and one side of it is made shorter, a twist action will occur.

The timing for dropping the arm into the twist is very important. It must happen just as the heels are driven over the head, which is almost at the time of take off. The head should be left in a neutral position because it is not used in the twist action.

Some gymnasts will be able to see the floor as they twist; others will not. Landing positions will vary according to the exit from the move but if it is to standing position, the feet should land with the body leaning slightly forward.

SIDEHORSE

Below: Bart Conner of the USA, sidehorse finalist in the 1978 World Championships in Strasbourg. Note the extension of the body and the strong support on the left arm.

Front shears (front scissors), 1–3: The swing must come from the shoulders.

Back shears (back scissors), 4–5: The gymnast must swing from the shoulders and lift the front leg high for the back leg to come under.

The main requirements of the Code of Points regarding the sidehorse exercise are that double leg circles shall predominate, with all three parts of the horse being used; that front and back shears (scissors) shall be included with at least one of them being executed twice in succession; and that the exercise shall swing smoothly without stops and without the body touching the horse.

These are requirements that make sidehorse exciting for the purist and extremely demanding for the young gymnast who must develop sufficient conditioning to enable him to swing all the time in support.

Front shears (front scissors)

Although a sidehorse exercise is made up mainly of horizontal circling moves, it must also have a proportion of vertically swinging elements of which the front and back shears are examples.

At the top of a front support pendulum swing, the gymnast turns the hips towards the horse and swings the upper leg over the horse to the front, regrasping the pommel quickly. He continues the pendulum swing up the other side, extends and turns the hips towards the horse, swinging the back leg high over the horse to the front, and the front leg underneath it to the back. The release and regrasp of the pommel must be quickly done, before the swing begins once more up to the other side for a second shear.

The gymnast must initiate the pendulum swing from the shoulders, and not just from the hips. As the swing moves up to the right, all the body-weight is supported on the left arm, with the right hand releasing the pommel, and both legs swinging in a wide arc above the horse, with the legs being kept wide apart. The reverse is true for the swing up to the left, and the whole move must be performed rhythmically, with the legs

Front shears (front scissors)

1

2

3

Back shears (back scissors)

4

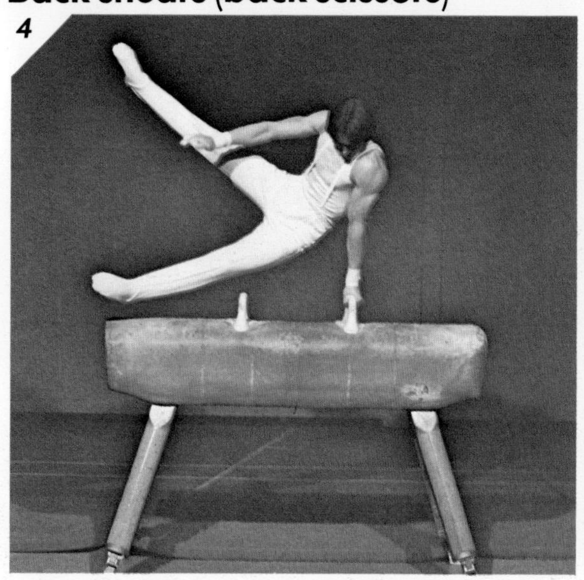

5

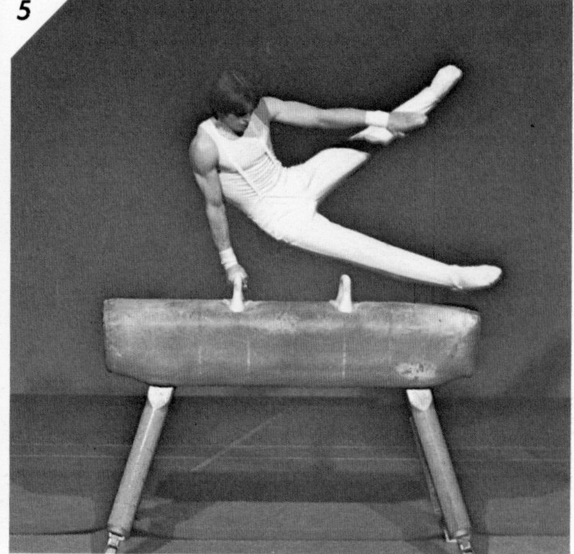

tight and the arms in a strong position of support.

The gymnast can practise by swinging the foot of the lower leg on to the end of the horse with good body extension before bringing the upper leg in, at both sides of the swing. He can progress to performing the shears with an intermediate swing in the straddle position. Then he can perform a number of shears in repetition, with the coach aiding the lift of the upper leg.

Back shears (back scissors)

The back shear requires a good, high pendulum swing, with the ability to widen the shoulder-angle, between the support arm and the chest, in order for the hips to lift above the level of the pommel handle.

The back shear needs to start from a straddle support swing, with the left leg to the front if the first shear is to the left. As the gymnast swings up to the left the support on the right arm must be strong, and the gymnast must concentrate on a high wide swing of the back leg which will swing under the front leg and to the front, with the front leg shearing to the back. The swing must come from the shoulders, with the widening of the shoulder-angle, and as the legs shear at the top of the swing the hips should make a slight outward turn with the shoulders remaining square. As the back underleg swings in forwards, the front upper leg should be lifted as it swings to the back. The gymnast then continues with a smooth, rhythmic swing into another back shear on the right side. The hand must regrasp quickly and firmly after each release.

The gymnast can practise this move by first of all swinging the back foot on to the end of the horse before exchanging the legs. He can also practise an undercut exercise, where from pendulum swing he undercuts the lower leg to the

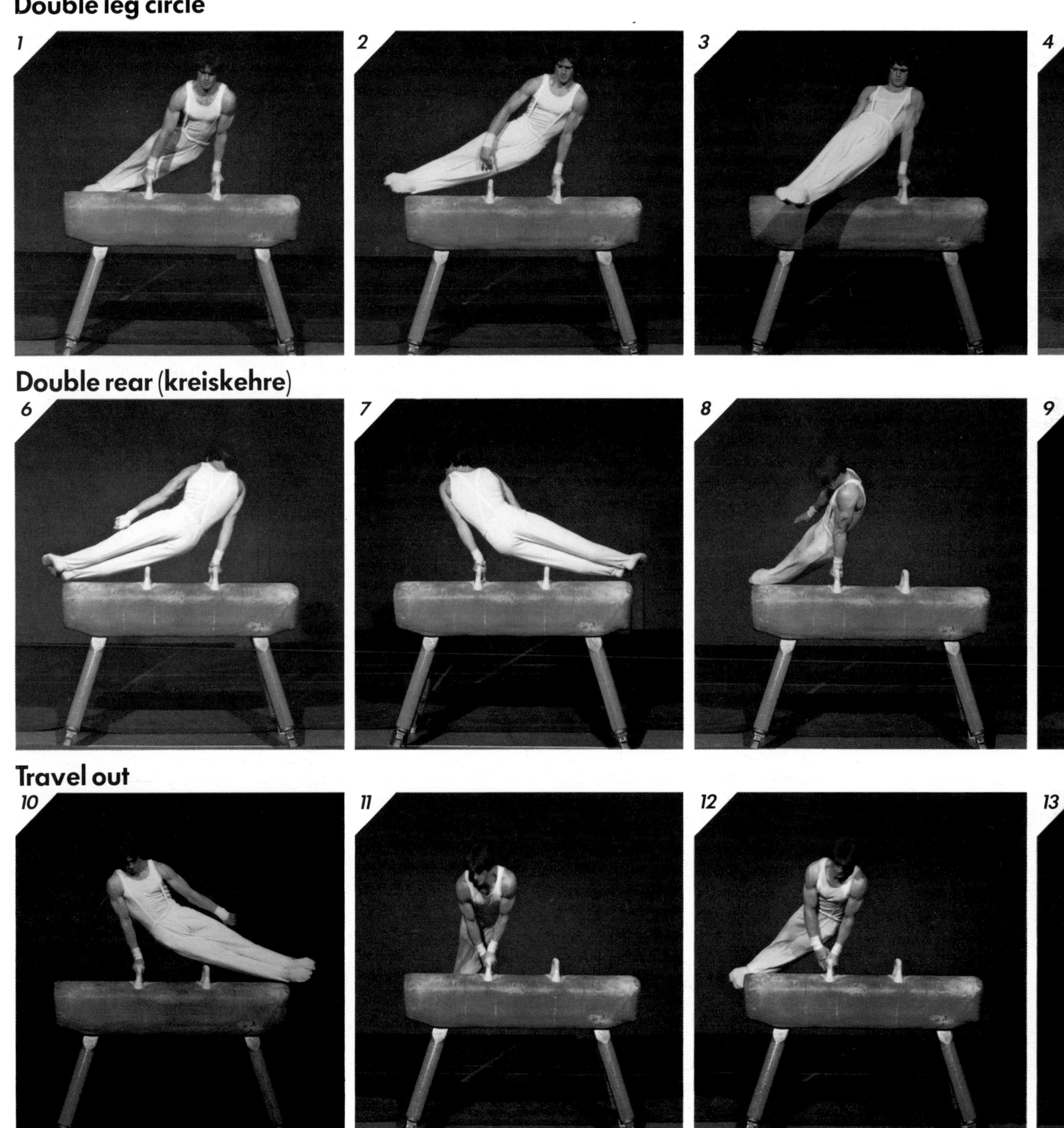

front under the upper leg (right under left if swinging up to the left), and continues the swing to take the undercutting leg back out to front support pendulum swing.

Finally, he can practise the back shears with the coach aiding the lift of the legs. The gymnast must practise these exercises on both sides so that the rhythm, strength and control builds up equally all round.

Double leg circle

The double leg circle is the most important basic move in sidehorse work, as most of the sidehorse moves are variations of the double leg circle, and in a full sidehorse exercise double leg circling has to predominate. Correctly speaking, the circle is made by the whole body, not just the legs, with the body extending out from the chest and the hips and legs circling in an horizontal

Double leg circle, 1–5: The circle of the body must be well extended, without any turn of the hips.

Double rear (kreiskehre), 6–9: The body must remain extended, with the

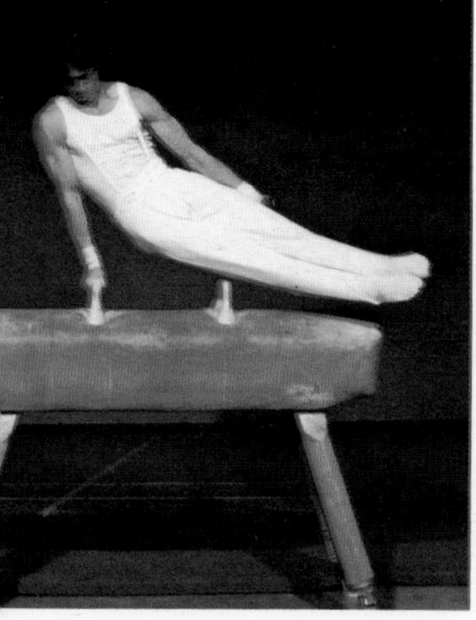

support shoulder leading the turn.

Travel out, 10–13: The gymnast must retain the shape of the double, and bring the hand across to initiate the travel.

plane, keeping the legs straight throughout.

At the beginning of the circle the gymnast must turn his hips slightly to the side from which he is starting his circle, with the legs extended, the feet facing upwards, and the shoulders parallel to the horse. As the legs circle under the first hand, regrasp the pommel quickly, and keep the hips extended outwards and a slight lean back of the shoulders. The whole circle extends out to the front, and as the legs pass over the second pommel, which must be quickly regrasped, the hips must remain slightly turned. As the circle is completed, returning to the front support position, the upper back must be rounded, with the body remaining straight and the legs and hips making as big a circle as possible.

The double leg circle is worked on all parts of the horse, and needs to be practised both on the handles and on the ends. It is easier for the gymnast to learn it on a buck, or a 'mushroom-shaped' apparatus. Concentrate first on a half circle, with the hips and legs extended, and the hips slightly turned. Then move on to a full circle, to return to front support with the upper back rounded, and the hands moving fast back into support. The gymnast can also perform a half circle to place his feet into the hands of the coach who will guide the second half of the circle back to front support.

It is essential to spend much time on learning this move correctly as it is the whole basis of sidehorse work. When the gymnast can perform one circle, he must aim to progress quickly to performing them in repetition, rhythmically and with good technique. A good test of the technique of the double leg circle is to be able to perform it on the floor.

Double rear (kreiskehre)

The double rear is performed both from the pommels to the end of the horse, and from the end of the horse into the middle. In other words, it is a travelling move, from one part of the horse to another.

The double rear normally starts from a double leg circle, and turns in the same direction as the double leg circle. The gymnast turns his head in the direction of the circle, and begins to lead the rear with his supportive shoulder, with the arm in a strong position of support, and the hips close to the supporting arm and extended. The gymnast pushes off the other arm, with the upper body almost upright during the first quarter turn, the supporting hand under the seat, and the chest slightly extended. During the second quarter turn the hips extend out, and the free hand reaches for the end of the horse under the seat to come to support for the following move. At no stage during the rear should the body be too piked, with the hips behind the supporting arm. The move must be smoothly performed throughout the circle.

The gymnast can practise the rear out to sit on the end of the horse, with the coach supporting the leading arm and the hips. Start this exercise from a jump with the waist turned slightly away from the direction of the rear, and finish in an extended sitting position with strong support on both arms. When the rear out can be smoothly performed it should commence out of a double leg circle into a double leg circle.

The gymnast must also learn to rear in from the end of the horse onto the pommels. He can learn it from a jump in, the hips slightly turned away from the direction of the circle, with a strong push off the free hand, leading the circle with the supportive shoulder. The feet must be kept low with the hips extended, and the side of the body kept close to the supporting arm. Once again, the move must be smoothly performed.

Travel out

This move is used frequently, to travel out from the pommels to the end of the horse, and also to travel back into the middle of the horse. A gymnast will travel in the same direction as he doubles, i.e., if he doubles to the left he will travel to the left. The gymnast starts from a well-extended double leg circle. As the body begins to circle back in, the shoulders must be leaned towards the direction of the travel, and the second hand, instead of regrasping the original pommel, moves across to grasp the pommel in front of the first hand in a strong position of two-hand support. The body continues its circle, over the neck of the horse, and the first hand then comes to support on the end. The body must maintain the extended shape of the double leg circle throughout the travel, with no turning or lifting of the hips during the travelling circle. The travel comes from the movement across of the second hand to the first pommel, together with the slight sideways lean of the shoulders.

The gymnast can practise the travel from a small pendulum swing, starting on the pommels. If he is travelling to the left as he starts to swing down to the left he leads outwards with his left shoulder and moves his right hand onto the left pommel in front of the left hand, and then as the swing passes through the vertical he moves his left hand with the swing on to the end of the horse.

He can also practise by circling his feet into the coach's hands at the front, and the coach then guides the double leg circle round while the gymnast concentrates on the transference outwards of the hands and shoulders. In any case, this move cannot be learned until the double leg circle is perfected.

When the travel out has been learned the gymnast must also learn the travel in from the end on to the pommels.

Stockli and tramlot
These two moves are combinations of the rear out and the travel out with a rear back in to the middle. So, both the stockli and the tramlot are not only moves which travel but also moves which change direction. In fact, although both moves contain what is known as a 'rear', the rear position is more akin to a flank position, as it is the side (flank) which passes over the horse rather than the back (rear).

Stockli The gymnast must be able to perform both the rear out and the rear in before attempting to combine them for the stockli. As the rear out extends on completion into a half double leg circle the head should already be turning inwards in anticipation of the rear in. The supportive shoulder then begins to lead the turn, with the body leaning close to the supporting arm as the outer hand pushes off the end of the horse. During the transitional phase from the rear out to the rear in the waist should be facing downwards.

Tramlot The gymnast must perform the travel out as a double leg circle with the hips and legs circling horizontally. Upon completion of one full double leg circle on the end, the supporting arm for the rear in must be quickly established, and once again the head anticipates the turn, with the supporting shoulder leading it as the outward hand pushes firmly off the end. The body leans close to the supporting arm, and as the rear in is completed the hips and chest extend outward for the following move with the free hand firmly grasping the pommel handle.

Czechkehre
The czechkehre is basically a double leg circle with a 180° face vault turn to rear in, and it can be done in different combinations on different parts of the horse. It is generally learned in the middle of the horse on the handles.

The gymnast must fully extend the outward circle before the turn, and the shape of the double leg circle must be maintained throughout the move with the shoulders leading the turn. The supporting shoulder leads the first part of the turn as the far hand pushes off and regrasps beside the supporting hand in undergrasp, with the upper back rounded and no dropping of the hips. The gymnast must maintain the two-arm support as long as possible while continuing to lead the turn with the shoulders. The body then extends out into a double leg circle as the first hand quickly moves into support on the other pommel.

The gymnast can practise the move from straddle support swing, by circling the front leg out to the back and the back leg to the front as he makes the first half of the turn, joining the legs for the second half as he double leg-circles the

Tramlot

4

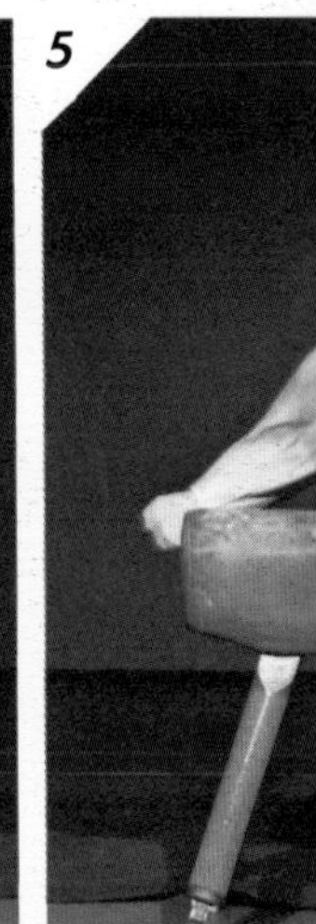
5

Czechkehre

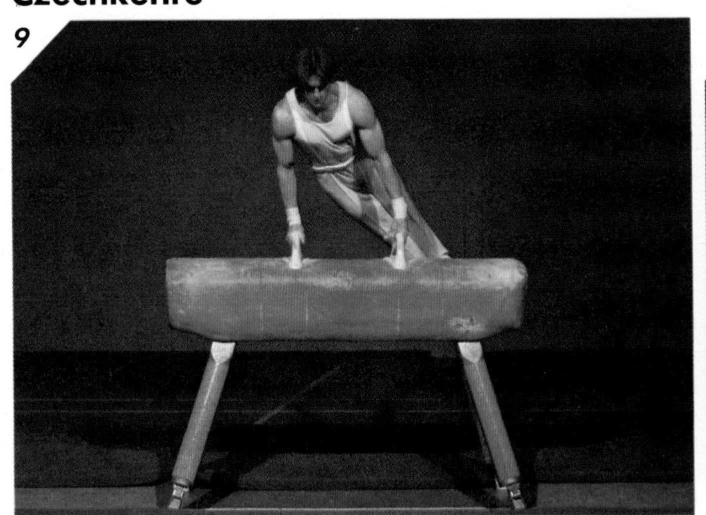
9

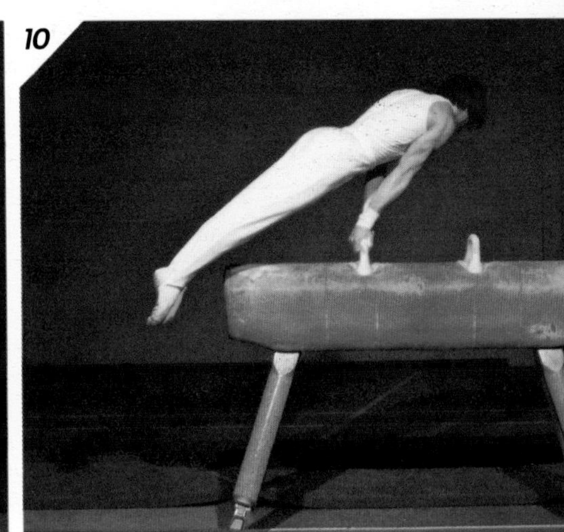
10

Stockli, 1–3: The gymnast must lean the body close to the supporting arm and lead the turn with the support shoulder. The move continues with photos 7 and 8.

Tramlot, 4–8: The body must remain extended throughout the combination, with the moving across of the hand and shoulder leading the travel and the supporting shoulder leading the rear in.

Czechkehre, 9–12: The hands must move fast to maintain good two-hand support and the shoulders must lead the turn, with the body remaining extended throughout.

legs into the front. It is important to move the far hand on to the pommel beside the near hand as quickly as possible to maintain the two-handed support for as long as possible. He can also practise a half-czech from jump in on the back, as well as the full czech on the buck, once again moving the hands into a strong support position as fast as possible. When he tries to move on the handles for the first time, the coach can take the feet at the back and guide them round, allowing the gymnast to concentrate on the correct position of support with the upper back rounded particularly as the body moves over the horse.

When the move is perfected the gymnast can try a number of czechs in sequence, with an intermediate double in-between.

Stockli

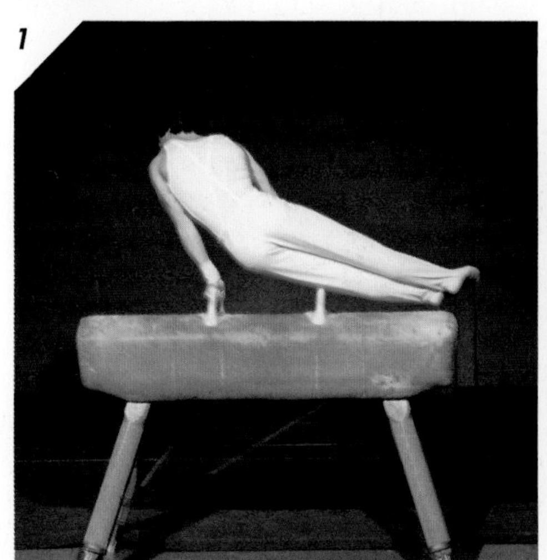

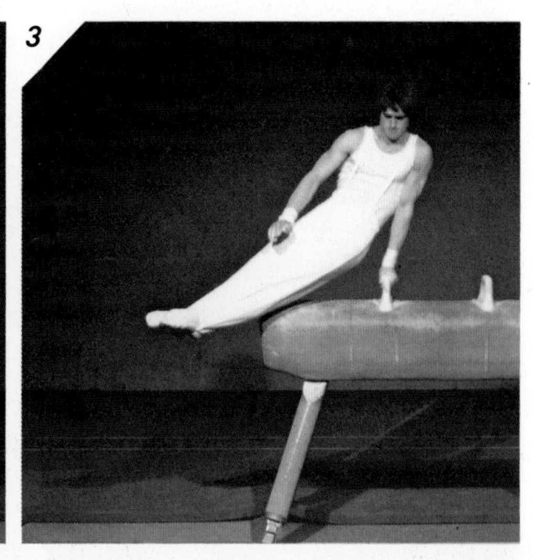

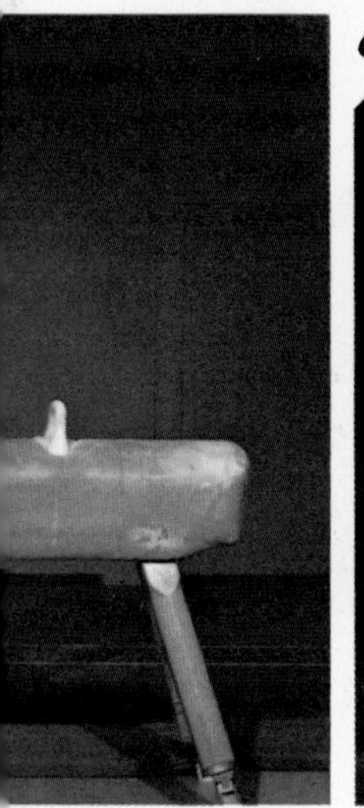

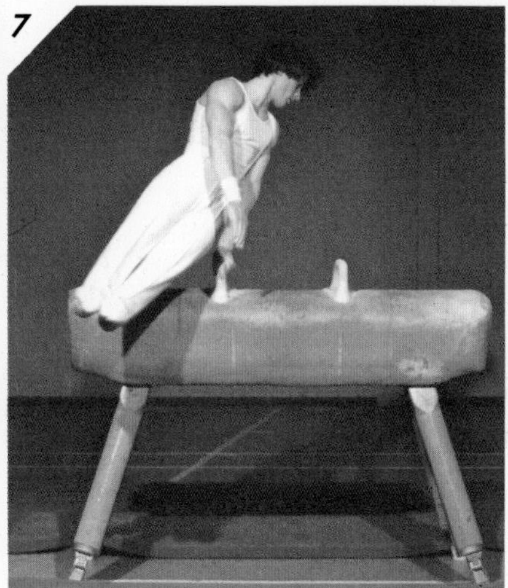

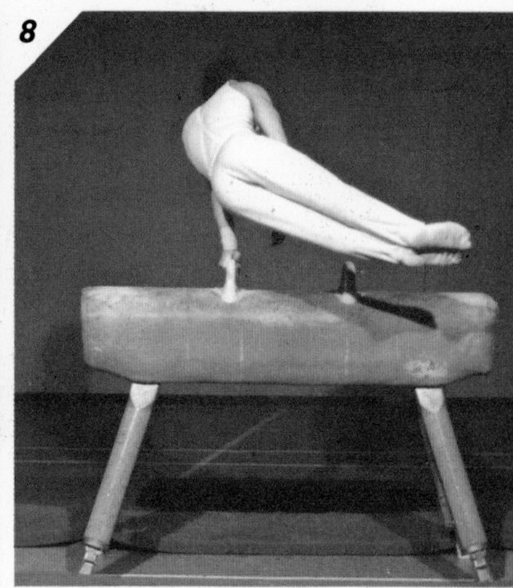

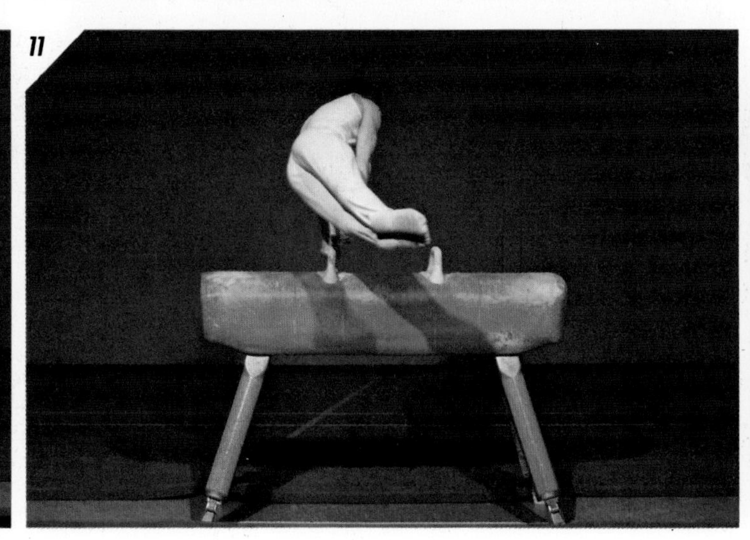

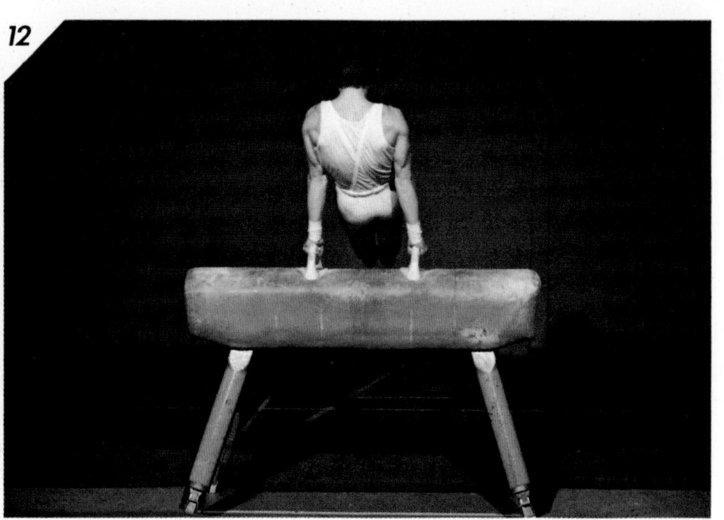

Double swiss

Back travel

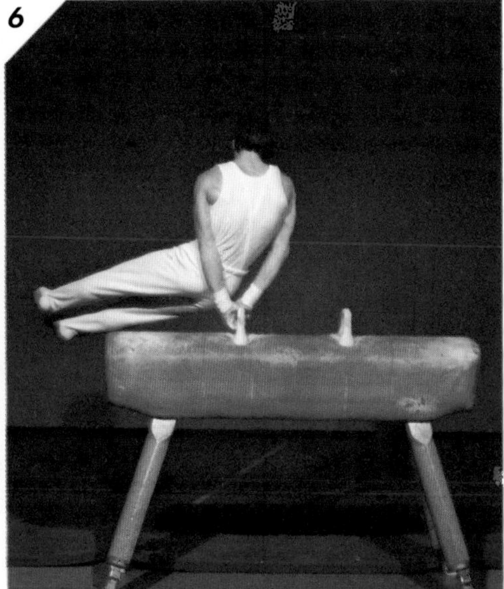

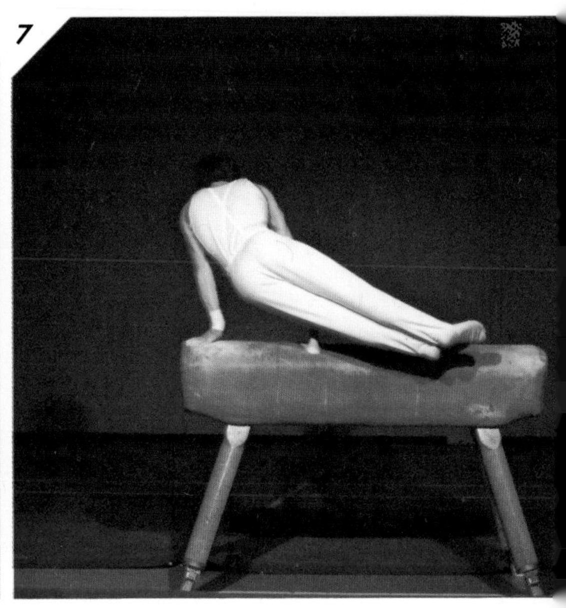

Double swiss, 1–2: The gymnast must retain the shape of the double, while turning with the shoulders and moving the hands very fast.

Back travel, 5–8: The gymnast must be fully extended in the double in order to travel the right hand out under the hips.

Double swiss
This is a double leg circle with a jump half turn, and is included in the set exercises for the World and Olympic Championships of 1978 to 1980.

If the gymnast is circling clockwise, he quickly regrasps the right pommel as he completes the double, and turns his head to the right, at the same time moving the left hand on to the right pommel in strong overgrasp support. His back must be rounded during the turns, and he immediately moves his right hand on to the left pommel, leading the turns with the shoulders and then moves into a double leg circle. The hand changes must be very quickly performed with the body retaining the shape of a double leg circle.

The gymnast can practise this move, at first on the buck, by jumping off the floor with a face vault with half turn to land the other side, concentrating on the quick hand changes and the lead of the shoulders. He can then do the face vault round from a double leg circle, to land on the other side of the buck, concentrating on changing the hands support coordination with the circle. When the gymnast can happily perform these exercises on the buck, he can try them on the pommels. When he is able to coordinate the hand changes with the circle, he can practise the full move from double leg circle into double leg circle.

The photo sequence shows the early turn of the shoulder and the hand moving across.

Back travel
This is similar to the travel out with the hands in front support but it is considerably harder, as the hands lead out during the back support position and the gymnast is unable to see the travel movement of his hands. In addition, the move requires a very good, extended double leg circle.

End-facing doubles

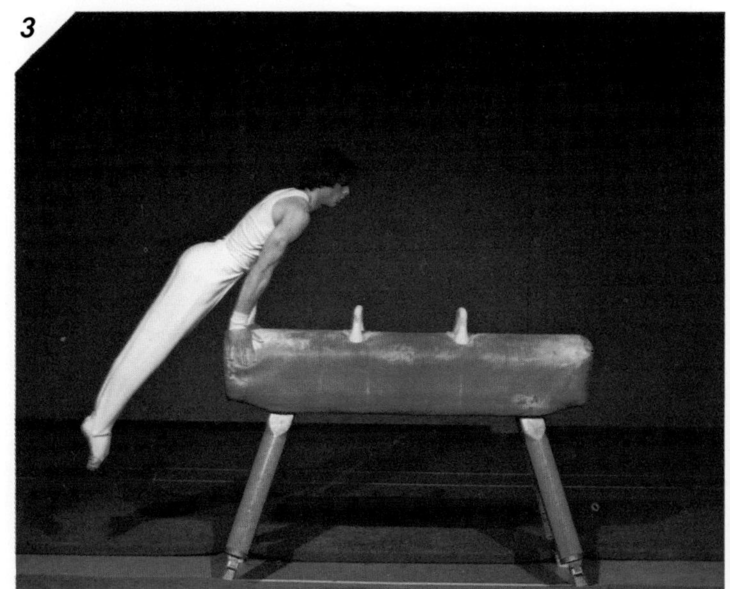

End-facing doubles, 3–4: *The gymnast must double with the hips circling well forward of the hands.*

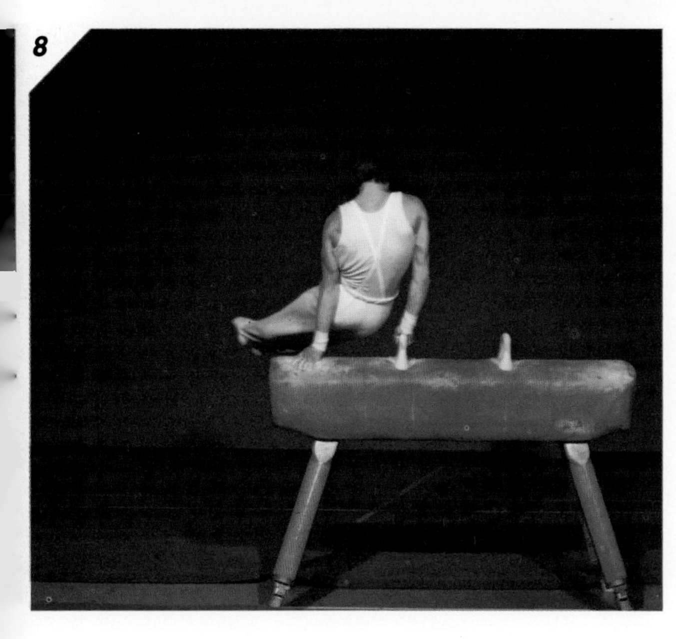

During the outward circle of the double, the gymnast leads with the travelling-side shoulder, at the same time moving the far-side hand quickly across to the near pommel alongside the support hand, in overgrasp. The gymnast must keep the hips extended throughout, and as he moves over the neck of the horse the near hand must move quickly on to the end as the hips face downwards for the inward circle. The shoulders must face slightly away from the direction of the circle.

The gymnast can practise the back travel out from the back support pendulum swing. As he swings downwards in the direction of the travel, he moves the far hand across on to the near-hand pommel in overgrasp and moves the near-hand on to the end of the horse. The gymnast can also practise making a back travel out to sit on the end of the horse, aiming to keep the support over the pommel as soon as the travel out has been completed. Once the gymnast has acquired the feeling of the travel out, he can try doubling his feet into the coach's hands at the front of the circle, and the coach can guide the legs while the gymnast concentrates on the travel out.

End-facing doubles

End-facing doubles are being used more often today by top-class gymnasts. Zoltan Magyar of Hungary originated end-facing doubles which travel up with the whole length of the horse.

The gymnast must begin the circle from a strong position of front support, with the upper back rounded, the shoulders slightly forward and the body extended. As the gymnast circles out to the front, he must regrasp fast and keep the legs as low as possible with the hips extended ahead of the hands. The hips must not turn with the circle, and during the inward part they must be faced downwards, with the shoulders coming forward for the front supporting part of the circle.

The circle of the legs and hips must be as horizontal as possible if the gymnast is to perform these end-facing doubles in sequence or in combinations, particularly on the pommels.

The gymnast can improve his doubles on the end of the buck or on the 'mushroom' before trying end-facing doubles on the horse. When he first tries them on the horse, he can remove the pommel handles to concentrate on extending the hips and keeping the legs low at the front of the double.

At first he should try one double, taking off from the floor and returning to front support before jumping off and concentrating on facing the hips downwards without turning them during the inward circle. The hands must be moved back fast into support.

When the gymnast has mastered the double he should train it with high repetitions and also in combination with normal doubles on the end of the horse which will require the quarter turn into and out of the end-facing doubles.

Thomas flair

1

2

Schwabenflanke dismount

5

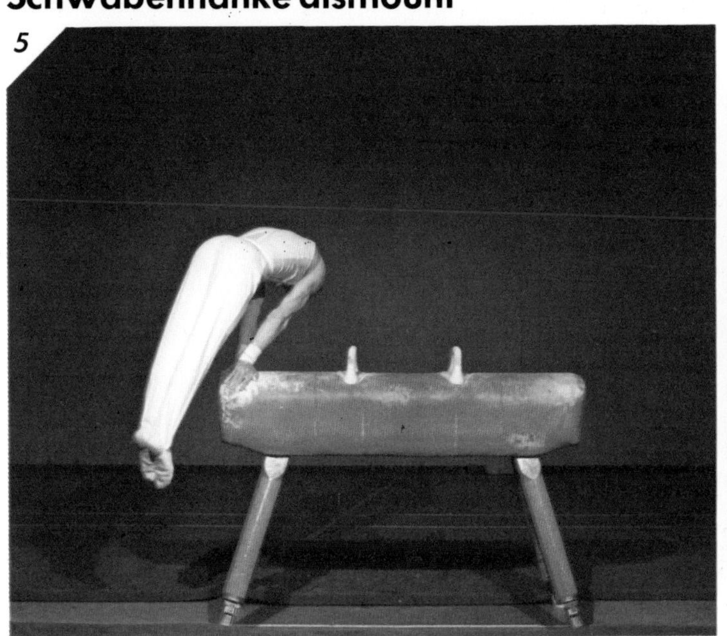

6

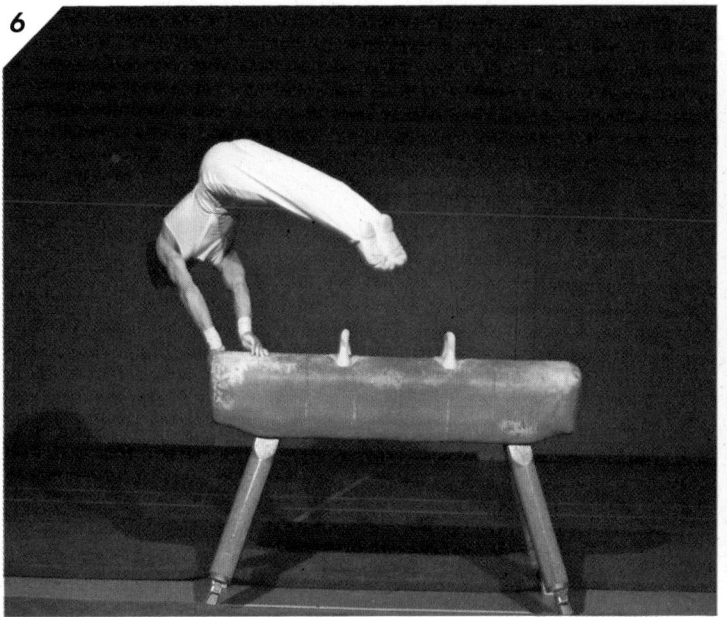

7

Thomas flair
This is a flamboyant new move introduced first into the international repertoire by Kurt Thomas of the United States at the Montreal Olympics. Since then it has been copied in various forms and combinations by many of the world's top gymnasts.

In simple terms, it is an alternating single leg circle of each leg, but it requires a high degree of flexibility, strength and good circling techniques. It is, therefore, an advanced move.

If the gymnast circles to the right from front support swing, he swings the right leg up high and circles the left leg under it to front, and then swings the left leg up high and out to back circling the right leg round and under it back to front support, keeping the legs wide apart during the whole move.

At no stage should either legs drop below the horizontal in its swinging, and in fact a good test of the move is to be able to do it on the floor, as Kurt Thomas does in his floor exercises.

To prepare for the flair, the gymnast can practise the circling and undercutting of each leg separately. First, from front support he swings the right leg up high and circles the left leg underneath it for a complete circle, and indeed should perform a number of undercutting circles of the left leg. Then he should practise circling the right leg undercutting the left leg at the front.

Finally, he can practise circling the right leg undercutting the left leg at the back, on the inward circle. When the gymnast is capable of undercutting with each leg circling horizontally, he can practise the full flair, first on the buck and then on the pommel handles. In addition, the gymnast must practise hips and leg flexibility

exercises in order to bring out the full virtuosity of this exciting move.

Schwabenflanke dismount

The schwabenflanke dismount is in fact a turn around the end of the horse with a face-vault over the horse, and is performed very frequently as a dismount or as the end part of a dismount move. It is normally taken from a double leg circle on the end of the horse.

As the gymnast swings outward into the double and starts to make the quarter turn to end-facing support, he must replace his outer hand facing forwards at the far corner of the horse, leaning the shoulder towards the end of the horse, rounding the upper back and leading the turning with the shoulders, the second hand coming into support on the other corner of the horse facing outwards.

The gymnast must lift the hips and keep the feet low as he continues the turn round the end of the horse in preparation for the face vault, with strong support on both arms. The gymnast must now lift powerfully with his hips and legs, and extend his head and chest as he pushes off his first hand, support remaining on the second arm. The reason for keeping the feet low during the turn around the end of the horse is to react with a high face vault over the horse.

When the gymnast performs the schwabenflanke dismount from a double leg circle, the preceding double leg circle must be fully extended so that the whole combination is performed with a wide circling of the body.

The gymnast can practise the move first of all by face-vaulting from a jump over a buck or at the end of the horse. He can start facing the end of the buck or horse, and then move further round to the normal starting position, vaulting over at first with the knees bent. He must concentrate on the correct hand support positions, the lift of the hips and upper back with the feet kept low during the turn around the end, and the leading of the turn with the shoulders.

When he can do the turn and the face-vault over the horse with body extended, he should add the preceding double leg circle.

When the move is perfected the gymnast should precede it with a travel out to make a simple finish to his exercise. In addition, he can practise the chaquinian dismount, which is a schwabenflanke round the end of the horse into an outward-facing czechkehre into a schwabenflanke dismount.

In fact, the Schwabenflanke dismount is merely the ending of any number of combinations which the gymnast can devise as an end to his exercise. However, it all starts with the perfection of the double leg circle which forms the basis of almost all sidehorse work.

Thomas flair, 1–4: The circling leg must be circled horizontally and the lifting leg raised high.

Schwabenflanke dismount, 5–7: The turn must be led by the shoulders, and the feet must start low and then lift high over the horse.

Above: Martin Davis of Great Britain has circled up to a straddle support position. This is a beautiful and dramatic move requiring considerable strength and flexibility.

RINGS

The Code of Points requires that rings exercises combine swinging, strength and held elements. It also states there must be at least two handstands, one coming from a swing move and one from some form of strength element.

Dislocate backward

This move is one of the essential basic elements of rings work, and is also an important preparation for the long swing. The term 'dislocate' is in fact a misnomer, as when the move is correctly performed the shoulders do not dislocate but, rather, rotate around the axis of the grip on the rings.

The gymnast starts in inverted hang, then pikes and extends, as in an upstart, in order to raise the body, and in particular the shoulders which should circle forward, up and back. As the body extends from the pike, the gymnast must apply pressure on the rings through the arms and chest in order to achieve this shoulder lift with the upper back rounded, circling the rings until they are straight out in front of him.

The gymnast must now hyper-extend the shoulders and lead the downward swing with the chest, in order to swing smoothly through the bottom without jerking the shoulders. As the gymnast swings through the vertical, he must kick through with the feet to lead the forward upswing.

The gymnast must first practise the move on the low rings, with support, as well as ensuring he has sufficient front support strength to safely handle the circling of the rings without injuring the shoulders. From inverted hang, he can practise the co-ordination of the pike and extend with the circling of the rings, to land on a crash mat. He can also practise the complete body extension and circling of the rings, with the coach aiding the lift of the chest and legs.

When the gymnast can co-ordinate the move on the low rings, he can practise it on the high

Dislocate backward

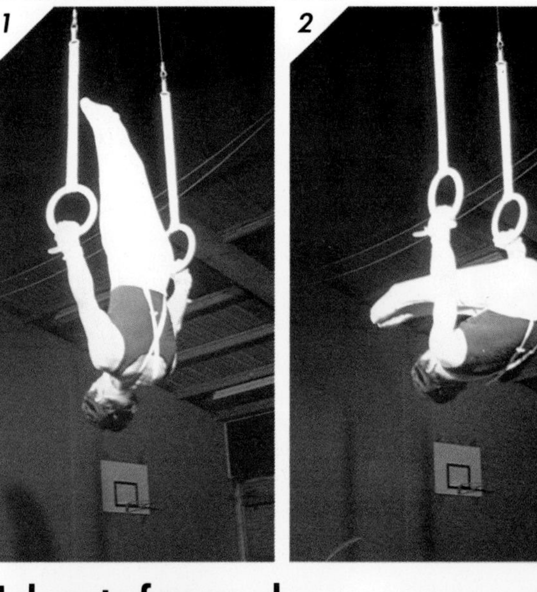

Inlocate forward

rings, again with the assistance of the coach. As an intermediate exercise, the gymnast can practise the dislocate to jump off with a crash mat.

It is essential to learn this move correctly so that there is no injurious jerking of the shoulders at the bottom of the downswing.

Inlocate forward

This is also an essential element of ring work, circling in the opposite direction from the dislocate, and leading on to the longswing from handstand to handstand.

The gymnast starts in inverted hang, and casts out forward by piking and extending with a rounded upper back, at the same time pulling on the rings and then pushing them out behind him, in order to lift the body for a big downswing with the head forward.

As the downswing begins, the arms must be extended, with the rings pushed back away from the feet and with the back leading the swing. The gymnast must lead the upswing into the inlocate with his heels as he swings through the bottom and on the upswing, he must press the rings outwards to lift the shoulders, and then lead over the top with the upper back. He must try and swing through between the wires without piking at the hips, and with the body tight.

The gymnast can practise the inlocate on the low rings, by pressing down on the rings with straight arms and doing a forward roll. He can also perform a piked onlocate from a small pendulum swing on the high rings, reaching from the heel-lead of the upswing to flex the hips and drop the head forward into the inlocate.

Before doing the straight inlocate from inverted hang, he must perfect the timing of the cast out with the pendulum swing. Once he has fully mastered this, then, with the coach to help the lift of the legs, he can attempt the full move. It is important for the gymnast to master the leg whip-action at the bottom of the swing as this aids the lift both for the inlocate and for other moves later on.

Dislocate backward, 1–4: The gymnast must extend the hips back and up at the same time as he presses down on the rings, circling them back, sideways and forwards.

Inlocate forward, 5–8: The gymnast must kick up the back with the heels and press down on the rings as he swings up the back.

Back stemme (uprise)
This move can finish in a variety of balances, the ultimate being handstand. The most common way to learn it is into a half-lever.

During the preceding downswing, the gymnast must push the rings away from the feet and lead the swing with the upper back. As the swing reaches the bottom the legs whip through for the heels to lead the upswing, with the shoulders relaxed. The gymnast must then press down on the rings to lift the shoulders, circling the rings out to the side and under the hips with arms straight, coming into support. The hips then pike, bringing the legs into the half-lever position, with the rings parallel and under the hips, and the arms straight with wrists pressing down.

The gymnast must practise the pendulum swing, arriving to put sufficient pressure on the rings on the back swing in order to raise the shoulders above the level of the rings. If not, he will be unable to come to support with straight arms which is an essential requirement of this move.

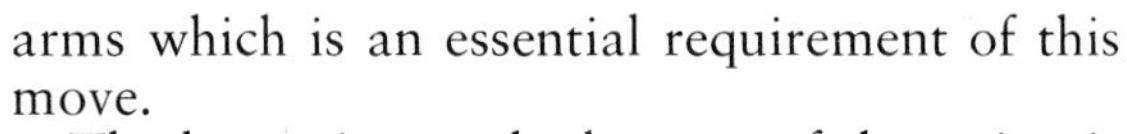

The leg action at the bottom of the swing is also an important element for this move.

When the gymnast can swing well, he can learn the full move with the aid of the coach who assists the lift of the legs until the body is in support. The gymnast should also practise half-levers on the little rings, with the legs parallel to the ground, the arms locked at the elbows with wrists pressing down on parallel rings, and with the back straight and shoulders pressing down. The full move must be learned with straight arms.

When the gymnast can perform the back stemme correctly, he can combine it with a straight inlocate.

Front stemme
The front stemme is one of the moves in the set exercise for the Moscow Olympics, and when performed well it is a beautiful smooth movement, coming into half-lever. It is an unusual

Back stemme

1

2

Front stemme

4

5

6

Back stemme longswing

7

8

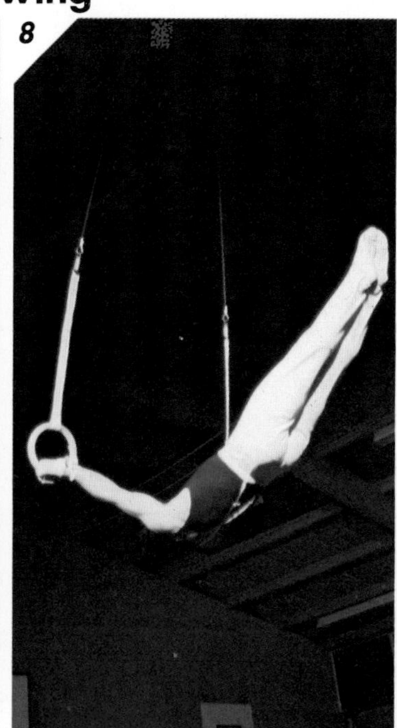

9

Back stemme (uprise), 1–3: The gymnast must kick hard through the bottom with the heels, and press down on the rings to uprise.

Front stemme, 4–6: The gymnast must lead the upswing with the chest, and press the rings out to the side.

Back stemme longswing, 7–10: The gymnast must lead the downswing with the upper back kick hard through the bottom with the feet and press hard down on the rings for the upswing to handstand.

move in that it leads up the front with the chest, requiring a precedent double action-reaction of the body at the bottom of the swing.

The gymnast leads the downswing with the chest and shoulders and as the shoulders relax at the bottom of the swing the feet kick through, but there is an immediate reaction from the chest and shoulders which stops the forward momentum of the feet, and leads the upswing. The gymnast must then turn out the rings and press them sideways and downwards with straight arms in order to lift the shoulders above them. As the hips rise to the level of the rings, the body pikes into the half-lever balance.

The gymnast must practise the double action-reaction bounce at the bottom of the pendulum swing, in order to get the correct chest and shoulder lead, together with the stopping of the feet, for the upswing. He can practise the upward action into half-lever on the low rings by hanging with the feet out forwards on the floor and the hips flexed, and then dynamically extending the chest and pressing the rings down and out to the side, and lifting into half-lever.

When the gymnast is familiar with these aspects of the move, he can try the whole move on the high rings with the coach to aid the lift of the chest and stopping of the feet.

Finally, it is good practice to work the move from a dislocate.

Back stemme longswing

This is a longswing similar to the undergrasp longswing on the high bar, apart from the problems of dealing with the moving rings which have to be pushed away from the feet in order to extend the radius of the swing. Correctly, the move must be performed with straight arms.

From handstand, the gymnast must start to lead the downward swing with the feet, turning the rings out and pushing them back. Then, as the shoulders come level with the rings, the upper back leads the swing to the bottom, with the head in, before the legs whip through to lead the upward swing. As the gymnast swings up the back, he must press hard down on the rings pushing them out to the side slightly behind the shoulders. Then, as he comes towards handstand he starts to turn the rings in to a position of parallel support, pressing hard down on them and straightening out the body with a stretched handstand position.

The gymnast can practise the downswing from handstand on the little rings with a thick crash mat just below the level of the rings, concentrating on the turning out and pushing back of the rings at the beginning of the downswing, and the lead of the upper back by the time he lands on the crash mat.

The upswing can also be practised on the low rings, with the coach lifting the feet into the handstand position. The gymnast must also practise the dynamic leg-whip at the bottom of the swing in order to lead the upward swing correctly, and must be able to perform a high back stemme.

When the gymnast is ready to try the full move, the coach can aid the leg lift up the back, and the gymnast himself can cheat at first by slightly bending his arms to get to handstand.

Dislocate longswing

This move today is performed in a similar fashion to the longswing on the high bar, although there are additional features to the move due to the necessary forward and backward displacement of the rings. However, to be performed correctly the arms must be kept straight throughout, with the body moving from handstand to handstand.

Before swinging down, the gymnast must stretch the hand-stand through the shoulders, with the body tight. The feet initiate the swing, but almost immediately the chest and shoulders must lead the downswing as the rings are pushed

Dislocate longswing

Press to handstand

Honma

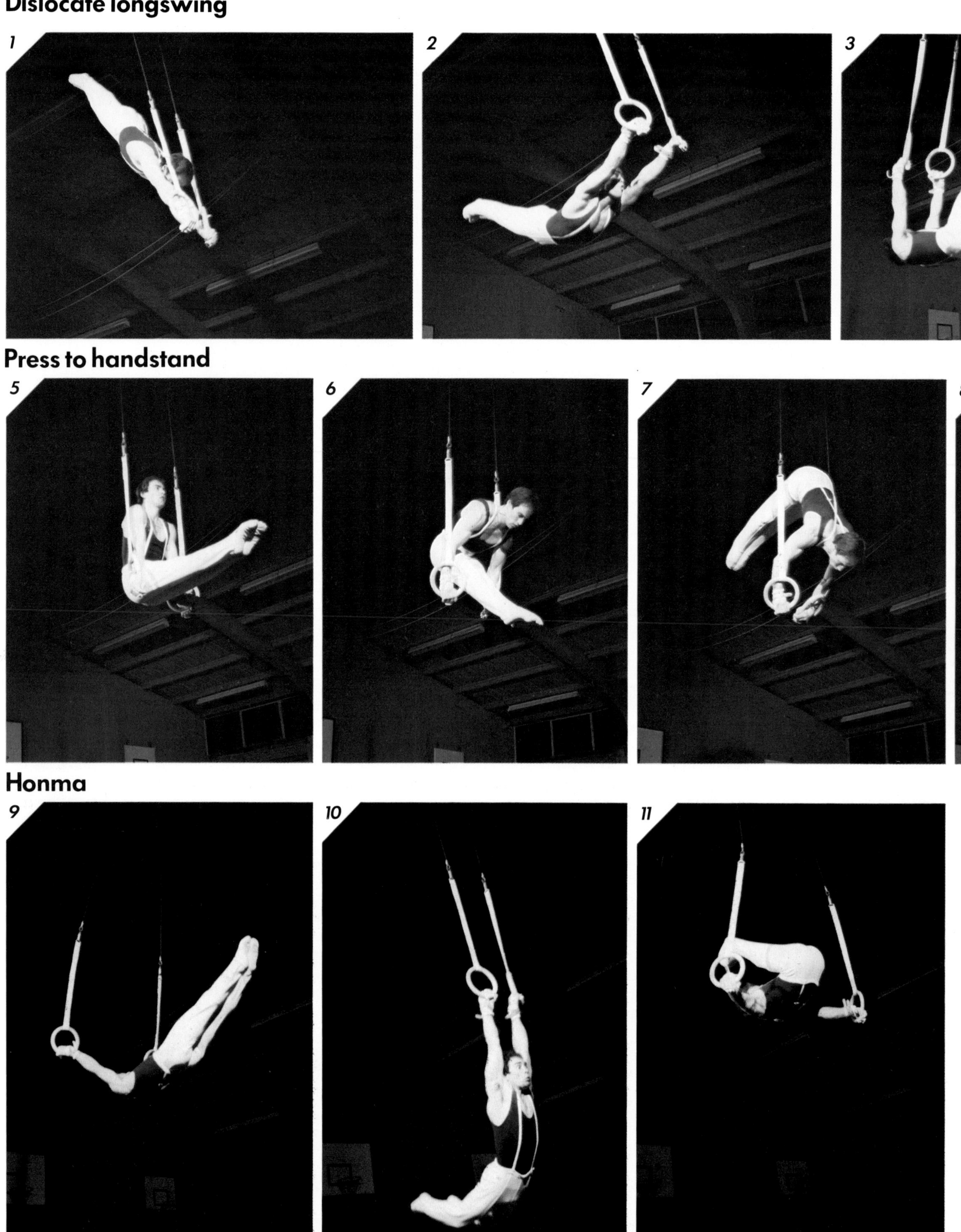

Dislocate longswing, 1–4: From handstand the gymnast must push the rings out forwards, kick hard through the bottom to lead the upswing and maintain firm straight-arm pressure on the rings, into handstand.

Press to handstand, 5–8: The gymnast must first lift the hips then straighten the body to handstand extending through shoulders and elbows, wrists pressing down.

Honma, 9–11: The gymnast must kick through hard, fold into the pike and press hard down on the rings.

out to the front to shoulder-width apart. As the swing comes through the bottom, the gymnast kicks the feet through for the upward swing to handstand, and turns and pushes the rings out, pressing hard down on them to lift the shoulders. The body then straightens, with a slight chest lead for the final lift to handstand, as the rings are pressed in under the shoulders. The gymnast must straighten the body and lock out the shoulders and elbows as he reaches handstand.

There are a number of exercises the gymnast can do to prepare for this difficult move as well as building up the necessary strength during his periods of conditioning training. The gymnast can practise the straight-arm backward roll to handstand and continue with the drop down, with straight arms and chest leading, into a crash mat. He can practise a similar exercise on the low rings, with the rings just above the level of a thick crash mat, starting in handstand and pushing the rings out to the front to swing down and land on the crash mat.

With a similar set-up, the gymnast can practise the upward swing from lying on his back on the crash mat, and the coach taking his feet and lifting the gymnast into handstand. Before trying the full move the gymnast must be able to perform the swing down from handstand, and to be able to hold handstand.

During the early stages, the coach must check the swing down.

When the gymnast first works the full move, he can swing the feet up on to the ring wires to check the rotation, and then press in the rings to handstand.

Press to handstand

This is one of a large number of strength elements that can be performed on the rings; it is also an essential requirement for a voluntary exercise on rings. The press can be performed in a number of different ways, but the most basic is with bent arms and piked body, either with legs straddled or together. The move normally starts from a half-lever position.

From a good half-lever position, the gymnast begins to bend the elbows, leaning the shoulders forward and lifting the hips, sucking in the stomach. The lift must now be continuous, and as the hips come over the shoulders the arms and legs begin to straighten out towards the handstand.

The gymnast keeps the upper back slightly rounded, and as he comes to handstand he extends the body in the shoulders and the hips, with the rings slightly turned out from the thumbs and the wrists pressing down for good support. In a good handstand, the arms do not rest on the ring straps. The gymnast can either straddle the legs, circling them together as he straightens at the hips, or keep them together throughout.

The gymnast can practise pressing on the floor, on the parallel bars or on the low rings lifting or kicking to handstand and placing the feet on the wires at first to steady the balance. He can also practise pressing on the low rings from half-lever to shoulder stand, keeping the rings in under the shoulders, and arriving for a 90° angle at the elbows. Gradually, this press can open more at the elbows, until the arms are straightened. When first practising the press on low rings, the gymnast can have two spotters to hold the rings steady while he presses. This move requires a lot of practice, not just for the pressing but for the holding of a good handstand.

Honma

This move is named after the Japanese gymnast who first conceived it. In essence, it is a front 360° circle from pendulum swing to support, and it is normally taken to half-lever. However, it can be taken into a variety of other positions or moves, such as lowered into crucifix or swing to handstand. It is an advanced move.

The gymnast must perform a dynamic leg whip-action as he swings through the bottom, in order to get heel-lead for the upward swing and for the following hip-pike reaction into the forward circle. The gymnast achieves this reaction by bending the head forward and piking to lead with the hips, at the same time pressing hard down on the rings, turning them and pushing them out to the side, in order to lift the shoulders above them.

As the gymnast completes the circle, he maintains the pike keeping the legs up high, and bringing the hips to the rings. Once he feels himself in support he lowers the legs and brings the body into the half-lever position. If the gymnast intends to perform any move out of the Honma, he must first of all achieve the half-lever position before continuing on.

The gymnast can practise the high inlocate, arising for the shoulders to lift above the rings, with the turning out of and strong pressing down on the rings. He can also practise a high piked front somersault dismount, using the inlocate action, as well as practising the upstart from inverted hang, concentrating on bringing the hips to the rings.

Crucifix (cross)

Crucifix (cross)
The crucifix is a spectacular strength element commonly shown in top-class rings exercises. It is normally lowered into from positions such as handstand or half-lever, and it requires a considerable amount of specific strength training. It is therefore not a suitable element for a gymnast to work seriously until he has reached maturity.

If a gymnast is working crucifix out of half-lever, as he straightens at the hips he must turn the rings out and lean the shoulders slightly forwards of them. As he slowly lowers to the crucifix position, the rings must be pressed out to the side with the grip well over the top of the rings. The crucifix position is not achieved until the shoulders are level with the rings, and the shoulders should then be turned slightly forward but not lifted, with the elbows locked out and the chest extended. The body must remain straight.

To build up the necessary strength to hold the

1

Crucifix (cross), 1: The shoulders must be level with the rings and turned slightly forward, the elbows locked out and the chest extended. This is a superb example of the move by the Japanese gymnast, Kajiyama.

Full twisting back somersault, 2–6: The gymnast must throw the rings before wrapping into the twist. The body must be kept tight and the head in.

Full twisting back somersault

2

3

4

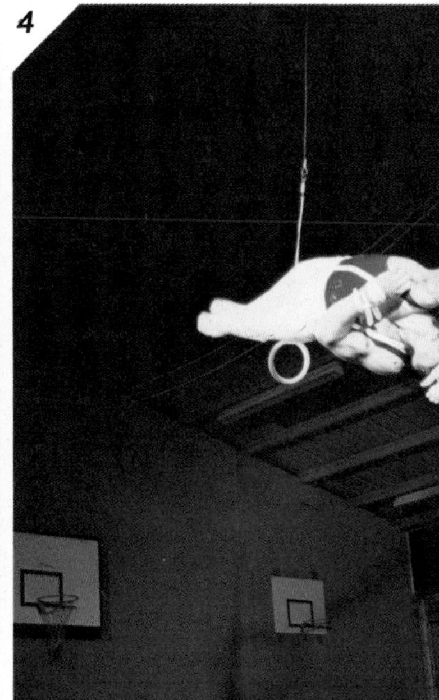

Double back somersault dismount

7

8

9

crucifix position, the gymnast can work on the various types of rings-trainer machines. He can also use an elastic strand, holding on to its end as he grips the rings, placing it under his feet as he lowers from support and presses back up to support a number of times. As his strength increases he can loosen the strand, thereby taking more of his own body weight.

Another exercise is to use the low rings, placing the arms through the ring straps and gripping the rings with the straps close to the elbows, and then lifting and pressing off the ground a number of times. A gymnast can also lower from support into crucifix with the coach holding his feet and helping him to press back up to support, after holding the crucifix position for at least three seconds.

Full twisting back somersault

The full twisting back somersault dismount is a complex dismount requiring good technique in both somersaulting and twisting. However, it is a swing move not requiring great strength, and so it can be learned by good young gymnasts.

As the gymnast swings through the bottom he must kick through hard with the feet for a dynamic upswing, and pull on the rings to lift the shoulders with the head being kept in. The gymnast must release before the body swings through the wires, and as he releases he must throw the rings out to the side. Then, keeping the body tight, he turns the head in the direction of the shoulder leading the turn and pulls in the arms across the chest. As the turn is completed, he raises the arms out to the side to prepare for the landing, maintaining the stretched body position.

The gymnast must practise and perfect the straight somersault and the full-twisting technique separately, before attempting the complete move. The somersault can be practised on the high rings, with the gymnast concentrating on a strong kick through at the bottom, a tight body with the head in, a strong pull on the rings and throw-away of the rings at the point of dismount, and releasing the rings in front of the wires in order not to over-rotate the somersault. All landings should be into a crash mat.

The gymnast can learn the back full-twisting technique, as for the floor and the other apparatus, by making a full twist drop out his back with a crash mat from a small jump; by a full-twist back somersaulting off a trampette to land in a thick crash mat; by a full twist turning from back drops to back drops on a trampoline; by doing a standing full-twisting back somersault with full support from his coach; there are many ways of learning to full twist.

When the gymnast first tries the move, he must have the coach standing by to safeguard his landings. At first, after releasing the rings, he can try just a half twist, and then progress to the full twist. It is important to co-ordinate the point of release with the full-twist action.

Double back somersault dismount, 7–9: The gymnast must kick hard through the bottom. As he throws the rings he must pull into a tight tuck. Photo 9 shows the second rotation.

Double back somersault dismount

Although an advanced move, this is quite a common dismount, being done tucked or piked, or hollow, as by World and Olympic champion Nicolaï Andrianov. It is also done with a twist in the somersaults. However, it is important to start with the tucked version, as it is the easiest to rotate, although it requires technically good dislocate swings.

As the gymnast swings through the bottom, he must put in a dynamic leg-kick to lead the feet up the front, and as the shoulders start to lift the gymnast must begin to tuck. As he releases the rings, throwing them away to the side, he must pull in the tuck rounding the upper back to speed up the rotation, with the head extending to spot the mat for the landing.

The gymnast then extends the body without hollowing, to prepare for the landing, taking the arms out to the side. A good double back will have the somersaulting completed while the gymnast is still above the level of the rings. It requires a high swing up the front, and fast rotation in the somersaults.

The gymnast should first practise lots of high, tightly tucked single somersaults, kicking them out early in order not to over-rotate. All landings must be made into a thick crash mat. He can familiarize himself with double back somersaults by working them off an inclined trampette into thick crash mats. When he first does this, he should have the coach to aid the lift off the trampette.

When the gymnast first tries the full move off the rings, he must have two coaches to aid the lift up the front and also safeguard the landings. He must concentrate on a dynamic upswing part for a high dismount as well as fast rotation after the throw-away of the rings.

Squat vault

1

Straddle vault

5

Above: Ludmila Savina of the Soviet Union performs a fine vault at the Champions All tournament at Wembley in 1975.

THE VAULT

Women vault on a broad horse standing 1.2 metres (4 feet) high. There is no set distance for the run up although in major competitions the length of the podium will govern length of run.

Women are allowed two vaults which can either be the same or two different varieties and the higher of their two scores count for the competition. But in the apparatus finals, they must perform two different vaults and the two marks are averaged to give the final score.

Vaults are not all marked out of ten. The handspring vault for instance is marked out of 9.20 which means that however well the gymnast performs it, she cannot exceed that mark. But the more difficult vaults such as the tsukahara are marked from ten.

The vault is a very dynamic piece needing speed, power and superb muscular reactions. A complete vault takes less than five seconds and is the fastest of all the apparatus.

The number of different kinds of vaults can almost be counted on one hand but generally the tsukahara, the handspring twist and the handspring front are amongst the most common in top competitions.

The squat vault

A powerful, even run and good board take off is required for this vault as for all others. However, it is not necessary to accelerate the heels from the board with quite so much speed, as the body does not have to invert completely.

As the legs extend rapidly and straighten into the board, the arms swing forwards and upwards towards the horse, the body remains straight with the hips tight and as the shoulders rotate forwards the legs lift straight behind. Just before the hands make contact with the horse the body and legs will be in a straight horizontal line parallel to the floor.

Immediately the hands make contact with the horse the arms thrust strongly from the shoulder joint, elevating the top of the body upwards and forwards from the horse. As this occurs the knee

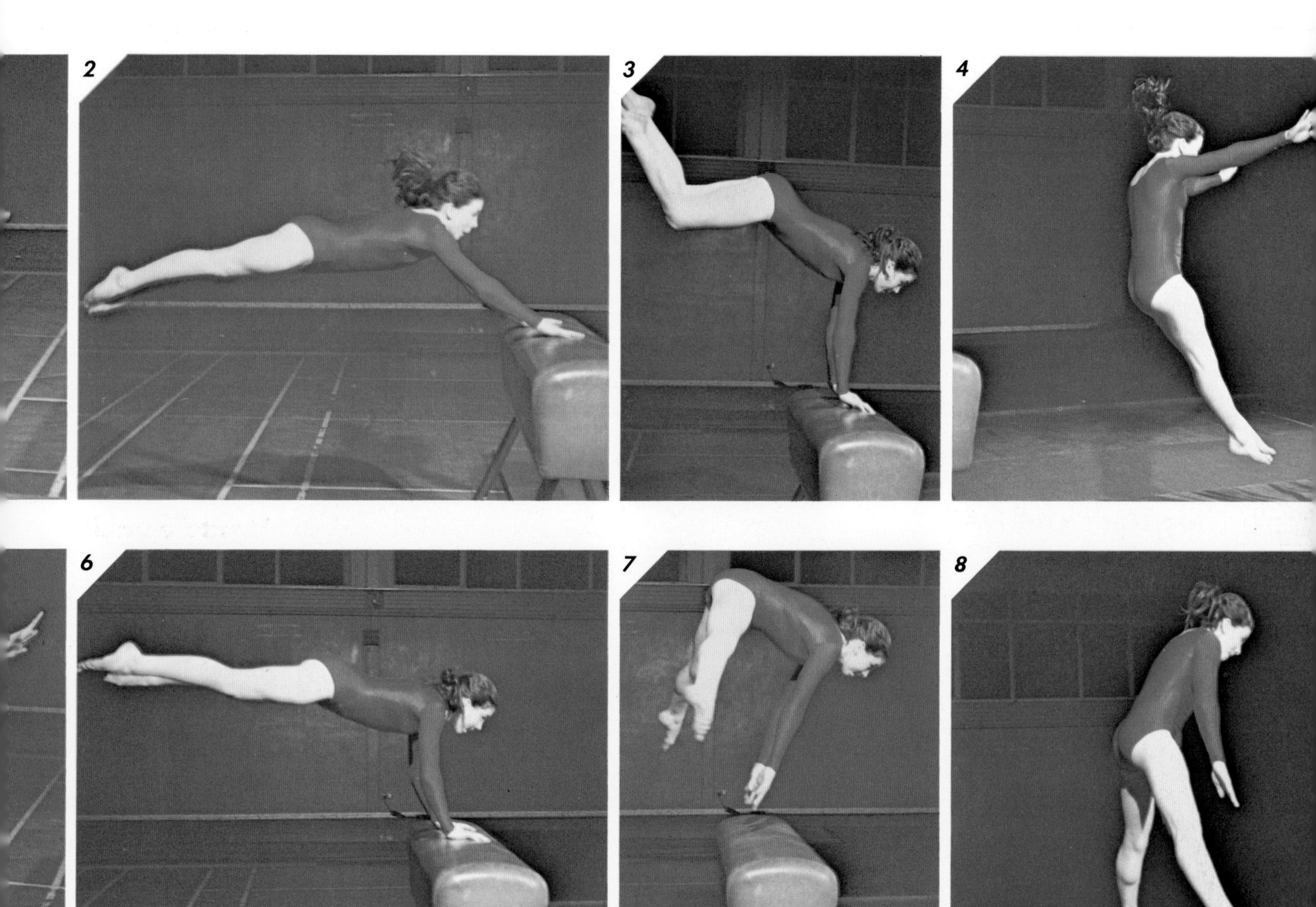

and hip joints flex, enabling the legs to bend in front of the body as it passes over the top of the horse.

The body continues to rise aided by the lifting of the arms upwards as the body moves in to the second flight. Once the horse has been passed, the legs and hips extend forwards ready for landing, the arms remaining upwards with the back straight. The toes touch the floor first and as the whole foot comes in contact with the floor the ankle, hip and knee joints flex to absorb the landing.

The squat vault as with other vaults needs a very quick and powerful reaction off the top of the horse. A good squat vault will have a much higher and longer second flight than first flight, although it is necessary to show a completely stretched body during the first flight.

Straddle vault

The straddle vault is from the same category of vaults as the squat and has many similar features. It does not involve the body inverting and for this reason is ideal for the younger and less experienced gymnast.

The preparation is as for the squat vault until the point that the hands make contact with the horse. The same thrust through the shoulder girdle and hands occurs, lifting the upper body off the horse, and as the body passes over the horse the legs remain straight and part into a straddle position. The body continues to rise in the second flight as the arms lift upwards and the legs join slightly in front of the body in preparation for landing.

The arms remain upward as the ankles, knees and hips flex to absorb the impact of landing.

The second flight should be much longer and higher than the first flight, although the body should be completely stretched with good body tension and straight legs before the hands make contact with the horse in the first flight. Contact with the horse should be of a minimal length of time and needs to be used as an aid to second flight. The landing is the same as for the squat vault.

Squat vault, 1–4, and straddle vault, 5–8: Landings are the same for these two vaults. In the straddle below, the legs straddle as the thrust starts. These are the two most basic of all vaults.

Handspring vault

1

2

3

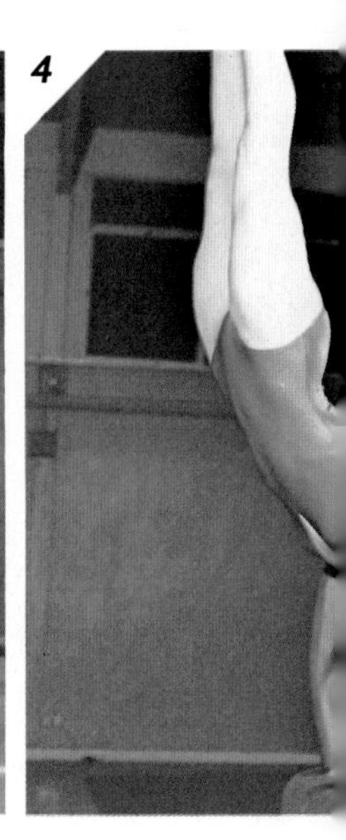
4

Handspring full twist

7

8

9

10

Handspring with one and a half twists

11

12

13

Handspring vault, 1–6: The gymnast runs to the board and springs through handstand on to the horse and thrusts off to land in the same direction.

Handspring full twist, 7–10: In the full twisting version of the handspring vault, the gymnast's right arm drops to initiate the twist.

Handspring with one and a half twists, 11–13: In the last photo of the one and a half twist handspring (13), the right arm swivels with the left arm, to complete the last part of the turn.

Handspring vault
A gymnast needs the fastest controllable speed when she hits the board for take-off. The distance of the run depends on her size and power. There is no official limit to the run up but small gymnasts or those without quick acceleration usually take the longest.

The gymnast needs to stay on the floor as long as possible to conserve linear speed and minimize the deceleration that immediately occurs when in the air. The step on to the board should be as low and short as possible and really the gymnast should run right on to the board and at the very last moment make a late pick up of the second leg for a two-footed take-off. It then means the back leg is driving at all stages thus cutting deceleration to a minimum.

The exact position of the trunk of the body will depend on the size of the gymnast but as a rough guide the body should keep at the same angle as in the running position, that is, it should be leaning forwards. During the run the arms should be gathered just behind the line of the hips. To make sure the body is in a strong position and mechanically correct for first flight, it is important that the chest and stomach are kept in and the hips tilted forwards.

From this position the arms should move directly at the horse with the heel of the hand making contact with the leading edge of the horse. The heels should lift as fast as they possibly can to create maximum rotation which is aided by tension to ensure that the whole body is in rotation.

Rotation and not linear speed is now the vital thing so it is important that the board should not be too far from the horse. It should be as close as possible without interfering with the efficiency of the first flight.

The hands should contact the horse well before the body reaches the vertical position and the shoulder angle should open and extend as quickly as possible so that the gymnast can leave the horse before the vertical. Through this phase, the arms should stay straight with the head in a neutral position. If the gymnast's timing is correct, her post flight should be very high with enough rotation for landing. During second flight the gymnast should appear to be in a handstand position right through to landing.

On landing, the gymnast should try to keep the trunk of the body straight and absorb the impact through the legs. Arms can be allowed to open to help the landing balance.

This vault is the first real progression to twisting handsprings and the one and a half front somersaulting vaults. If not 100 per cent sound and continually practised, the other, more sophisticated vaults will suffer.

Handspring full twist
This vault is a progression from the handspring but must not be attempted before the handspring is sound and well learned. In a good handspring there is plenty of time to rise from the horse, make the 360° twist, open out and land.

The run-up, hurdle (hop step), board take-off and first flight are as for a normal handspring. There are various ways for the subsequent twist. It can be done by turning the hands while in contact with the horse but some thrust is lost by this method and the gymnast risks a lower score than one who uses a better technique.

Again, it is possible to use a pike extension which in practice looks like a wriggle, but it is not a recommended technique.

The most successful method used by most leading gymnasts involves making the twist in second flight. It allows for concentration on a good handspring to maximize the thrust phase and, with the twist in second flight, the body can stay perfectly straight.

As soon as the thrust has finished and the hands are off the horse, the gymnast drops one arm either directly to the corresponding hip or to the opposite hip. The principle of the twist is the same, that is, shortening one side of the body while in rotation. If the right side is shortened in this move, then the twist will be to the left.

The only difference in the arm positions is the speed of the turn. To the corresponding hip the twist is slow, to the opposite hip it is faster. The difference in speed is due to the amount that one side can be shortened but both actions are acceptable and depend on the gymnasts' and coaches' preference.

The head should not look over the shoulder but stay inside the line of the extended arms. As long as the gymnast has completed a 360° turn before landing, the vault is successful. It should finish though in enough time to open out both arms to help stabilize the landing.

Handspring with one and a half twists
To perform this vault successfully a gymnast needs an exceptionally good handspring vault and must be very aware of twisting, as it is a

Yamashita

1 

2 

3 

progression from the handspring full twist. Before attempting the one and a half twists, the gymnast must be capable of a good full twist that finishes relatively early in second flight, thus allowing scope for the extra half turn.

The run and first flight of this vault should be approached exactly the same as for the handspring full twist. As soon as the gymnast has finished thrusting and the hands have no weight on them, the twist can be initiated. One arm is dropped to the opposite hip and kept there for one twist. When this twist is completed, the gymnast switches arms. This means the hand which is on the hip is driven hard above the head while the arm which is already above the head is simultaneously driven down to the hip.

The drop of the first arm initiates the twist by straightening one side of the body and lengthening the other while in rotation. The switching of the arms will aid the twist and at the same time help to stabilize the landing. Throughout the move, the head will do little to aid the twist and is used only for helping to judge a well-timed landing.

Yamashita

This vault is a handspring with a pike action in the second flight and it was named after the great male gymnast.

The run and hurdle technique to the board is exactly the same as for the handspring vault, although the angle of the take-off will be slightly less, to account for the different action in second flight.

When the gymnast makes contact with the horse there is no real necessity to put an arch in the back although some gymnasts do.

With this technique, there is an action reaction which takes place to put the body into the pike position for the second flight and as soon as the gymnast has completed the thrust, the pike action should occur. If the gymnast did a handspring and then put a pike in the second flight this would result in a great deal of over rotation.

Half twist on full twist off

7 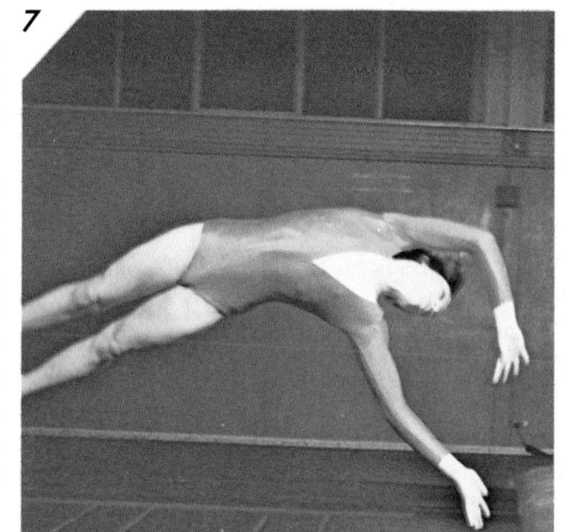

8 

9

The pike action will happen on the way up and should be completed by the highest point in the flight path, when the legs should be opened out so that the body is in a straight line for the downward flight and landing.

The deeper the fold for the pike action the better, but it is very dependent upon how much rotation has been created: if there is a great deal, there has to be less pike.

This vault also lends itself to twisting. Slight variations have to be made to facilitate the twist, and the first flight needs more rotation. The second flight, too, will need extra rotation, in order to include a twist.

The pike action cannot be as deep as for a normal yamashita because there will not be enough time to make the twist action which is aided by the extension from the pike. As well as dropping one arm to the opposite hip as in a normal handspring full twist, the hip extension makes the twist faster, and is the reason why it can be left so late in the second flight and still be successful. Extra rotation is needed because the body is in the shallow pike position for such a short period of time and in the straight position for so much longer.

Yamashita, 1–3: The full pike is reached in picture 2, and by the last photo the gymnast has come out of the pike and is close to landing.

Half twist on half twist off, 4–6: In the first photo of this the compulsory vault (4), the gymnast is making her first twist on to the horse, and by the next one (5) the thrust is completed and her shoulder is initiating the second half of the turn.

Half twist on half twist off

4

5

6

Half twist on full twist off, 7–9: Picture 8 shows the important arm action which enables the gymnast to rotate quickly and smoothly. In the last photo she demonstrates a well-balanced landing.

Half twist on half twist off

This is the 1978 World Championship and 1980 Moscow Olympic compulsory vault. It calls for a 180° twist in first flight and the same in second. As a compulsory vault, both twists must be in the same direction but as a voluntary vault, the turns can be in different directions.

This vault can be attacked as for a handspring but in general gymnasts either make the run a little slower to facilitate the turn in first flight or they move the board out a few centimetres.

Run down should be at the same speed as for the handspring and the same late pick-up of the feet should be emphasized in the hurdle step with the same board landing.

The turn is made from the board and the gymnast can be instructed to turn either the hips or the shoulders. It is important to know which to turn right from the start as the whole body and not just the shoulders must turn through 180°.

When the gymnast makes contact with the horse, she is, in fact, in a reverse handspring position with no apparent twist in any part of the body. To ensure a turn through the longitudinal axis only, the gymnast must think, before leaving the board, of moving one shoulder over and behind the other. It is vital for the head to be kept in a neutral position between the arms when the turn is made. A late turn will help the gymnast to concentrate on the take-off for good heel lift.

The gymnast should make contact with the horse with the arms shoulder width apart and the hands square with the edge of it. Contact must be made before the vertical is reached otherwise there can be no thrust in an upward direction.

The second turn should also be initiated from the apparatus. At the very last moment of the thrust phase, the gymnast pulls one shoulder back to initiate the twist. If the thrust is good and the second flight high, the turn can afford to be slow.

From the point when the hands leave the horse, the head should stay between the arms at all times. On landing, the arms can open to stabilize the body. The gymnast should land a little short of vertical with the body in a straight position; only the legs bend to absorb impact.

In the 1978 World Championships in Strasbourg some of the Eastern bloc gymnasts were trying to get more flair into the compulsory vault by arching the back in second flight and leaving the turn until the gymnast was in the air. The turn was made by moving from the arch to a pike position. The technique worked but in the opinion of the writer it was not truly successful. It seemed the hollow was put in to resist rotation and to maximize thrust. The problem with this vault is that a really good thrust can lead to over-rotation.

Half twist on full twist off

The half on and full off involves a 180° turn in first flight and a 360° turn in the second. It is assumed these days that a gymnast using this vault in top competitions is a weak vaulter with problems in the more dynamic vaults. However, if the gymnast can perform an average handspring vault and can twist easily, then this vault should present no problems.

If the gymnast attacks this vault in the same way as for a good handspring, there is every chance of her falling on landing. If the gymnast runs slower for this vault, she will have less power off the board, or if she has a greater distance between the board and the horse there will be deceleration in the flight due to the longer time in the air.

The technique for this vault is the same as for the half on, half off. One shoulder rotates behind the other, the chest is held in and there is no arching of the back. If the gymnast maximizes her thrust on making contact with the horse there is every chance she will fall over on landing.

The twist happens from the horse and the gymnast must put emphasis on that twist when she is at the top of the horse. She pulls one shoulder backwards very fast to initiate the twist and the arms can be drawn together to make a smoother faster action. The head has little effect on the twist and it stays between the arms in a neutral position.

When the twist is complete the gymnast opens the arms to slow the twist down and to help stabilize the landing. When she makes contact with the floor, the body should be kept straight, allowing the legs to bend to absorb the impact of the flight.

It helps if the legs are slightly apart and the feet turned out a little. This will help particularly when short landings occur and when the gymnast stands up to present herself to the judges. The heels are drawn together to show a good finishing position.

Tsukahara, tucked and piked

The tsukahara vault is a quarter or half turn on to the horse followed by a one and a half back somersault in second flight. It was first performed in major competitions by the Japanese male gymnast of that name.

Until recently gymnasts have had to nominate either a quarter or a half turn in the first flight. Now they only have to state whether the vault is going to be tucked, piked, straight or twisted. In the first flight they must make between a quarter and a half turn on.

The gymnast must run at the fastest controllable speed right on to the board for take-off. The second leg catches up to the first at the last possible point before making contact with the board. This action keeps deceleration to a minimum. As for most other vaults, the board needs to be as close as possible to the horse but proximity must not be allowed to impair the vault.

When the gymnast leaves the board, she seeks maximum heel lift and a turn. Good heel lift will come through late pick up and correct body position on the board. For the turn, the chest will be kept in as she leaves the board, with no arch in the back and her arms will move above the head.

The turn will be caused by moving one shoulder behind the other and the speed of that movement determines how much turn is made. Some world-class performers have used the quarter or half turn on very successfully but most commonly the turn is somewhere between the quarter and half. It is far better for the leading hand to go on the leading edge of the horse. Wrist angle is less and it helps the body pirouette on to the second hand.

The angle of the body to the horse on contact must be short of vertical but the actual angle depends on speed, size and the power of the gymnast. The latest position the gymnast wants to leave the horse is vertical because after that she can only go down leaving her insufficient time for a good one and a half rotations before a correct landing.

When the gymnast leaves the top of the horse, she should be straight; when a body is rotated in a long lever position (straight) and the lever is shortened, the rotation will accelerate. As soon as the gymnast is in the air in a long position, she can tuck to accelerate the somersault to the point where she can complete the move. If she comes off the horse in a semi-tuck position, she will not have enough rotation to complete one and a half somersaults.

When the gymnast is about to land, the legs should open out, the back must be straight and the arms out for balance. If anything goes wrong with the move the result is usually a short landing. If the landing is short, the gymnast usually experiences pain at the front of the ankle and a stretched achilles tendon: to guard against these injuries, it is better to teach the gymnast to land with the legs slightly apart and the feet turned out a little.

There is very little difference between the tucked and piked tsukaharas and if the gymnast can do a high and efficient tucked tsukahara the pike should be no problem. When the gymnast leaves the horse in the straight position, she immediately pikes the feet to the face and holds on behind the knees. Rotation will be a little slower but if the first flight and timing of the pike

Tucked tsukahara

1

2

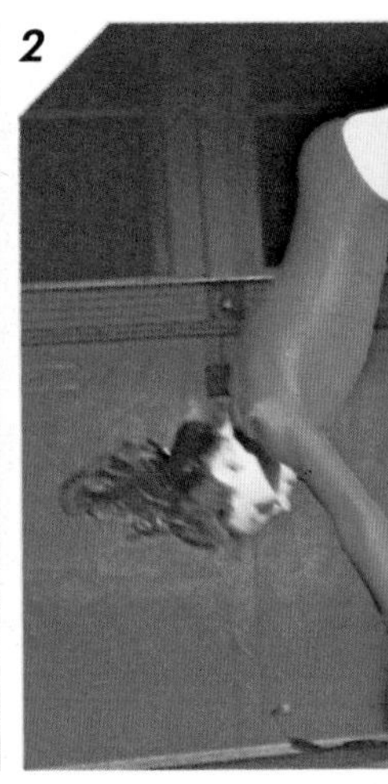

Handspring front somersault

5

6

Tucked tsukahara, 1–4: First the gymnast turns on to the horse, and in the last picture (4) she is seen completing the one and a half back somersault prior to landing. By the second photo (2) the thrust is complete and as she leaves the horse her legs begin to tuck. The tsukahara is also performed piked and straight.

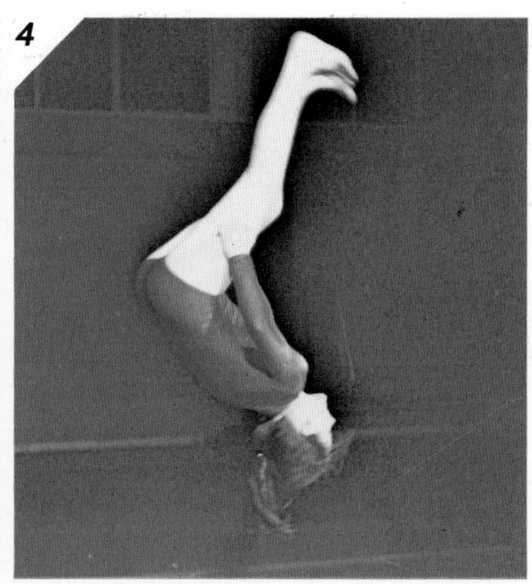

Handspring front somersault, 5–7: Starting as for the handspring vault, it goes into one and a half front somersaults in second flight. A complete somersault occurs between the second and third photos (6–7).

Overleaf, above: Ludmila Tourischeva performs on the bars at the European Championships at Wembley in 1973.

is correct, the vault will be successful. The landing position will be the same as for the tucked tsukahara.

Straight tsukahara

The perfect straight tsukahara should be a turn on to the horse followed by a one and a half back somersault with the body staying very straight. In practice this does not happen as the second flight always tends to be a little piked or arched. This is inevitable, considering the height of the horse, the length of the gymnast and the amount of rotation that can be achieved.

The run for this vault should be the same as for the handspring – very powerful, very fast. For the tucked and piked tsukaharas, the gymnast can afford to be a little incorrect on take-off and still complete the vault, but for the straight tsukahara take-off has to be perfect. This is the point which will initially decide if the vault will be a success. After take-off, the rest of the vault is determined.

First flight should be the same as for other tsukaharas. The gymnast should make contact with the horse in exactly the same manner as before, but from that point on more rotation is generally needed than can be obtained by thrusting off in a straight position.

While making the thrust, the gymnast puts a slight pike into the hip. It is important that this happens while the hands are still in contact with the horse and the effect created should be one of transfer of momentum.

The slight pike is put in and the feet are suddenly stopped, transferring the momentum created to the rest of the body. From this position, the gymnast arches the top half of the back and drives the arms down to the hips. As soon as this arched position is reached, the gymnast immediately moves through to a piked position.

It is almost impossible for a gymnast to complete this vault successfully in a straight position. She has to gain rotation by going through the pike-arch-pike sequence. The very best gymnasts will pass through an almost imperceivable pike-arch-pike uplift. Not so good gymnasts have to over-emphasize these actions.

There is another technique which some Russians use which works but may not be so good. They do not pike when their hands are on the horse, but go straight to the arched position, stay there for as long as possible, then put in a considerable pike for landing. The movements required to do the move are so far from the straight position that the other technique should score higher in competition.

Handspring front somersault

This vault starts the same as a handspring vault and it has one and a half front somersault in second flight. It needs a good handspring vault which the gymnast can over-rotate with ease.

The run and bounce take off is as for a normal handspring and the most efficient gymnast at this stage should have the best vault. Dombek (a well-known East German gymnast) for instance does it piked and, after an almost perfect first flight her body is straight on contact with the horse. It is the best first flight technique for this vault and although there are three other methods they are not so good from the judging angle.

Gymnasts often use these three to achieve more rotation but usually it means they have not got a good enough handspring.

The first of the three techniques on to the horse is a tuck to give more rotation and greater upward thrust than for the straight handspring.

The second method is a pike in first flight for faster rotation and greater height. When contact is made with the horse, the gymnast accelerates the heels out of the pike to leave the body in a straight line.

The most popular technique is to move the heels off the board very fast without stomach tension to give the gymnast a hollow position on contact with the horse. Again the advantage is faster rotation. On contact the gymnast thrusts hard through her shoulders and extends the body through the straight position to the tuck in second flight. The back acts as a spring for thrusting in the hollow position but it can cause back damage if not done correctly. Strictly speaking, the handspring in first flight should be better marked by the judges.

From the start of second flight, the gymnast can tuck for the somersault. In all techniques, the idea is to start a long lever rotating then to shorten it for rotation acceleration.

Once in second flight the gymnast is on a parabolic curve to the floor which cannot be altered, so only rotation is left for consideration.

Some gymnasts cannot get enough rotation in the tucked position so they resort to 'cowboying'. This means they split the legs to get parts of the body closer to the axis of rotation.

Landing is the difficulty, for this vault has a blind opening with the gymnast guessing when to open. The sooner she opens, the easier the landing but the final decision depends on the rest of the vault.

Forward hip circle

1 2 3 4

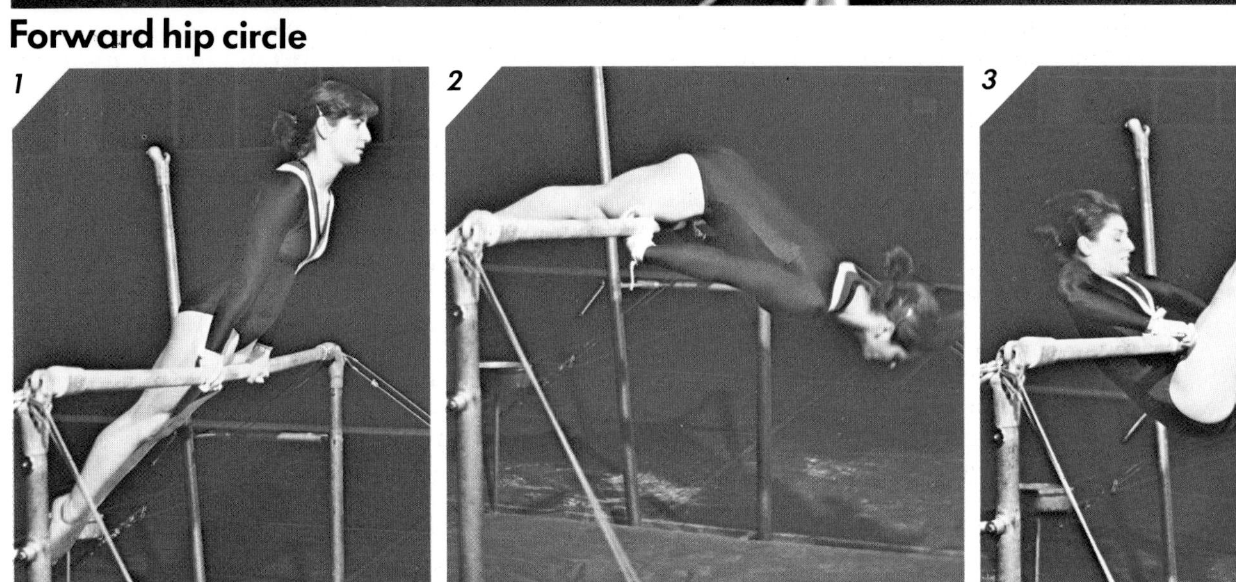

Backward hip circle

5 6 7 8

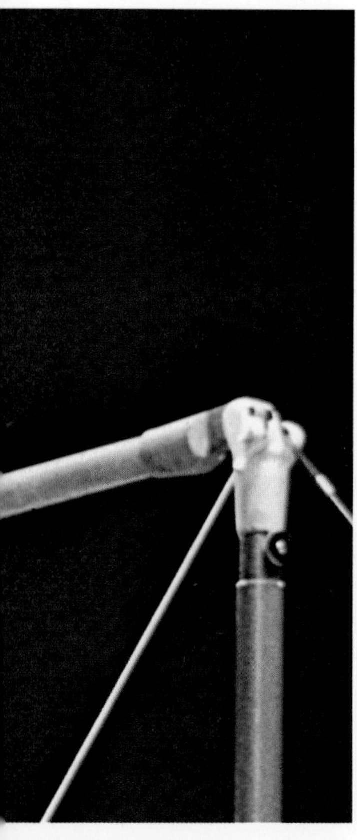

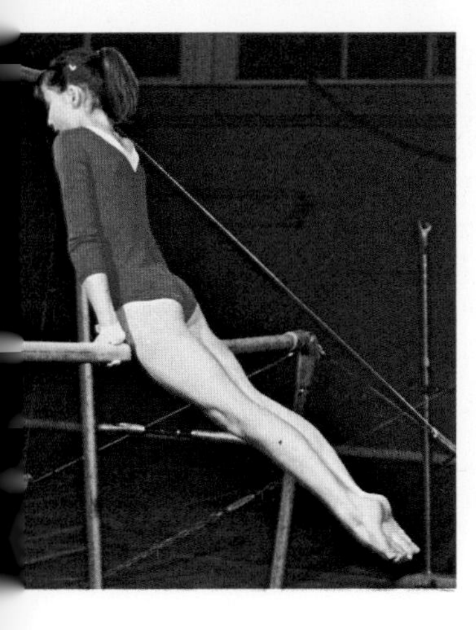

ASYMMETRIC BARS

The asymmetric bars (also known as the uneven parallel bars, or high and low) were being developed in the 1930s and first appeared at the Olympics in 1952. Before they were introduced, women shared the parallel bars with men.

The asymmetrics are a complex apparatus all of their own. Although they replaced the parallel bars for women, the movements for asymmetric bars are in fact derived from the men's horizontal bar. Increasingly, top women gymnasts are adapting the more advanced men's moves, and at many big international events daring innovations can be seen.

At this apparatus the woman gymnast has to train for a predominance of swinging movements and frequent bar changes to include connections with changes of grip and elements executed on both bars. On the asymmetrics changes of support and hanging elements are frequent together with changes in the direction of movement. The gymnast must avoid stops and interruptions in swing – in fact, stops and pauses are almost certain to be penalized.

Elements of difficulty include suspended hanging positions through circling movements, elements with swing to handstand, turns around the longitudinal axis (pirouettes) and around the horizontal axis (somersaults) and counter swings with grip changes (passing from one bar to another).

Dismounts must come only from swinging movements and under no circumstances from a standing position. A gymnast does not jump off the bars. When she falls accidentally, she may continue the exercise within thirty seconds, for the minimum penalty.

Care of the hands is vital on the asymmetrics. Gymnasts wear handstraps for protection. Also watch any gymnast working the bars and you will observe a constant 'washing' of the hands in bowls containing a white powder. The substance is magnesium carbonate and not chalk as often supposed. It reduces the possibility of hands slipping around or off the bars through perspiration. A firm grip is essential for all work on the asymmetric bars.

Forward hip circle

The forward hip circle can most easily be described as a forward roll around the bar. The exercise is never used for its own sake; it is a preparatory move for a more difficult element. This circle is used for moves that need a great deal of leg speed such as a handstand or perhaps a radochla (somersault between the bars).

The forward hip circle is taught to gymnasts very early in their career and it is important at this very early stage to teach the skill correctly. It should be taught in isolation first and then joined by an upstart at one end and another move at the other end.

The gymnast should start in front support on the bar. Shoulders should be pressed down and, depending on arm length, the body may also need a slight curve to it. This should bring the bar to a position on the thighs perhaps four inches below the hip.

At this point, the heels are lifted to put the body in a straight line and by lifting the heels, the gymnast will put herself into an off balance position. The principle in use is to start moving a long lever and then shorten it quickly, thus producing the effect of accelerating the body around the bar.

The gymnast stays in this off balance position and starts to rotate around the bar slowly. The bar will have started to roll up the leg towards the hip and, at a certain point, the friction of the leg on the bar will not be sufficient to stop the gymnast from sliding. Just as this is about to happen, she should pike the shoulders around to the feet and, at the same time, take a new hand position back on top of the bar.

The action should have been forceful enough to rotate the shoulders in front of the bar and, this being the case, the hip should be in contact with the bar and the arms should be slightly bent.

From here the heels can be driven backwards very hard and the arms straightened to give a cast from the bar that is potentially good enough to go to a handstand. If the gymnast fails to get back on top of the bar, it is generally caused through piking too early or too late.

If the move is going to come from an upstart, then the bar should not finish in the hips and then be pushed out to the correct starting position. When the bar passes the thigh at the position that the gymnast wants to start the circle, the bar is stopped. The shoulders continue to finish the upstart and, when they are in the right position to start the circle, the gymnast lifts the heels so that the body is straight and the forward circle can commence. Care must be taken in the move to straighten out of the upstart before moving into the circle.

Backward hip circle

The backward hip circle is used by young and inexperienced gymnasts. The aim of the move is for the body to go around the bar in a straight line with the hips in contact with the bar. It is only used by beginners because it has very few exits indeed and therefore a full swing would be needed which constitutes a penalty.

The backward hip circle can come out of almost anything because all that is needed is a good lay away or cast position. Taken to its ultimate, the gymnast will start the move from handstand but failing this, any lay away that is on balance.

This means the gymnast will not be falling away from the bar, the shoulders will be forward, the legs as high as possible. When the move is finished, the legs have to stop in the vertical position and, this being the case, very little speed is required at the beginning.

From the cast position the feet move in a circle, the hips move towards the bar and the shoulders must go backwards so that the body stays in a straight line. The shoulder angle closes to nothing and the body should complete the circle.

If too much speed is used, the gymnast will go past her finishing position and if too little is used, the gymnast will finish up in a piked position on top of the bar. To begin with, younger gymnasts may need some practice before acquiring perfect control of speed.

Float upstart (glide kip)

The float upstart is one method of getting from a hang position under the bar to a support position above it. The upstart can either be done from stand as a start to an exercise or from a drop action from the top bar. Alternatively, it can be practised with a short run under the bar, as in chapter two. The principle is the same for both so let us examine the technique from a standing position.

The gymnast should stand facing the bar a little more than an arm's length from it. As she jumps forward from there to catch the bar, her head should be between her arms and there should be no angle either at the shoulder or at the hips, but as soon as the legs move towards the floor, they pike very quickly to form an angle at the hips.

The feet should be kept close to the ground but obviously not touching it, and as the body goes underneath the bar, the angle at the hip starts to diminish. Finally the body should end up in front of the bar as far forward as possible.

The idea of starting the body in a straight line and then piking it, uses the long lever in rotation principle, being shortened. This accelerates the body under the bar and through to the other side.

After the extension has been made, there is a very fast piking of the feet back to the bar. Ideally, the feet should be at the bar while the hips are still as far from it as is possible. At this point, the arms come into their own for the first time. They make a very strong forward and downward action at the same time. The bar should travel from the feet along the leg and stop in the hip. It is important to emphasize that the best upstarts are achieved when the bar stays in contact with the leg at all stages in this section.

The arm drive causes the shoulder angle to close very quickly. If it is done correctly, then the first part of the body to pass over the bar will be the shoulders.

At the point when the legs piked back to the bar, the feet should have started a circular action. When the bar gets to the hips of the gymnast, the legs stop for a split second to gain transfer of momentum to the shoulders so that they can get over the bar to their correct position.

The gymnast should now be in a piked position, the shoulders forward of the bar, the

Float upstart (glide kip)

1

2

3

Straddle on undershoot

7

8

9

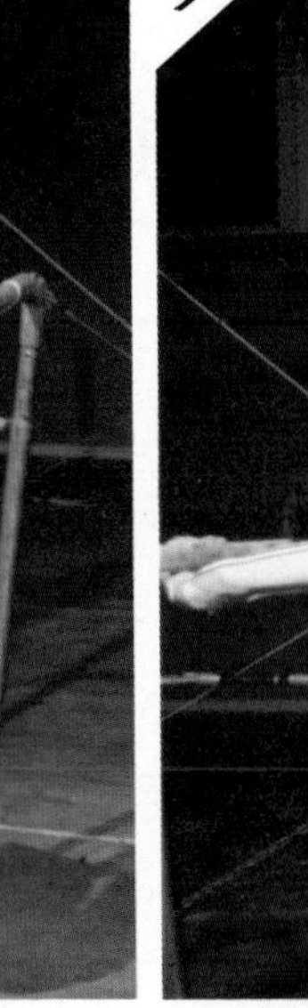

Straddle handstand half turn

10

11

12

4

5

6

13

feet forward of the bar and the hips on the bar. At this point, all that is left for the gymnast to complete the move is to swing the heels back as fast as possible to complete the circle and for the body to finish in a handstand.

Straddle on undershoot

This move can be a medium or a superior element if it is used correctly. For a medium it needs to be completed with a half turn with a double hand change: for a superior, it needs to be completed by going up to handstand, or the undershoot may be completed with a one and a half twist to re-catch the bar which is in itself also a superior.

The ultimate starting position of this move is from handstand, but the junior gymnast should just lift the hips up and place the two feet on to the bar.

If the gymnast goes from handstand, and this is what she is aiming to do, she will take her shoulders forward of the bar and pike at the hip so that the feet come in contact with the bar. At this point the hands are in contact with the bar, the arms are straight, the head is kept between the arms, and the back will be rounded with the chest pulled as far in as possible. The hips should be positioned directly above the bar, with the legs straight and feet as close to the outside of the hands as possible, and the only part of the foot which should be in contact with the bar is the toes. The ankles should be extended so that the gymnast is as high above the bar as possible. At this point the gymnast will move backwards around the bar gaining as much speed as possible by the time she is underneath the bar. The rest of the move is governed by deceleration. The hips will move upwards in the circle to the point where the toes release from the bar. Depending on the strength of the gymnast and the move which is going to follow, the feet will leave the bar when the hips have passed the bottom of it and passed the horizontal point with the bar.

The two most common exits from the undershoot is a dismount and also a half turn to re-catch the same bar.

For the undershoot to be used as a dismount, the feet leave the bar in an upward and forward direction. They are stopped by the gymnast so that a transfer of momentum can happen and a rotation will transfer to the shoulders. The gymnast will also pull hard on the arms to aid the rotation and so complete the move.

If a half turn is required, the gymnast will push the legs out in the same direction as before but will not stop the legs. At the point of release of the legs from the bar there will be an angle at the hips. As it decreases, it aids the half turn.

Straddle handstand half turn

In a routine the straddle handstand can come from an upstart or a forward circle. As the gymnast leaves the low/high bar the arms should be straight, shoulders forward of the bar and the legs moving from a forward position. The gymnast should initially think of lifting the heels behind her, keeping the shoulders forward.

As soon as the body moves off the bar in an upward direction, a pike can occur at the hips to bring them forwards over the bar and the legs will straddle at this point as well.

From here the heels move strongly towards handstand and as the heels move so the right hand is turned outwards for a right pirouette. The turn happens on the spot and the hand moves neither in nor out, but rotates on the spot.

Timing is vital. The second hand should have completed the turn at the same time as the legs come together. When the turn is made, the supporting shoulder extends and turns while the moving arm must turn behind the head and not in front of it. This means the head must be in a neutral position and not lifted to look at the bar.

There are in fact many different methods of head change which are all successful in making the 180° turn. Most of them must wait until the gymnast has reached handstand before turning. At the best the gymnast will have completed the turn while falling into a long swing which must limit the number of possible exits.

The technique described here uses the idea of making the turn on the way up and finishing it in handstand. This has the advantage that many more exits can be capitalized upon which are not possible when using other techniques. They include late toe on, short clear and the stalder.

This technique has the added advantage that the full pirouette is a natural progression, but there is no chance at all if the pirouette is started in the handstand position.

Wrap hecht full twist

1

2

3

4

Wrap dislocation catch with full twist

6

7

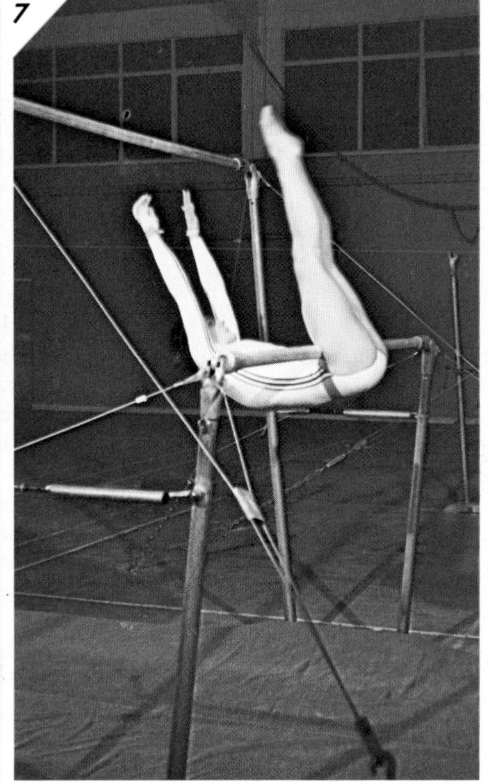

8

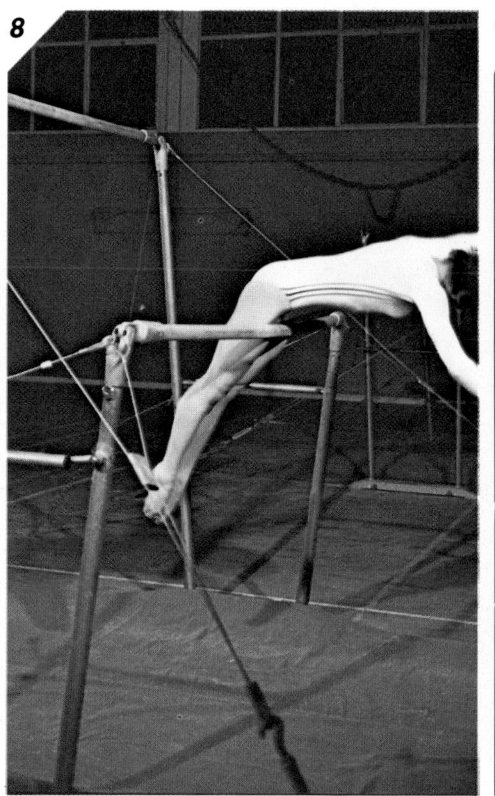

9

Straddle on undershoot, 7–9 (previous page): Note the rounded position of the back, hands and toes together, as the gymnast swings backwards.

Wrap hecht full twist, 1–5: In picture 2 the gymnast is squeezing the bars together just before she lets go of the high bar. As she leaves the high bar her body is

Wrap hecht full twist

The gymnast starts from a handstand on the top bar and moves backwards into a long swing. The body should be straight, head in, chest tight, stomach tight. The feet should not be in front of hips when the hips make contact with the low bar.

The hands and hips are fixed at this point though the legs continue to circle the low bar. The two bars should be squeezed together as much as possible before releasing the top bar and when it is released, the gymnast should start to open out the angle at the hip.

At this point, it is better to think about lifting the heels rather than the shoulders as well, because the shoulders are already moving in the right direction and should not need any help from body muscles.

This 'popping' action of the body should be aided by energy stored in the bar by the compression that happened earlier. Angle of projection from the bar depends on the timing of the opening of the body. If too early, the gymnast will go head first towards the floor and if too late, then she will over rotate on landing and will probably sit down. The gymnast will work out very quickly when to open – it should start almost as soon as the hands have let go of the top bar.

There are various ways of putting a twist in the hecht and one is now described. As the gymnast is about to leave the bar, she pushes one

piked round the low one (3).

Wrap dislocation catch with full twist, 6–10: In the third photo (8) the left shoulder and hips initiate the twist and between the last two photos (9–10) she turns to catch with a mixed grasp (i.e. fingers pointing in opposite directions).

hip into the bar and rotates the other in the direction of the required twist. When she actually leaves the bar, the arms can be brought into the body to accelerate the twist and so complete the 360° required. It is possible to leave the bar straight and put the twist in the flight phase but this is very difficult and needs a gymnast of exceptional quality.

Elvira Saadi, the Russian gymnast, used to perform this move and her arm action was to leave the left arm raised above the head and to drop her right one down by the right hip. This action has the effect of twisting the body to the right. The principle being used here is to lengthen one side of the body and shorten the other. If this is done while the body is in a backward rotation, then a right twist will happen. The technique was helped slightly though by a twisting action off the bar.

The wrap dislocation catch with full twist

To gain the highest marks, this element should start from a handstand position. The gymnast should stay very straight and make a long swing into the low bar. The hips should make contact with the bar before the feet move in front of the bar. The chest and stomach should be held in tightly so that no arch can occur in the back. The head should be kept in line with the arms.

When contact with the bar has been made the feet will continue around the bar to a point where they will stop automatically. The arms and the hips in their fixed positions on the bar will pull the two bars together and so make a spring for the next part of the move. When the hands release from the top bar, the body continues to rotate around the low bar in a pike position. When the gymnast's hips are on top of the bar, the gymnast must 'pop' off the bar. This will be aided by the spring action of the bar which has been created by the two bars being pulled together in the early stages. The hips will be thrust into the bar and the shoulders and heels will be lifted backwards off the bar. As the pike extension action of the hip occurs, the gymnast will press one hip into the bar and turn the other hip off the bar so that a turn will be created.

At this point the rest of the body should be as straight as possible. If the whole body is kept very tight then the whole body will turn in the required direction. If the body is not tight the top half will turn but not the bottom half of the body and a very disjointed action will occur. The shoulder can turn in conjunction with the hip and this will aid the turn, but it must be stressed that both shoulders should be kept parallel and one must not be lifted higher or lower than the other.

If the move has been made successfully to this point the gymnast should have made a 180° turn or more and be facing the top bar. The body should have lifted off the bar to a position where the shoulders are at the same height or above the top bar. If this has not happened all the gymnast has to do at this point is catch the bar in a crossed mixed grip and pull on both arms. The rest of the turn will be made on the bar and the gymnast should have made the turn and again be facing the low bar.

This move is more difficult for the smaller gymnasts, who have to lift off the bar higher and travel further between the two bars to make a successful catch. The gymnast in the photo sequence has judged the lift well, which has put her in a good position for the catch.

A general point: as long as the gymnast can 'pop' off the bar successfully and remembers that the turn must be made through the whole body and not just part of the body turning at one time, this move is relatively simple.

Straddle on undershoot one and a half twists to re-catch

1

2

3

Late toe on toe off to handstand

6

7

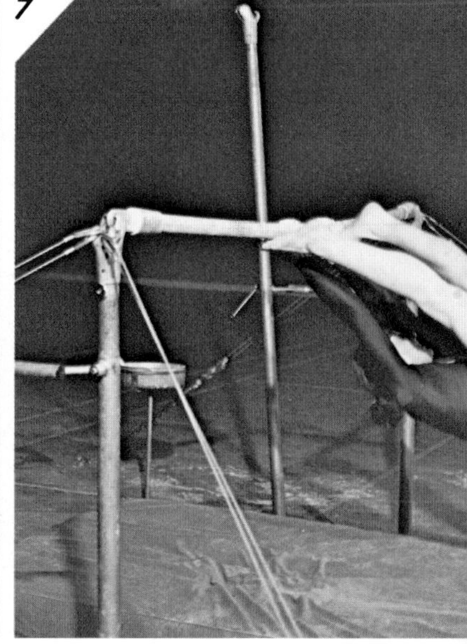

Straddle on undershoot one and a half twists to re-catch
This move should be done at or just above the height of the bar.

The gymnast should think of this move as a half turn followed by a full turn, and not as a one and a half turn.

From the straddle on position, the gymnast moves underneath the bar and the hips move forward for the second part of the sole circle. The feet should be on the bar with just the toes touching so that a good fast release can occur.

The gymnast pushes the feet off the bar as hard as she can, at the same time from this pike position moving the hips into the twist to maximize the twisting action.

The feet should point to the left if the twist is going to the left so that at the end of the twisting action the gymnast is straight and in line with the bar again. If the gymnast pushes the feet off straight and makes the twist, after the re-catch has occurred, the legs will be out of alignment with the rest of the body.

The twist action is set up through the pike extension of the hip. Once the twist action has started it cannot be accelerated and it must finish while the gymnast is horizontal to the bar; if it is left much later than this, the gymnast will have great difficulty in re-catching the bar.

When the gymnast does the first half turn she should finish in mixed grip. This stops the body moving away from the bar while twisting and ensures that it moves across the bar with the hands still in contact with the bar. From here the back of the leading hand moves across the bar while the second hand comes from its mixed grip position, across the bar to a normal grip. This move is spectacular done in either direction but especially when done between the bars.

The late toe on toe off to handstand
This move must start from handstand, and so the gymnast has to be of a fairly good standard to attempt it. It needs much courage because of the speed involved. The gymnast moves backwards in a long circle, staying in a very strong tight handstand position all the time. There must be no counter balance of any kind at this point, and this means that the shoulders or the hips must not go forwards of the bar when the rest of the body is moving behind it.

To explain it to the gymnast, ask her to think of a piece of glass vertical to the bar and she is touching it. When moving backwards to do the move, no part of the body must go through the glass and break it. The body should now be accelerating downward around the bar. When the gymnast has moved about 10° past handstand the feet should be kicked towards the bar itself. I say kicked and not piked to the bar because this is exactly the necessary action. If the legs have travelled more than 10° before they are kicked to the bar, it is too late for the move to be completed because the legs would never have time to reach the bar. If this action is done correctly, the feet will just reach the bar by the time the hips have travelled around the bar and are just short of being vertically underneath it.

The principle in use here is moving or rotating a long lever and then shortening it very quickly. This action has the effect of accelerating the angular velocity of the body. It is important at this point for the gymnast not to allow any angle to be created at the shoulder from handstand through to the bottom of the bar. If this happens when the hips go through the bottom of the circle the angle will very quickly be decreased and the hands will rip off the bar.

The chest should be pushed as far away from the bar as possible on the down swing to allow

Straddle on undershoot one and a half twists to re-catch, 1–5: Starting in the straddle position, the gymnast moves under the bar by the sole circle, and the twist to re-catch occurs in the layout position. Note in the first photo (1) the arms and shoulders are fully extended, chest in and back rounded. Picture 3 is the position before release; the half turn is completed in the next photo. By the last (5), the gymnast has done the full one and a half twists.

Late toe on toe off to handstand, 6–8: From handstand to handstand through a long circle, this move needs much courage and is certainly not for the novice. In the first picture (6) the shoulder angle stays open and the feet begin to kick into the bar. No counter-balance is needed at this stage. All the weight is on the hands in the second photo (7) with the hips under and lifting.

the feet room to reach the bar. There should not be a hard thump as they hit the bar. If this occurs it is because of an angle at the shoulder.

For the right action to occur on the second side of the circle it is important that the hips are in the correct position on the downward swing of the circle, with the pelvic girdle tilted forwards so that the hips are kept underneath the body rather than stuck out at the back. This will have the effect of rounding the lower half of the body.

Throughout the whole of the move the weight of the body should be kept on the arms. At no point through the move should weight be transferred to the feet, as it would be very difficult to take the feet off at the correct point and move them towards handstand.

If all these points have been adhered to correctly the late toe on should have been completed and the gymnast will go through the bottom of the circle very successfully. If there has been a counter balance of any kind, when the gymnast reaches the bottom of the circle the feet will rip off and the gymnast will not be able to do the late toe off and finish in a handstand position.

Depending on the speed, size and strength of the gymnast, the feet will be taken off the bar when the hips have passed the bottom and have not quite reached a horizontal position to the bar. This will vary with each gymnast and her effectiveness on the second side. When they leave the bar the feet are kicked directly towards the ceiling to complete the handstand. The hip angle will open very quickly and the shoulders will press backwards. If this is done successfully the handstand should have been completed.

This move can be done in a pike position and it can also be done in a straddle position. The technique differs only in the placing of the feet on the bar in relation to the hands.

The late toe on action is not used only for the late toe off to handstand. It is also used for many dismounts which need a great deal of rotation for the move to be completed. Moves such as the one and a half front somersault in a tuck position could be done from a normal toe on but it is more successful and can be taken higher from a late toe on. When moved to a piked one and a half front somersault or a one and a half front somersault involving a twist, this action is of paramount importance for the success of the move. Marcia Frederick, the USA gymnast and World Champion on asymmetric bars, uses this technique very effectively during her exercise and also for her dismount.

The stalder circle

The stalder circle is very similar to the late toe on toe off to handstand. The principles involved are the same, but the legs are held in a slightly different position going through the bottom of the circle.

The gymnast should start in handstand. From this position she should move backwards making a large circle around the bar, the body extended as long and as tight as possible. When the gymnast has moved about 10° from handstand a movement towards the bar will occur. As for the late toe on toe off to handstand, the gymnast must not allow any counter balance to occur from the handstand position. This means that the shoulders or the hips must not move forwards in front of the bar which decreases the rotation necessary for the move to be successful.

The principle used for this move is rotating a long lever and shortening it very quickly, which has the effect of increasing the amount of rotation around the bar so that the gymnast can open out and make the handstand on the second side.

When the gymnast is 10° past handstand the legs are kicked towards the bar. They do not in fact touch the bar, but move to a position just above the bar so that the heels are above the bar.

The gymnast must make sure that there is no angle at the shoulder at the start of the move and that the chest and head are kept in line with the arms. When the pike occurs at the hip, the pelvic girdle must be tilted forwards so that the gymnast can go through the bottom of the circle with the hips leading.

When the gymnast is at the bottom of the circle she should be in an inverted figure four position. The arms will be vertical, the back rounded and the legs parallel to the floor. The hips lead the movement up the second side, lifting as high as they can, with the stomach pulled well in. The arms begin to open and the legs are kicked out towards a handstand position. The angle at the hip should decrease to a point where the gymnast finishes the move in handstand on top of the bar.

Radochla

1

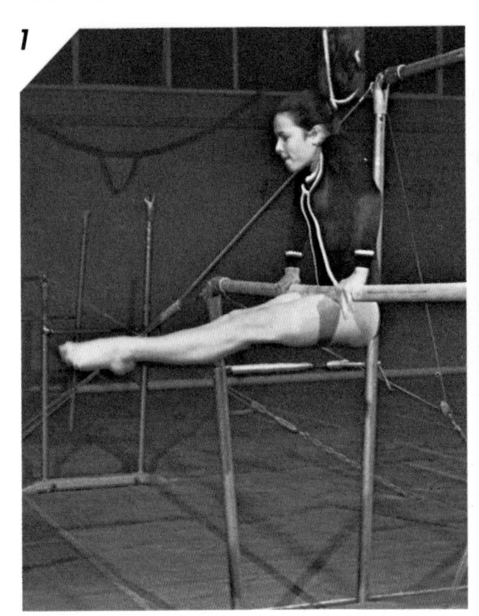

2

3

4

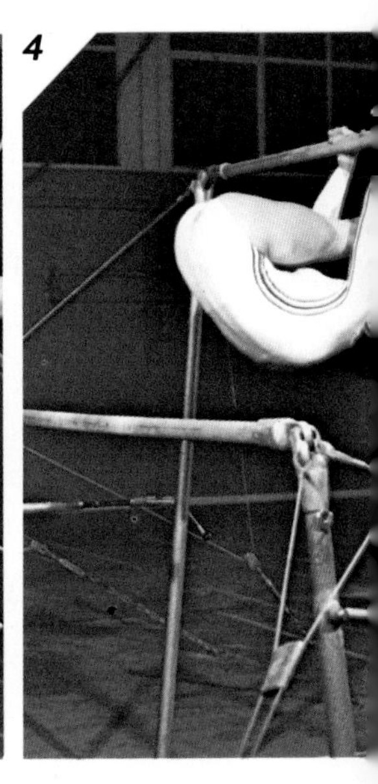

Radochla to re-catch the same bar

7

8

9

Shoot front dismount

11

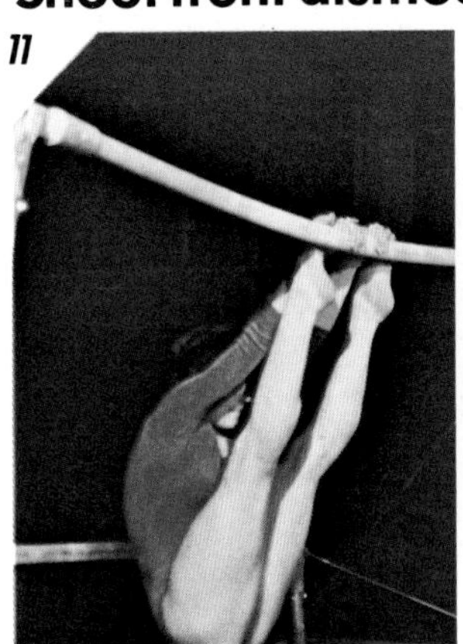

12

13

14

Radochla, 1–6: Photo 4 shows the piked position, though normally this move is performed straddled as in the rest of the picture sequence.

The radochla

The radochla, sometimes known as the brause, is a forward somersault between the bars, starting on the low bar facing out and finishing on the high bar. It is generally done in a straddle position but it has been known in a pike position. The move generally comes out of an upstart or a forward hip circle.

The gymnast starts on the low bar with the shoulders well forward, as deep a pike as possible at the hips, and the feet as far forward as possible. From here the heels are driven backward and upward towards the top bar. The hips will also lift upwards and backwards towards the high bar to allow the gymnast to catch the bar when the legs are parallel to the floor.

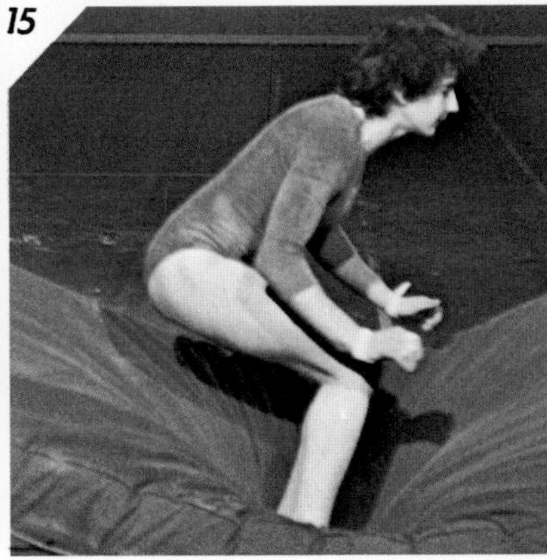

Shoot front dismount, 11–15: A sudden stopping of the legs whilst the hands are still in contact with the bar (12) gives the momentum for the somersault.

When the gymnast leaves the low bar the chest and stomach will be held in so that no arch can happen in the back. The shoulder angle will be decreased and the shoulders pushed backwards towards the top bar. As soon as the gymnast's hands leave the low bar the legs straddle and the top half of the body pikes as deeply as possible between the legs so that the hands can regrasp the top bar. From here the legs are driven backwards out of the pike position in readiness for the start of the next move.

The radochla to re-catch the same bar

This kind of radochla starts with the gymnast beating from the top bar the short way, before releasing from the top bar to complete a front somersault either in a straddled or tucked position and then re-catching the top bar.

For this move the gymnast starts with a handstand on the top bar, swings down to beat the low bar and squeezes the two bars together using the hands and the hips. To get the right reaction from the bar it is important that the gymnast makes sure that the chest is kept in and is not allowed to drop forward and have an arch in the back. From this position the heels are driven backward and upward as hard as possible, utilizing the spring which has been stored in the bar. If the chest and back are kept tight the legs will stop automatically at a certain point. At this point the hands pull the bar up then release the top bar, the legs straddle and the gymnast pikes the top half of the body through the legs. There is a transfer of momentum effect of stopping the legs while the hands are in contact with the bar which will aid the top half of the body to rotate and therefore help the somersault.

The gymnast needs ideally to catch the bar with the body as far away from the bar as is possible. This will allow the legs to drop down between the bars and given enough swing for the next move.

The shoot front dismount

The move is in fact a straddle on undershoot with a one and a half front somersault to land on the feet. The late toe on technique is ideal for this move but it is not absolutely necessary. The advantage of the late toe on technique is that the gymnast can release from the bar that much later and the somersault will rotate well above the height of the top bar. If the gymnast uses the normal straddle on technique or pike on technique, the rotation point will be around bar level.

The gymnast should gain as much speed as she can before she leaves the bar. When the feet leave the bar they should be driven very hard to a straight position so that there is no angle left at the hip. If the legs are stopped very violently at this position with the hands still in contact with the bar there will be a transfer of momentum effect from the legs to the shoulders, which will aid the rotation of the somersault. The shoulder angle will be opened out as violently as possible to get the chest and shoulders up above the legs, and as soon as the hands have released from the bar the gymnast should make as tight a tuck as is possible. The amount of rotation that has been obtained and the height of release for the somersault will affect the timing for opening out the body to a straight line and for landing.

Long upstart (underswing kip)

1

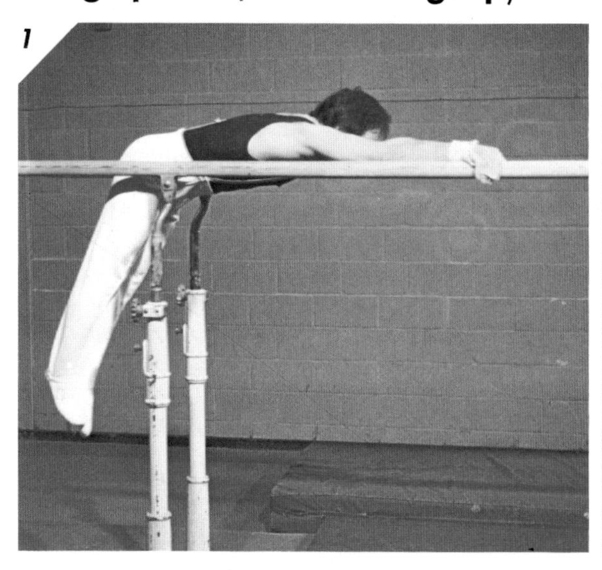

2

3

Above: The Soviet gymnast, Detiatin, performs a flying back to handstand (back toss). Note how the hips and thighs are leading the swing and the arms are circling fast over the top to re-grasp the bars.

PARALLEL BARS

The Code of Points requires that a parallel bar exercise must be made up of swinging, flight and held (balance) elements, with the swinging and flight elements predominating. Flight elements are those where the gymnast releases and re-grasps the bars, and every exercise requires at least one element which releases and regrasps with both hands simultaneously. Every balance, of which there must not be more than three, must be held for 2 seconds.

Long upstart

This is an essential basic move that takes the body from below to above the bars. There are many ways of leading into it and out of it, and if performed correctly the gymnast should be able to swing to handstand from it. It is best to learn the move from the ground, jumping off a reuther board.

As the gymnast jumps off the board he grasps the bars well forward, lifting the hips high with the jump, and with the upper back rounded. The

body will therefore be piked at the top of the jump but, as it starts to glide forwards with the feet kept low, it opens out until it is fully extended at the hips with the body slightly dished. The gymnast then pikes the knees to the face and pulls and presses hard on the bars to lift the shoulders and hips above the bars in the reacting back swing. As the body comes towards support above the bars, the gymnast should extend the hips up and out to get a good swing back to handstand.

The gymnast can practise the glide by reaching forwards to grasp the bars ahead of the shoulders and, jumping off a box-top, lifting the hips with the jump, and then gliding forwards and back to bring his feet back on to the box-top. He can then practise grasping the bars and running through between them, piking at the end of the extension, and then being guided into support by the coach. Another practise is to grasp a low bar, run under it and stoop the legs between the arms under the bar and extend the legs and hips over the top of the bar, pushing off to land in a crashmat. When the gymnast practises the full move the coach can assist the upward swing through the bars, while the gymnast concentrates on holding in the pike and pressing down on the bars.

Cast to upper arms

Long upstart, 1–4: The gymnast must extend, pike deep, and pull hard on the bars, before extending the hips up and out into the swing.

Cast to upper arms, 5–8: As the shoulders drop back into their circle, the gymnast must pull hard on the bars, and not release too early, extending the hips up through the bars.

Cast to upper arms

The cast is one of the fundamental moves on parallel bars. In its simpler form it is taken to upper arms, but it can also be taken to straight arms support, as in the World and Olympic set exercise for 1978–80. It can lead from support swing or be used as a mount from the ground. The gymnast should learn it from the ground.

Grasping the bars in front of his feet, the gymnast jumps up to a position of near-support, pressing on the bars with straight arms and his upper back rounded, lifting the legs quickly between the bars with knees towards the face and the shoulders as far away from the hands as possible. As the shoulders swing down the gymnast must pike tight, and when the shoulders reach the bottom of the swing he must extend his hips forward and up through the bars, pulling hard with his arms, which remain straight until the point of release. As the shoulders swing towards the bars, the gymnast releases and regrasps in upper arms, with his hips extended and his feet high, ready for a long and powerful downward swing. Throughout the 'basket' swing of the cast, under the bars, the head must be facing the knees and the upper back rounded, with as big a swing of the shoulders as possible.

The gymnast can practise the underswing part of the move on the low bar by jumping up to a position of near-support and immediately dropping the shoulders back with the hips coming to the bar and underswinging to dismount. He should also practise the 'basket' swing part of the move on the parallel bars by jumping up and immediately lifting the legs into the piked position with the upper back rounded, rocking the swing under the bars back and forth.

When the gymnast first works the full move, the coach should support the back so that the gymnast can concentrate on the long arm-pull on the bars, in order to bring the shoulders up close to the level of the bars before he releases and regrasps in upper arms. This is a swinging move, and the gymnast must learn to underswing dynamically.

Undersomersault (felge)

Stutzkehre

Undersomersault, 1–5: The gymnast must keep his upper back rounded as he pulls hard on the bars. The feet drive up through the bars towards handstand.

Forward pirouette, 6–8: The gymnast must swing tight and lead the turn with the supporting shoulder, transferring the weight on to the second

Undersomersault

The technical name for this move is a *felge*. It is, by definition, a back somersault under the bars to a position of support above the bars. Ultimately, the gymnast should be able to perform it to handstand. It is a development of the cast and, like the cast, it is perhaps best to learn it from the ground to straight arm support.

The gymnast starts from stand on the ground or on a reuther board, with the hands grasping in front of the feet. From a light jump, the gymnast initiates his rotation by lifting the feet fast towards the point of grip and extending the head back, with the upper back rounded. He then begins to extend the hips, driving the feet upwards through the bars and, pulling strongly on the bars, he starts to open the angle between the arms and the chest. He must retain his grasp on the bars for as long as possible as well as keeping his upper back rounded, and as the shoulders come up level with the bars he releases and regrasps with straightened arms. By this time the body should be fully extended and tight, ready for the following downswing.

This move is similar to the short clear circle on the horizontal bar, which the gymnast can practise on the low bar. On low parallel bars he can practise the rotation and strong pull through the arms, releasing the bars to land between

Forward pirouette

supporting shoulder for the second quarter of the turn.

Stutzkehre, 9–13: The gymnast must accelerate into the swing from handstand, releasing and regrasping quickly, with the body being extended during the turn.

them, without attempting to regrasp. He can build on this, adding the extension of the hips and keeping them forward of the point of grip, again to land between the bars but regrasping as he lands. The gymnast can then practise the full move with the coach supporting the chest to aid the lift through the bars. It is more suitable to learn the move by gripping the bars from the inside, although gymnasts occasionally work the move from the floor with an outside grip.

Forward pirouette
The Code of Points defines this as a basic move, but it requires a good swing to an extended handstand, and lots of practice. It is one of the moves in the set exercise for the World and Olympic Championships 1978–80.

The gymnast must approach handstand with the upper back leading and no hollow in the lower back. As he moves into the first quarter turn, the shoulder of the supporting arm must be extended and leading the turn as the free hand pushes off the other bar, the head in by the supporting shoulder. When the free hand regrasps the opposite bar, the gymnast transfers his weight on to the supporting arm, and pushes off with the first supporting hand into the second quarter turn, regrasping and extending into handstand. This transferring of the support from the one arm to the other is of essential importance, as is the extension of the body in the handstand position.

The gymnast should practise the pirouette at first on the floor, using parallel lines to simulate the bars, and on mini-parallel bars. When he first tries it on the parallel bars he should swing at the end of the bars facing outwards, and swing towards handstand and pirouette to land on a thick crashmat. He must be able to turn square within the lines of the bars before trying the move in the middle of the bars. He should then try the move with the coach to guide the turn. Although not difficult, it requires precision.

Stutzkehre
This is one of the essential swing moves in parallel bar work, although it is a difficult move to perform correctly from handstand to handstand. Again, it is one of the moves in the World and Olympic set exercise, 1978–80.

The gymnast must start to accelerate into the move, leading with the feet from handstand with the upper back rounded during the downward swing. As the gymnast swings through the bottom, the feet continue to accelerate up the front causing a slight pike at the hips. As the hips reach shoulder height, without the shoulders leaning back, the gymnast pushes off one bar, at the same time straightening the body at the hips. The gymnast immediately pushes off the second hand, regrasping quickly with both, the body tight and the upper back rounded in order to regrasp firmly with straight arms.

The gymnast can practise the turning action from back support on the floor with his feet up on a box-top, straightening the body as he makes the first quarter turn and moving the hands fast to complete the turn in from support. The coach can also lift the gymnast through the move on mini-parallel bars. The gymnast should first try the move at the end of the parallel bars facing outwards, to land on a crashmat regrasping the bars as he lands. He must aim to land in between the lines of the bars. He can then try the move with the coach supporting and guiding the chest and legs in the turn, taking it from a reasonable swing.

When the gymnast first does the move on his own he can pad the bars with mats. He can take it from an increasingly higher swing as he gains confidence, but it is essential to accelerate through with the feet from the starting point.

Press to handstand

Russian lever press to handstand

Press to handstand (straight arms and bent body), 1–5: The gymnast must lift the hips over the hands before encircling the legs to handstand.

Russian lever press to handstand, 6–9: From Russian lever, the gymnast continues the lift of the hips until they are above the hands.

Press to handstand (straight arms and bent body)
There are a number of ways of pressing to handstand, but the most common one is the straight arms and bent body press. However, the press can also be done with bent arms and straight body, with straight arms and straight body, and on both bars or off just one bar.

The gymnast starts in a half-lever position, with the legs parallel to the bars, the back straight and head high, the hips between the arms and not too piked. He must begin the lift by leaning the shoulders slightly forward at the same time as he begins to lift the hips and tighten the pike by contracting in the stomach. He must retain the pike position until his hips are over his hands in a position of balance, and he can then lift the legs, straddling them as he extends at the hips and bringing them together in the handstand. As he gets to handstand he must push the shoulders back over the hands and tighten the body, extending in the shoulders to lock out the handstand. If the gymnast wishes, he can also do the lift with the legs kept together.

The gymnast can practise the press, and build up the correct conditioning for it, by using mini parallel bars, and lifting first from half-lever to straddle the feet on to the bars, and then pressing the second half from there. The coach can assist by aiding the lift of the hips, first from straddle stand and then from half-lever. The gymnast must also work to improve his piking flexibility.

Flying back to handstand (back toss)
The flying back, or back toss, is an advanced and beautiful move if taken from handstand to handstand, and it is often worked in combination with the stutzkehre. The main problem in learning the move is to get sufficient acceleration from the feet for a dynamic swing and yet to stop the feet in handstand.

The gymnast starts from a stretched handstand, and begins to accelerate his feet-lead right from the top of the downward swing, with his upper back rounded and minimal lean forward of his shoulders. As the feet swing through the bottom, the chest must be extended to lead the upward swing, thus checking the momentum of the feet. As the gymnast swings up the front with the chest leading, he must hold on until his shoulders are fully extended and pushing forwards, and then he pushes strongly off the bars taking the arms over the top to regrasp quickly and firmly. He immediately tightens into a straight handstand. Some gymnasts prefer to drop the head back early as the feet lead through the bottom; others extend the head in conjunction with the chest lead off the bars.

The gymnast can practise the chest lead from a light pendulum swing, placing his feet on the bars at the front of the swing and extending his chest and shoulders. He can also practise the chest-lead to handstand from seat drop, and extend to handstand on the trampoline.

To build up confidence in somersaulting between the bars, he can place a thick crash mat under the bars, with the bars low and mats over them. He then performs tucked somersaults from a light swing to land on the mat between the bars, not allowing the shoulders to drop back as he releases. He gradually extends the hips and chest more, lifting the somersault higher off the bars. When he first works the full move to handstand, the coach must support the back and shoulders.

Russian lever press to handstand
This is a specialist press requiring great flexibility combined with strength, especially for a good Russian lever with the hips up high and the knees on the face. The gymnast retains the pike of the Russian lever until his hips are above his hands, and he then presses out from there.

The Russian lever can be practised by sitting with the upper back leaning against the wall, hands on the floor with knees bent, and then straightening out the legs and holding the position for three seconds or so.

Gymnasts with the right body shape and good flexibility can achieve this balance with reasonable practice, but for most gymnasts it takes a great deal of work. However, when it is done well, the Russian lever press to handstand is a very beautiful move.

Flying back to handstand (back toss)

Flying back to handstand (back toss), 10–12: The gymnast must accelerate hard through the bottom with the feet, and then drive hard with the hips and thighs, swinging the arms fast over the top into handstand. The photo of Detiatin on page 96 shows this part of the move.

Straddle clips to half-lever

Straddle clips to half-lever
This move is normally done from swing, although the set exercise for the World and Olympic Championships, 1978–80, uses it as a mount from the floor on to the end of the bars.

The gymnast swings down with a slight hip lead, and as he swings through the bottom he reacts with a whip action of the legs to lead with the heels. Then, keeping the back swing no higher than head-height, he pikes at the hips, pushes off the bars and straddles the legs around forward of the shoulders, regrasping quickly slightly behind the hips and stopping the legs in half-lever. When he pushes off the bars the gymnast must not allow the shoulders to travel forwards, and he must stop in the half-lever position without any waver of the legs.

The gymnast can practise the straddle clips action from front support position on the floor, hollowing, piking and straddling the legs round fast to back support, driving the feet forward and pushing the shoulders back. He can also practise straddle clips at the end of the parallel bars, jumping from the floor and clipping one leg around at a time and then, with both legs, with the coach to support the lift at the hips.

Another useful exercise is for the gymnast to clip off the end of the bars to land on a crash mat, concentrating on keeping the backswing low and pushing hard off the bars. Before doing the full move, the gymnast can clip the legs around to straddle sit on the bars and then lift off into half-lever.

There are many other ways of moving into and out of the move, including preceding it with a back uprise and following it with a pump-swing to handstand.

Front stemme

Front stemme
This is a common and useful move for parallel bar work and it is often used by gymnasts to precede a front somersault dismount. It is another of the moves contained in the set exercise for the World and Olympic Championships, 1978–80. The gymnast does best to learn it from support swing to support swing.

As the gymnast begins to lower from support to upper arms at the back of the swing, he must push the shoulders back as he bends his arms, with a slight piking of the hips. When he reaches upper arm support he leads through with the hips and then reacts with a whip action of the legs to lead the upward swing with the feet. As the legs lead forwards the gymnast must push hard through the arms, driving the shoulders,

Straddle clips to half lever, 1–4: The gymnast must keep the back swing low, and drive the feet round hard, releasing and regrasping quickly.

Front stemme, 5–7: The gymnast must drive the hips and legs through hard, pressing forcefully forward, and up off the bars.

Back stemme to support

Back stemme to support, 8–11: The gymnast must put in a strong leg whip-action at the bottom of the swing, and lead the upswing with the heels, pressing hard off the bars.

chest and hips forwards. In fact, the whole body must be driving forwards as well as upwards, until it is in support with the hips and legs extended ready for a strong backswing. When the gymnast is in upper arm support the angle at the elbows must be no less than 90°.

The gymnast can practise the forward upward drive of the body on low parallel bars, starting with his feet on a box-top and reaching forwards to grasp in upper arm support, and then driving through with the whip action of the hips and legs to uprise, straddling his legs to sit on the bars with the body extended at the hips. The coach can help by assisting the drive through of the hips and chest. The gymnast can try the same thing, but without straddling the legs on to the bars, with help from the coach in the early stages. He must also practise the lay-away from support to upper arms at the beginning of the move, with the coach guiding the drop down.

The gymnast must be accustomed to swinging in upper arms before learning the move, and he must perfect the whip action and the drive forwards and upwards of the whole body.

Back stemme to support

Raising the body from upper arm hang to support is one of the essential basic moves of parallel bar work. The correct leg-whip action must be learned from the start if the gymnast wishes to take the move to handstand. The learning of the correct upper-arm swing is therefore of extreme importance.

At the beginning of the downward swing, the gymnast must be in upper arm support with the elbows in front of the shoulders and pressing down so that the shoulders are above the level of the bars, and he must extend the body with the hips above the bars to lead the downward swing with the heels. As he approaches the bottom of the swing he must lead through with the hips and then react with a strong heel kick to lead the upward swing, pressing the elbows down to lift the shoulders as well. As the body lifts up through the bars with the action of the legs, press off the bars straightening the arms to support, turning the wrists on top of the bars.

The gymnast must first learn to swing in upper-arm support, with an approximate 90° angle at the elbows, which should be pressing down. In order to teach the leg-whip action through the bottom of the swing, the coach can stand between the bars at the front and take the gymnast's feet with the gymnast extending his body forwards. The coach then releases the feet and the gymnast leads first with his hips and reacts with the leg-whip for the upswing, and swings forward again leading his feet into the coach's hands. The gymnast can practise the swing on his own, pressing slightly off the bars on the upswing, and swinging down again to repeat the swing. He can also practise the leg-whip action on the high bar, by swinging in pendulum swing. When the gymnast first tries the stemme, the coach should aid the upswing from under the bars. The gymnast can also try the back stemme from a forward roll with the body extended.

Front somersault dismount

This is a common dismount, although top gymnasts normally perform it either with some degree of front or, less often, as a double front. The set dismount for the World and Olympic Championships, 1978–80, is a front with half turn.

The gymnast must lead the downswing with the hips, and as he swings through the bottom he reacts with a strong heel-kick to speed up the swing. As the body reaches the horizontal the gymnast reacts with the hips to lead into the pike, with the head coming between the arms and, with a slight lean over the dismounting bar, he thrusts hard off the bars pushing the shoulders under the hips, tightening the pike and then extending for the landing. It it important for the gymnast not to release too early; he must learn to co-ordinate the pike with the push off the bars.

The gymnast must learn the swing with the reaction of the heels and hips, practising until the hips lift over the shoulders, placing the feet on the bars. This action-reaction can also be practised on the floor, with the gymnast in front support and the coach taking the gymnast's feet. The gymnast then hollows and pikes, and as he pikes the coach thrusts the feet hard upwards and the gymnast performs a front somersault to land on a crash mat. The gymnast can first practise the front somersault at the end of the bars facing outwards to land on a crash mat, with the coach to support on the arm. When the gymnast first tries the move out of the bars, the coach must support the arm and make sure the gymnast travels out of the bars. All landings should be into thick crash mats, and the dismounting bar can also be covered with a mat.

Back somersault dismount

This is also an essential dismount, once again normally performed with a twist or as a double back by the best gymnasts. The gymnast should learn it thoroughly until he can perform it with straight body, from handstand.

The gymnast must swing down with the feet leading, as for the flying back to handstand. The feet continue to lead as the gymnast swings through the bottom and up the front, leaning slightly towards the dismounting bar. The gymnast must continue to lead the upward swing with his feet, allowing the angle between arms and chest to open up, without the shoulders leaning back before thrusting strongly off the bars with the head extended to look for the point of landing. After releasing, the gymnast tightens the body to prepare for the landing.

The gymnast can practise the same exercise within the bars as in the preparation for the flying back to handstand. He must remember, though, that the dismount is a 360° rotation, not stopping in handstand. With the bars well padded, he can practise the dismount to land on

Front somersault dismount

1

2

Back somersault dismount

6

7

Front somersault dismount, 1–5: The gymnast must utilize the heels-hips action to get height and rotation, leaning slightly over to the side on which he is dismounting.

a crash mat, with the coach supporting the arm on the dismount side to aid the travel out.

At first he can practise it tucked, concentrating on opening the angle between chest and arms, and on keeping the arms straight and not leaning back. However, he should quickly progress to doing the move without bending at the hips, although he can bend the knees at first. He must learn not to release too early. When the gymnast does the move from handstand he must start the acceleration at the beginning of the swing, and try to utilize the whip of the bars to assist his lift off them.

When the dismount is high and straight, the gymnast can practise the somersault with full twist, wrapping in the arms and dropping one shoulder into the twist after releasing the bars. This must be practised into a crash mat.

Back somersault dismount, 6–10: The gymnast must accelerate with the feet from the top of the swing, and lean slightly over to the side on which he is dismounting, without dropping the shoulders back.

Back longswing (back giant)

Right: Kurt Thomas of the United States, sixth overall in the 1978 World Championships, showing immaculate form as he prepares to regrasp the high bar, the most exciting piece of apparatus worked by the men.

Back longswing – overgrasp (back giant), 1–4: The gymnast must relax the shoulders at the bottom of the swing, and kick through with the feet for the upswing. The body remains straight as the gymnast swings through handstand, with no angle in the shoulders.

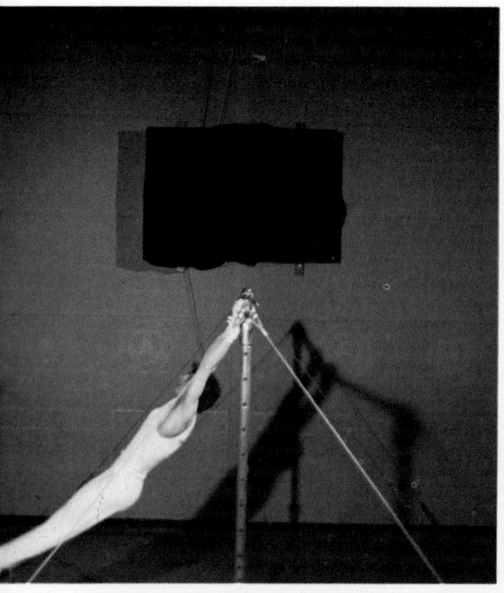

shoulders and immediately reacts with a kick through of the feet to accelerate the upswing.

The head remains between the arms, and as the gymnast approaches handstand he straightens the body at the shoulders and hips and turns the grip on top of the bar, so that he is extended and ready for the following move.

In the beginning, the gymnast will need to put in a clear leg action at the bottom of the swing and straighten out the body as he comes to handstand, but when the longswing is proficient the actions will be minimal.

The gymnast must learn first to beat up high and prepare himself for the downswing, which he can do on the low bar, with the coach to aid the lift and support the downswing into a crash mat. The gymnast can also practise straight arm backward rolls to handstand with minimum pike at the hips.

Forward longswing (front giant)

Forward longswing – undergrasp (front giant), 5–8: The gymnast must put in a leg-whip action at the bottom of the swing, and lead with the shoulders and upper back over the top of the bar, straightening out to handstand.

HORIZONTAL BAR

This is the most exciting piece of men's apparatus, and consists entirely of swinging elements around the bar without any stops. A full exercise requires changes of direction, changes of grip, and many variations of move with at least one release-and-regrasp move.

Back longswing – overgrasp (back giant)
This is as essential to horizontal bar work as the double leg circle is to sidehorse. Many of the moves on the bar emanate from either the back or front longswing, so the gymnast must learn them correctly early in his career. It is best for the gymnast to first learn the move from a beat-away from support.

As the gymnast reaches the top point of the beat-up he must extend the body through the arms, shoulders and hips, with the upper back rounded and the feet ready to lead the downswing. During the downswing the shoulders must be extended with the head between the arms, and as the gymnast swings through the bottom he leads through with his chest and

The kick through at the bottom of the swing can be practised on the high bar from pendulum. He should then learn the full move in loops to prevent his hands coming off the bar. The coach should stand up on a box to aid the gymnast round the bar, emphasizing straight arms and no shoulder angle as he swings over the top.

Forward longswing – undergrasp (front giant)
This is as important as the back longswing and forms the basis for many of the more advanced moves. It must therefore be learned in perfect style, and in order to learn it the gymnast must be able to beat up to handstand in undergrasp from support.

The gymnast starts from support, pikes the legs and moves the shoulders slightly forward and then dynamically casts up to handstand, pushing the shoulders back over the hands. He brings the head between the arms, and extends and tightens the body for the downswing. To increase acceleration for the upswing, as he swings through the bottom he puts in a leg-whip action and immediately reacts with a dishing of the body to lead the upswing with a rounded

Upstart (kip)

Top change

Blind change

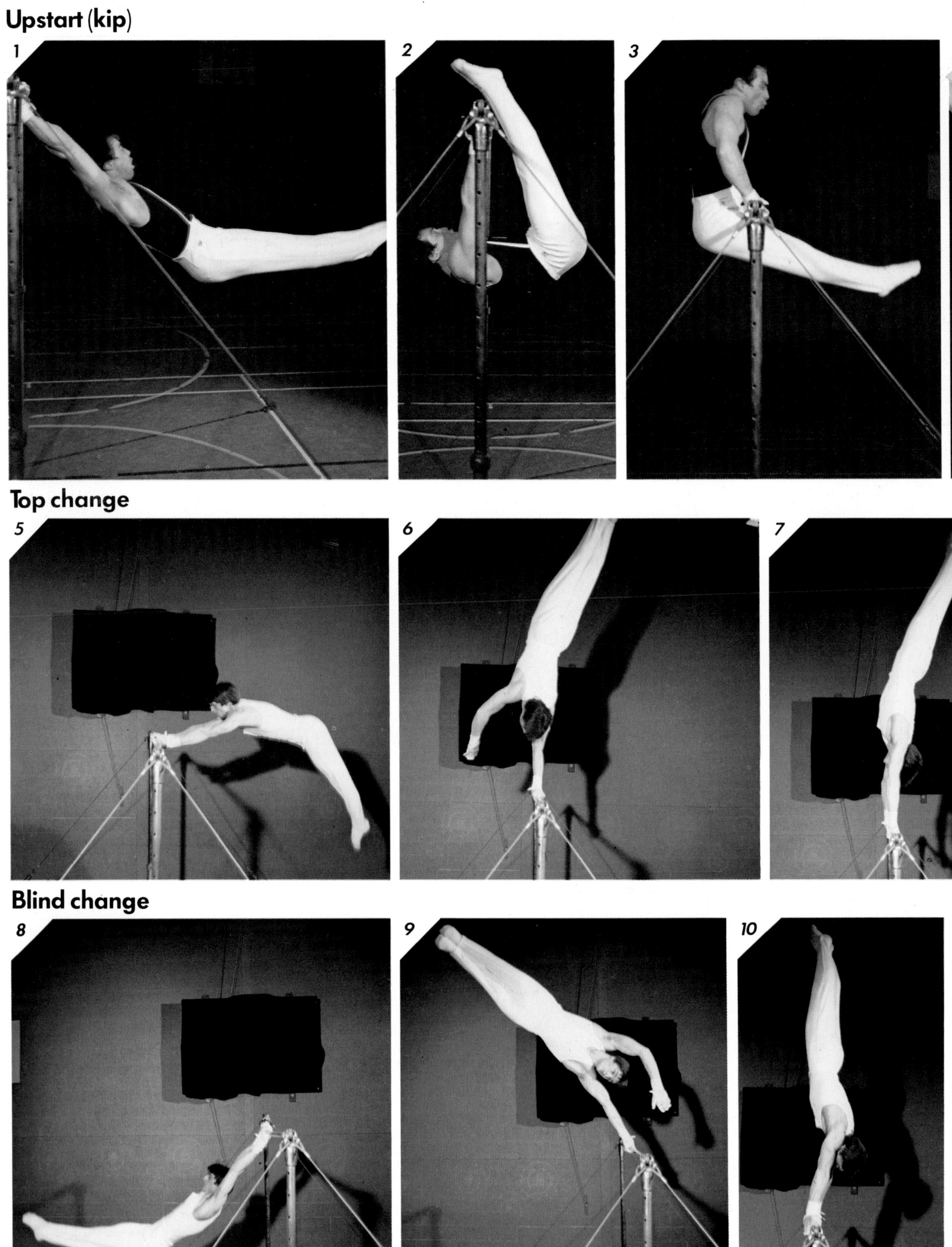

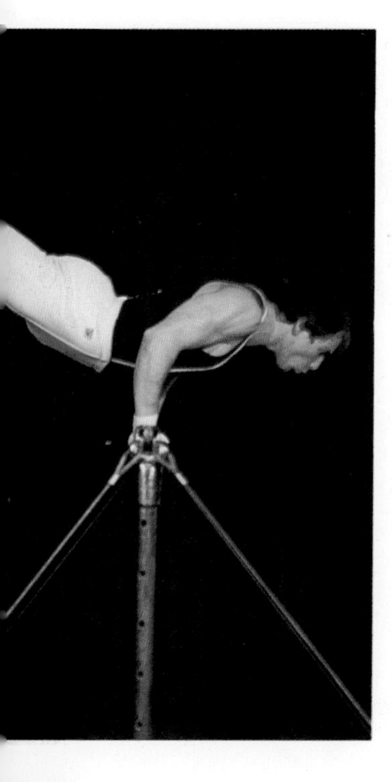

Upstart (kip), 1–4: The gymnast must pike his legs to the bar and press the bar up in front of the legs to the hips.

Top change, 5–7: The gymnast must lead into the turn with the shoulder of the released arm, turning over the top of the bar into overgrasp handstand ready for the down swing.

Blind change, 8–10: The gymnast must have good acceleration for the upswing into the turn which must be completed by the time he reaches handstand. The shoulder of the axis arm must remain extended.

upper back. As he swings up the back he puts in a little more pike, leading with the shoulders and upper back to handstand and straightening out the body as he swings over the top of the bar, once again bringing the head in between the arms.

The gymnast must first learn to beat up to handstand in undergrasp, on the low bar. In the early stages he can do this by bending at the elbows (no more than 90°) as he pikes the legs and straightens the arms in co-ordination with the upward swing of the cast, so that the whole body is extended as he reaches handstand. He then brings his head between his arms and swings down to land in a thick crash mat.

At first, the coach can aid the lift. The gymnast must also practise the leg-whip action on the high bar before proceeding to attempt the full move, preferably using the loops. The coach can assist the swing over the bar as the gymnast concentrates on sucking in the stomach to lead the upward swing with the upper back, and straightening out the body over the top of the bar.

Upstart (kip)
This is one of the essential moves for getting from hang to support and can be worked in a variety of different ways. It is best to learn it in overgrasp, at first to support and then beyond support to handstand.

As the gymnast swings under the bar he leads through with his feet for the upward swing and pikes his legs to the bar and, with his upper back rounded, begins to press the bar towards his hips, narrowing the angle between the arms and chest by straightening at the hips as the shoulders circle upwards.

As the gymnast comes to support he should turn his grip slightly forward and over the bar, with the body still slightly piked and the upper back rounded, and continue with the swing of the body up off the bar towards handstand. The pike of the legs and the press of the bar towards the hips must be continuous and smooth, and if the technique is correct the gymnast should be able to continue the swing up and off the bar in preparation for the following move.

The gymnast can practise the press action on the bar by lying on his back on the floor holding a bar above his head, piking his feet to his hands and pressing the bar down the front of his legs to his hips, lowering his legs to a sit position.

The move is best learned on the low bar, with the gymnast running through under the bar, piking his legs to his hands and pressing the bar to the hips. The coach can assist the lift by supporting under the legs and back. The gymnast can then practise gliding under the bar and performing the move, also with the coach assisting in the early stages. The coach should also assist when the gymnast first works the move on the high bar. The gymnast should then practise the move in repetition – upstart back hip circle underswing, and repeat.

Top change
The gymnast must learn to change direction in a number of different ways to satisfy the requirements for exercises on the horizontal bar, and one of the basic turns is the top change from forward to backward longswing. The gymnast must be able to perform the two types of longswing before learning this turn.

The gymnast takes the top change from an undergrasp longswing, and as he swings with good speed with the last quarter of the circle before reaching handstand, the upper back leading, he begins the turn by leading with the shoulder of the releasing arm, keeping the head in by the supporting arm with its shoulder extended. As the turn is made the body must be straightened, and the turn completed by the time the gymnast has reached handstand. The gymnast is then ready to begin the overgrasp longswing.

The gymnast must be well aware of how to turn on his hands with his weight over his support arm so that the turning is square. He can practise this on the floor and on mini parallel bars from a kick to handstand. He can also practise it on a low bar, kicking off from a platform level with the bar and turning through handstand from undergrasp to overgrasp, and jumping off into a crash mat. He must try to get the turn completed by the time he reaches handstand.

When the gymnast is confident of making a square turn over the bar he can try it on the high bar, from undergrasp longswing into top change, and jump off the bar into a crash mat. Then he can proceed to try the turn with the following overgrasp longswing. In the early stages the coach must stand in under the bar.

Blind change
This is another important turning move which enables the gymnast to turn from overgrasp to undergrasp longswing, with one arm being used as the axis arm through the turn and the other arm releasing and regrasping in undergrasp.

The gymnast performs the move from an overgrasp longswing, and as he swings through the bottom he puts in a strong leg-whip action for good upward acceleration, with the head kept right in. As he swings up the front the gymnast leads with the feet into the turn, straightening through the hips and extending through the axis arm and shoulder, looking for the bar to regroup in undergrasp with the push-off hand, with the body straightened into handstand for the following undergrasp longswing. The turn must be completed by the time the gymnast is over the top of the bar.

From forward pendulum swing in overgrasp the gymnast can try first making a half-turn into mixed grasp, leading the feet into the turn. He can then practise making a hop turn, releasing the axis hand from undergrasp to overgrasp immediately after making this turn, so that the following swing is in overgrasp. He should build this up from an ever-higher pendulum swing,

Short clear circle to handstand

1

2

3

4

Straddle on and off

5

6

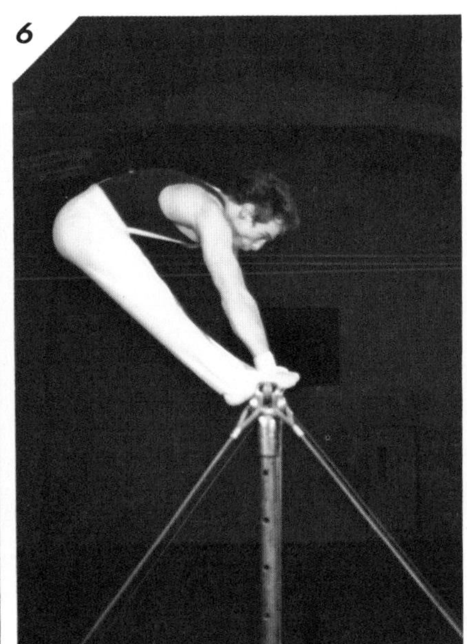

7

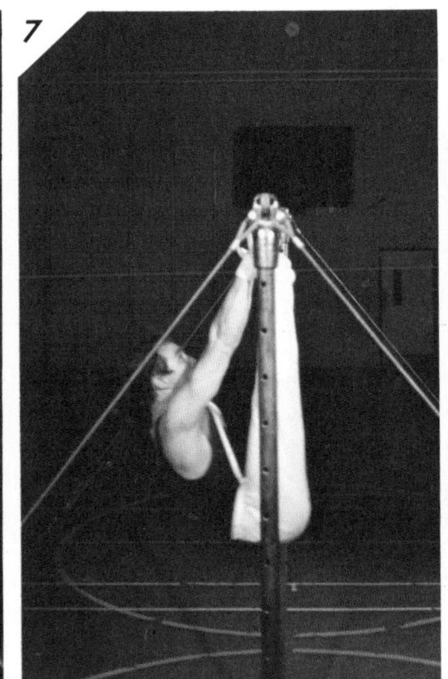

8

Squat dislocate

10

11

12

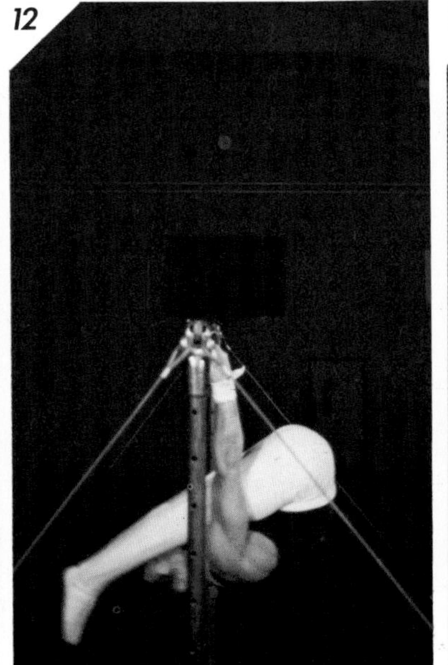

13

Short clear circle to handstand, 1–4: The gymnast must drop the shoulders back into the circle, with the chest in and body tight.

Straddle on and off (overgrasp), 5–9: The gymnast must circle the feet on by the hands, and then pull open with arms straight, to handstand.

Squat dislocate, 10–13: The gymnast must stoop in from handstand, fold deep, and then drive the hips and legs up towards handstand at the same time pushing out in the shoulders for the dislocate.

keeping the axis arm and shoulder stretched.

When he is confident of the turn, he can beat up from support into the swing, lead the feet into the turn as he reaches the top of the upward swing with the axis hand remaining in grasp, and push off the bar when the turn is complete to land on a crash mat, regrasping for a moment in undergrasp with the releasing hand before jumping off. Finally, with a good swing either from high beat-up or an overgrasp longswing, he can turn (regrasp in undergrasp, and continue on over the bar with an undergrasp longswing, with the coach on a platform to aid the gymnast over the bar).

Short clear circle to handstand

This move provides another method of getting into overgrasp longswings and is also similar in concept to the undersomersault on parallel bars, the felse action on rings, and indeed to the straight arm backward roll to handstand on the floor. The gymnast must perform the move with a tight body throughout.

As the gymnast beats up off the bar he must push his shoulders back over his hands to initiate the move from an off-balance position. This is essential, as the gymnast must circle very fast around the bar if he is to attain handstand, so the accleration must begin at the very start of the circle.

The gymnast then circles back in towards the bar with the upper back slightly rounded, the feet moving fast and the shoulders dropping back to lead the swing. As the gymnast swings down, the angle between arms and chest must remain closed, with the body tight and dished. After the shoulders have passed through the bottom of the circle, the gymnast must direct the feet upwards, opening the angle between arms and chest and straightening at the hips. During this extending stage, the chest must be kept in with the body remaining tight with no hollow in the back, and as the gymnast reaches handstand the handgrip must be turned over the bar.

This move should be learned on the low bar. First, the gymnast can learn to perform the back hip circle round the bar, beating up off the bar, and circling round it with the upper back rounded and the shoulder-angle remaining closed. As he circles round the bar he must always endeavour to keep the body clear of the bar until he returns to support.

He can then learn to underswing and dismount, by starting to open the shoulder-angle as he swings under the bar and directing the feet forward and up, away from the bar and releasing to land on a crash mat.

He can also practise the backward roll to handstand with straight arms to familiarize himself with the opening of the shoulder-angle and the directing upwards of the feet.

Finally he can do the full move on the low bar, with the coach on a low platform taking the feet as they move upwards and pulling the gymnast into handstand. The gymnast must keep his arms straight throughout the move. This move must be practised on the low bar until it is perfected.

Straddle on and off (overgrasp)

This is one of the more basic circling moves, which looks very elegant if it comes on high and lifts off to handstand. It can also be done as a stoop on with the feet between the hands. The move normally comes from an overgrasp longswing.

As the gymnast kicks through the bottom and swings up the front he starts to pike at the hips, but with the shoulders remaining extended. When the swing comes over the top of the bar, the gymnast must round the upper back and pike the feet towards the bar, still with the shoulders extended to keep the hips as far away from the bar as possible.

The gymnast places the feet on the bar just outside the hands, bringing the head forward and folding into a deep pike as he swings under the bar. During the upward swing the gymnast begins to pull open the angle at the shoulders and the hips, arms remaining straight as the legs circle towards a tight handstand position by the time the body is moving over the top of the bar into the following swing. The arms must remain straight throughout the move.

The gymnast can do much of his practise for this move on the low bar. First, he can beat up, straddle his feet on to the bar and circle under, pushing his hips away with rounded upper back, and underswing off into a crash mat. Then he can sole circle round the bar, starting from as high a beat-up as possible, and bending his legs at first on the upward swing to come back over the top of the bar.

He can do this exercise in repetitions of four or five and as he gains confidence he can practise opening the hip and shoulder angles to lift the feet off the bar.

When he is familiar with the move on the low bar, he can put it on the high bar, using loops, and straddling on from longswing. In the early stages it is better to lift the feet off too late rather than too early, and to learn to time the lift-off to handstand.

Squat dislocate

This is a complex move that can lead into a wide range of interesting combinations. Because of the dislocating action in the shoulders, it is performed best by those gymnasts who have supple shoulders and do not need to push their hands out wide when extending out of the move.

As the gymnast swings up the back in undergrasp he must put in a heel-whip action to lead with the heels, and as he approaches handstand he rounds the upper back and, with the shoulders extended away from the bar, he stoops the legs in deep between the arms bringing the knees to the face.

The shoulders should be circling fast and as the gymnast begins his upward swing he must start to drive the hips upwards and turn his grip over the

Pirouette to catch

Front somersault with half turn

Double back somersault

Pirouette to catch, 1–4: The gymnast must press strongly on the bar for the uprise, lead with the releasing shoulder into the turn, and regrasp fast.

bar and push the bar down and behind him, all in one smooth action. At the height of the extension the shoulders are dislocated, the head is in, and the gymnast begins to circle in an elgrip long-swing. The full extension should be attained just beyond handstand.

When learning this move the gymnast must work on shoulder flexibility as it requires supple shoulders. He should perform dislocating exercises at the wall bars or with an elastic strand.

Once again, much of the learning can be done on the low bar. First, the gymnast, in overgrasp, can run through under the bar, stoop the legs under the bar and, as he swings back up and forward, sit on the bar. He can then take this to shoot the hips and legs up and over the bar to land on a crash mat.

The next stage is to sit on the bar, in undergrasp, push the hips up off the bar until the angles are by the hands, and then do a stoop circle round and over the top of the bar to land on a crash mat. Then, beat up in undergrasp, stoop in, circle and extend out still grasping the bar to land on a thick crash mat, with the coach behind the gymnast to make sure the shoulders travel over the top of the bar.

The gymnast can do the same exercise with higher extension of the hips and put in the dislocation of the shoulders, again with the coach's assistance. When the hip and shoulder actions are smooth and co-ordinated, with the body extending in a higher position, the gymnast can try the move on the high bar, with thick crash mats and help from the coach.

Pirouette to catch

This is an example of a release and regrasp move that the Code requires a gymnast to have in his routine. It can be performed from either overgrasp or mixed grasp, and it is the first move of the

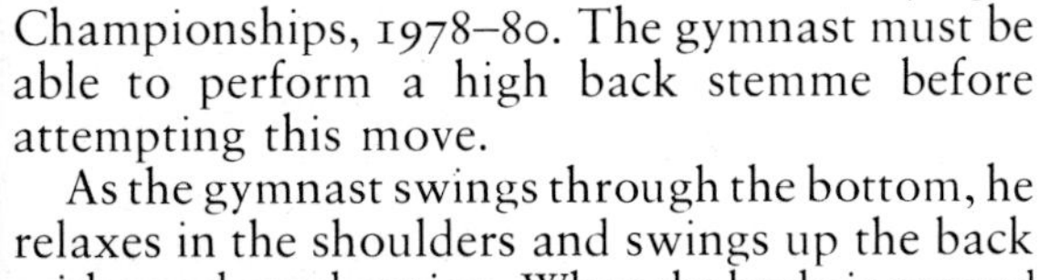

set exercise for the World and Olympic Championships, 1978–80. The gymnast must be able to perform a high back stemme before attempting this move.

As the gymnast swings through the bottom, he relaxes in the shoulders and swings up the back with good acceleration. When the body is around 45° from the horizontal, the gymnast leads his head into the turn, releasing one hand, putting the elbow into the turn and pulling down on the bar with the other arm straight. He almost immediately presses off the bar with the second hand, with the first arm tucked in by the body, spots the bar and regrasps fast with overgrasp.

The body must remain tight during the turn, with the shoulders tightened as the gymnast regrasps. He must keep the arms straight during the upswing and not pull the body into the bar.

To practise the turn, the gymnast can place a crash mat up against a wall, place the hands on it and lean away from it in front support, push off mat/wall and make the turn back to inclined front support. The gymnast must also practise the back stemme and press off the bar from a good pendulum swing, quickly regrasping and swinging back down.

When the gymnast is confident of the turning technique, he can try the pirouette from a large pendulum swing, and jump down on to a crash mat without regrasping, with the coach standing by. Finally, making sure the arms are kept straight on the upswing, the gymnast can practise the pirouette to regrasp. The coach should support the gymnast after the turn.

Front somersault with half turn, 5–9: The gymnast requires a good leg-whip into the upswing, pressing hard on the bar. After releasing, he leads the head and shoulder into the turn.

Double back somersault, 10–15: The gymnast must kick through hard for a high dismount, and after releasing pull into a tight tuck with the upper back rounded.

Front somersault with half turn

This is one of a number of moves which release the bar from an undergrasp longswing, and it is the dismount for the World and Olympic set exercise, 1978–80. It requires a strong leg-whip action during the swing under the bar.

As the gymnast swings over the top of the bar he puts in a slight leg-whip action, following the lead of the shoulders over the bar with a heel-kick to accelerate the downswing. As he approaches the bottom of the downswing he puts in a slight pike to lead with the hips, shoulders extended, and reacts once again with a heel-kick to lead the upswing, with the head in between the arms. As the gymnast presses off the bar he leads the turn with the head, spotting the point of landing, dropping the following arm across the chest, and then extending the arms and straightening the body in preparation for the landing.

The gymnast must first perfect the leg-whip action under the bar, from pendulum swing. He can then practise the front dismount, leading the heel-kick into a tucked position, with shoulders relaxed under the bar, to land on a crash mat.

The front dismount must now be built up until it can be performed with the body extended and taken from a longswing. The gymnast must concentrate on increasing the acceleration in the downswing, and on putting in a powerful whip-action under the bar. The gymnast can then put in the half turn, leading the turn with the head and straightening the body after releasing the bar, spotting the point of landing early.

When practising the move, the gymnast must have a thick crash mat for landing, and if necessary can learn it in a safety belt.

Double back somersault

The back somersault is the most common dismount, performed in many different forms. Variations of the double back are the most popular.

The gymnast must build up speed from the preceding longswing, and as he swings over the top of the bar he puts in a slight pike for the downswing with the shoulders extended. As he approaches the bottom of the swing he reacts by extending the body and leading through with the chest, with shoulders relaxed and head between the arms, and then reacts again with a kick through the legs to build up acceleration for a high dismount.

At the point of release the gymnast must extend through the shoulders and chest, throw the bar away, and then, dropping the head back, pull tightly into the tucked position with the upper back rounded. Once the first somersault is completed the gymnast must look for the mat to spot the landing, and then straighten out the body with the arms to the side to prepare for it.

The back away is an exciting but frightening move, and is best learned with a pit or an overhead spotting belt. First the gymnast must learn the whip-action under the bar, which he can do from pendulum swing with a pike-hollow-kick through and throw away of the bar without somersaulting, to land on a crash mat. He can then learn the toddler, or backaway from pendulum swing, making sure he extends the shoulders when releasing the bar. The coach can support on the upper back to aid the direction of release. The gymnast then builds up the backaway from beat-up off the bar, and, following that, from longswing, until he can perform a good high dismount, both tucked and straight.

Only then should he proceed to the double back, which he can do from a high pendulum swing, with the coach's support, into a thick crash mat.

Half turn (180°) on two feet

Full turn

1

2

3

BALANCE BEAM

The balance beam is so called because the essential requirement is balance or counterweight. Even the slightest inclination to one side must be balanced out on the other.

Difficult elements must be spread out through the exercise, with harmonious and dynamic link moves between every element of difficulty. Basic requirements are turns and pivots (at least one 360° turn), leaps, jumps, hops, skips and running combinations. Repetition of elements must be avoided and so should excessive sitting and lying positions.

A few momentary stops are permitted during a routine, but they must be planned pauses such as head or shoulder stands, support positions, or points in a routine where a pause enlivens the interest in the same way as a comma in a paragraph of text. The most common pausing fault is a deliberate stop before the standing back somersault or similar element. Such a pause hits you like a verbal announcement from the beam saying that the gymnast is about to attempt a movement of superior difficulty. Judges may penalize a gymnast by up to two-tenths of a mark for such an interruption.

Duration of the beam exercise is from one minute fifteen seconds to one minute thirty-five seconds, with a warning by whistle or bell at ninety seconds and again at ninety-five. Time penalties are incurred for under and over time and elements performed after the time is up are not evaluated.

Beam exercises are learnt on the floor, and apparatus progression is to a bench and a low beam before trying the four-inches-wide (10 cm) beam four feet (1.2 m) from the ground.

Below: The suppleness needed to perform gymnastic feats is evident here in this photograph of Nadia Comaneci.

Full turn, 1–4: The full beam turn is done in one movement, maintaining good posture, with shoulders over the hips through the turn. Note the supporting leg position through the move and the way it is lowered on completion.

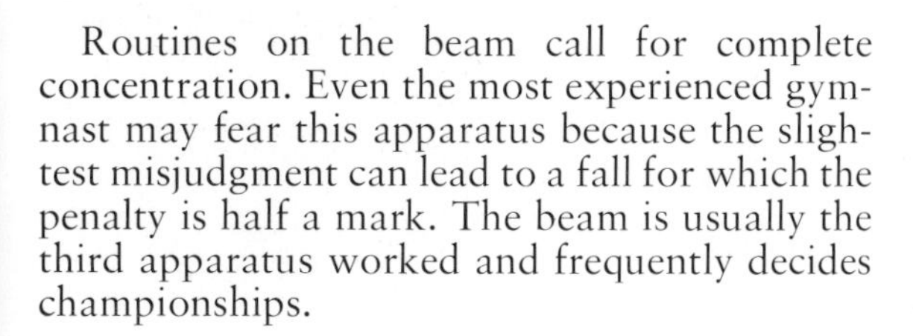

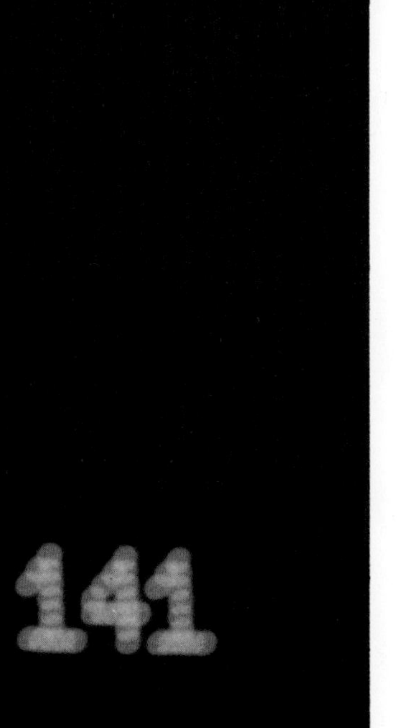

Routines on the beam call for complete concentration. Even the most experienced gymnast may fear this apparatus because the slightest misjudgment can lead to a fall for which the penalty is half a mark. The beam is usually the third apparatus worked and frequently decides championships.

Turns

Turns are an important part of work on the beam both as elements and as link moves. There are many variations to the basic turn on two feet. The 360° turn on one foot is vital in a voluntary routine and there will be a deduction if it is omitted.

Every turn must be executed on the toes and a gymnast will lose marks for failing to do so.

Half turn (180°) on two feet

Start by standing on the beam with one foot in front of the other, legs straight, hips pulled under, the stomach muscles tight. The back should be straight with arms by the side, shoulders down and head slightly lifted. There is no need to look at the beam because during this turn contact with the beam is never lost.

Maintaining this good posture, the gymnast pulls up on to the toes, fully extending the ankles. If it is a right turn, the left foot will be in front with the right tucked behind. The right shoulder and hip move simultaneously to the right to initiate the turn with legs and body maintaining complete tension. The head moves with the body until a 180° turn has been completed; the head is still slightly raised with eyes looking forward.

When the body has made the half turn, heels are lowered to the beam without any body control being lost. The same good posture at the start of the turn should still be apparent at the end.

Right turn on one foot

With good posture and body tension as for the half turn on two feet, a step is taken on to the toe of the right foot with the right leg completely straight. Arms stay by the side.

As the left leg leaves the beam, it gives a slight push and bends so that the left foot is touching the right calf. This is co-ordinated with the movement of the right hip and shoulder to the right.

It is essential that the body is held in a completely straight line with the head moving with the body. When 180° have been turned through, the right heel is lowered with control to the beam and the left leg extends for the next movement.

Full turn

The basic full turn is approached with the same technique as the half turn on one foot.

The heel of the supporting leg is lowered at the completion of a 360° turn.

Cartwheel on beam

Start facing forward along the beam. Raise the arms vertically upwards with no angle between the body and arms, and the head remains between the arms. The stomach muscles are contracted while one leg extends forward with the ankle stretched and the toes just lightly touch the beam. At this point both legs are straight.

The body moves forward in a straight line with the weight on the front leg. The foot makes contact with the beam and the knee bends into a lunge position.

The body continues in this forward motion maintaining a straight line between hands and back leg. The back leg leaves the beam straight with ankle extended.

As the hands are lowered toward the beam, a quarter turn is made, allowing the first hand to be placed on the apparatus, and the body keeps moving forward until the second hand is also placed on the beam. During this time, the back leg has continued moving while the supporting leg has gradually straightened again in order to move the body weight over the hands.

As the second leg extends and leaves the beam, the weight is taken completely on the hands with legs split overhead. When the hands make contact with the beam, the shoulder girdle extends and the surrounding muscles contract to give a firm base to support the body weight. The upper body, back and stomach muscles will be taut, holding the body in a straight line. Legs are, of course, straight and the feet stretched.

The movement does not stop in this position but continues its rotation so that the first leg is placed on the beam and, as this occurs, the knee flexed slightly to take the body weight. When the second leg reaches vertical, the first hand leaves

Cartwheel on beam

1

2

3

4

Complete split in leap

6

7

8

9

Upward jumps

10

11

12

Cartwheel, 1–5: In the second photo (2) the body weight is being taken on the hands, as the legs circle overhead in a splits position.

Complete split in leap, 6–9: Note the knee bend of 90° in the split leap – a method used by many gymnasts as a simpler way of achieving the leap.

the beam, creating again a straight body position between foot and hand.

The second hand then also leaves the beam with the head between the arms all rotating in the same plane as the beam itself. There should be no angle between either legs or arms and the body.

The first leg continues to bear the whole weight of the body as the second rotates towards the beam with arms moving sideways and upward. The first leg gradually straightens as the second reaches the beam and the finishing position is achieved.

The legs are slightly apart with feet across the beam; the legs are straight, the glutaeus (buttock) muscles are tightened, the back is straight and stomach muscles tight, the arms are vertically upward on either side of the head which is in line with the back. The shoulder girdle is relaxed.

Leaps

Leaps cover the category of jumps from a single foot take-off to a landing on the opposite leg. The most popular leap is the splits leap; indeed, the penalty for not showing this in a voluntary exercise is three-tenths of a mark. It is possible to use many variations of arm positions.

Start from an upright position with arms held horizontally sideways. Stomach and back muscles are taut and the shoulders pressed down. Step on to one foot, slightly flexing the knee and ankle in preparation for the jump with the body maintaining its position.

The other leg swings forward toward horizontal as the underneath leg extends, driving through the knee and ankle, leaving the beam and lifting backward and upward. The first leg must stay at horizontal until the back leg also reaches horizontal showing a split between the two legs of 180°.

During this, the arms remain horizontally sideways with the shoulders down, head in line with the back and the eyes directed down to the beam. As the first leg lowers to land on the beam, the body maintains its tension with the arms remaining in the same position.

The toes touch the beam first and, as the foot reaches the beam, the knee and ankle flex to absorb the impact of landing. The back leg remains lifted behind until the underneath leg straightens again and the back leg swings forward under control.

Complete split in leap

A slightly simpler way of achieving a complete split during a leap – and a method used by many gymnasts – is to lift the first leg with a bend at the knee of at least 90°.

In this method, the thigh lifts to horizontal and the lower leg extends quickly and in coordination with the extension of the underneath leg so that both legs arrive at a straight horizontal position at the same time.

Many gymnasts will vary this basic leap to complement the construction of their own routine. However, the method of take-off, landing and use of body tension remain essentially the same.

Upward jumps

Let us consider some of the many jumps that come from a two-footed take-off and involve the body in an upward flight rather than a movement along the beam.

One of the most complex upward jumps performed on the beam is the standing back somersault, but that will be considered on its own. First, we must look at the basic upward jump.

Preparation for any upward jump is important. Knees and ankles must flex, allowing the body to lower without leaning forward, the back remains straight with the hips rotated under. Arms are down by the sides, shoulders are pressed down, the head is in line with the back and only the eyes are directed towards the beam.

Keeping the back straight, the ankles and knees extend rapidly elevating the body into the air. Back, stomach and leg muscles should be contracted, with the toes leaving the beam last when they should be stretched towards it.

The arms, shoulders and head must remain in the same position with the height of the jump being measured by the distance between the toes and the beam.

As the body descends, toes make first contact, and the ankles and knees flex again to absorb the impact of landing. The back remains straight with the hips pulled under as on take-off.

As mentioned before, there are many variations of this basic jump. If arms are used, they must be lifted and held in position both during the jump and landing; it is important to appreciate that when arms are moved, shoulders must remain down and in line with the hips.

If the legs are moved, i.e., into a tuck or split position, they must extend fully through the ankles and knees as they leave the beam before they move to the required position.

If the jump involves landing on one leg, then the free leg must be held in a static position on landing while the body maintains its tension and the one leg absorbs landing in the same way as both do in the basic jump.

The coach and gymnast will use this basic technique to create many interesting and exciting jumps for inclusion in their optional beam routine.

Valdez

The valdez is a backward bending movement starting in a sitting position and lifting upwards and backwards into a handstand. It is completed when the feet continue down to the floor and the body lifts upward to a standing position.

Let us consider the valdez with the right leg leading. The gymnast starts by sitting on the beam with the left leg bent and the left foot flat on it. The right leg is straight forward resting on

Valdez

1

2

3

Straddle to handstand mount

6

7

8

9

Free walkover mount

11

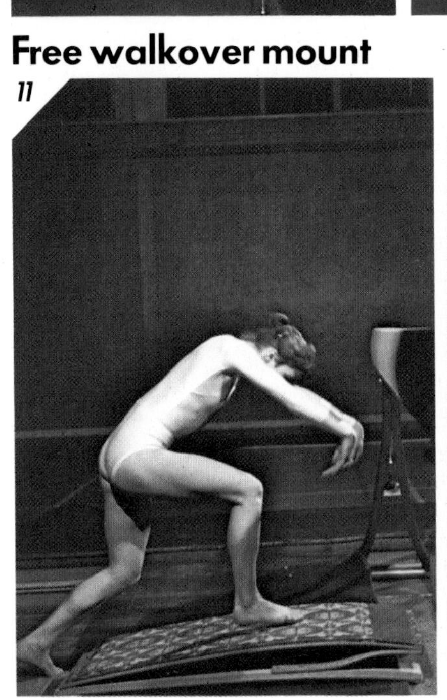

12

13

4

5

10

the beam with the knee pressed straight against it and the leg muscles contracted so that the stretched ankle is just off the beam.

The back must be straight and the right arm lifted vertically upward while the left arm is behind the back with the hand rotated so that it is pointing backwards but placed on the beam.

The right leg starts lifting upward as the left begins to straighten with the right arm and shoulders moving backwards to an arching back and head with the arm. This movement continues until the right hand reaches the beam and is placed just behind the left hand. By this time the right leg is pointing straight vertically upward, the left leg is only slightly bent, the back arched, the shoulder girdle extended and the surrounding muscles are contracted with the head between the arms.

As the movement continues the right leg moves over the head while the left leg straightens, the ankle extends and the foot leaves the beam. When the hips move vertically above the shoulders, the back straightens and the stomach muscles contract. At this time the legs should be 180° apart, showing a full split.

The legs continue to move until the right foot reaches the beam when the right leg bends slightly to take the weight of the body as the hands leave the apparatus. A straight line is kept between the left leg and arms as the head is lifted between the arms. The left leg reaches the beam at the same time as hands and arms arrive vertically upward.

The weight is moved on to the back leg, the hips are square, the glutaeus (buttock) muscles are contracted, back and stomach muscles tight, the shoulders down and arms pressed back. The head is lifted.

Straddle to handstand mount

There are many varieties of entry and exit for this beam mount and they all involve the basic 'elephant lift' action. Let us examine the floor 'elephant lift' and relate it afterwards to the various mounts on the beam that use similar techniques.

Both hands are placed shoulder width apart on the floor in front of the feet. The shoulder girdle is extended with the head between the arms and the arms pressing against the ears. The stomach muscles are contracted, with the back straight or possibly a little curved outward but never hollow.

The feet are slightly apart with the ankles extended and only the ends of the toes on the floor. Legs are straight and hips lifted as high as possible. As the hips lift forward over the shoulders, the toes leave the ground and the full weight is taken on the hands. At this point, the shoulders may move slightly forward of the hands but the arms are kept very straight and the pressure is taken on the finger tips with the fingers slightly bent.

As soon as an on-balance position is achieved with the hands, shoulders and hips in line and the back straight with shoulders completely extended, the legs move sideways and upwards into a split position in the same plane as the rest of the body. The legs continue to move upwards in this plane until they join together in the handstand position.

It is possible to use this lifting technique to mount the beam. The aid of a spring board is often used with the gymnast jumping with two feet on the board, placing both hands on the beam at the same time and the arms straighten and the hips lift vertically above the shoulders and hands. From the on-balance position, the legs lift as previously mentioned into handstand or any other desired position.

It is also possible to lift from a straddle-sit position on the beam. The hands are placed across the beam, the legs are straddled horizontally either side of the arms, which are straight. Shoulders are pressed down with the back slightly rounded. At that point, the shoulders are a little forward of the hands.

The hips move upward and as they reach vertical, the shoulders move back over the hands in to the on-balance position and the feet move over the beam with straight legs as the gymnast continues to lift into handstand.

Free walkover mount

This mount may be executed with either leg leading but for convenience we will consider it with the right leg leading.

Start facing the side of the beam with a spring board at right angles to the beam. Stand with the arms vertically upward, the back and legs straight and with the right leg pointed forward so that the toes are touching the top of the spring board.

The arms, shoulders and upper body move forwards and downwards as the right foot is placed on the board and the knee and ankle flex at the same time as the left leg bends and thrusts straight upward.

When the chest reaches the right knee, the left

Free cartwheel

1

2

3

Back flip

6

7

leg will be almost vertical. and it will continue moving upward and past vertical as the right knee and ankle extend and thrust off the board. Arms will work in co-ordination with the jumping of the legs and continue to swing downward circling backward.

As the body leaves the board the continuing motion of the left leg will swing the body forward making contact with the beam at hip level. The movement of the left leg is stopped at this point while the right leg continues its fast movement until the legs join straight together. Arms continue their circling movement and the hands make contact with the beam just as the legs join.

The sudden stopping of the movement of the legs aids the lift of the upper body and, as the stomach muscles pull tight, the body arrives in a straight position almost diagonally across the beam.

The leg muscles are tight with the ankles fully extended, arms straight, shoulders pressed down and the head lifted.

Free cartwheel

A free cartwheel is, as the name suggests, a cartwheel performed without the use of the arms as a support; the whole body rotates through the air from one foot to the other. This element may be performed on the floor or with greater difficulty along the beam. It is executed very similarly in both cases but with greater concern for direction when on the beam. It may be performed with either side of the body leading, but for ease of explanation we will take the right leg to be the take-off foot.

From standing with the body weight on the left foot, the leg straight and the body upright, the weight is transferred forwards on to the right leg as the left leg bends a little. The knee and ankle joints on the right leg flex preparing for take off. The body moves further forwards over the bent right leg and, as this happens, the left leg straightens and swings upwards from the beam. As the left leg approaches the vertical position the right leg straightens thrusting strongly from the beam, to give the cartwheel a good lift.

The right leg should reach maximum extension as the left leg creates at least a split of 180° between the two legs, this will of course differ from gymnast to gymnast dependent on hip mobility. The upper body and head are left in a position directly above the beam as the legs rotate above them. The left leg continues its motion circling downward toward the beam, the split between the two legs being maintained until the left leg reaches the beam.

As the leg reaches the beam, the toes arrive first and the ankle and knee flex to absorb the impact of landing. The body weight is taken wholly on the left leg as the upper body lifts upwards and backwards in co-ordination with the continued circling of the second leg. As the right leg reaches the beam behind the left leg the body is upright and the body weight is transferred on to a straight right leg.

The arms may be used as an aid during the take off of the free cartwheel, either swinging down the side of the body or across it. They should be lifted upwards to a precise position to increase stability on landing.

Straddle to handstand mount, (pages 118 and 119) 6–10: The first part of the photo sequence shows the 'elephant lift' action, which can be practised on the floor.

Free cartwheel, 1–5: The third photo (3) shows the back leg swinging rapidly upwards, whilst the underneath leg thrusts strongly from the beam. By the next picture (4) the legs have rotated overhead and the first leg is ready to land on the beam.

Back flip, 6–10: The gymnast lunges backwards through the handstand position. In the backward jump from the feet to the hands, the legs must be straight and must move rapidly overhead before landing.

Free walkover mount, (pages 118 and 119) 11–14: A spring board may be used for certain movements to assist the mount on to the beam. Here the extra spring gives the necessary lift into the free walkover.

The back flip

Just as with the back somersault, this move was first performed on a wooden beam with no covering. Beam work has now arrived at the point where a single flip is not looked upon as very much. In fact, the back flip is relatively simple as it does not incorporate a twist and is not explosive.

The gymnast starts with two feet together looking down the beam. Legs will be straight, hips tight, back straight and arms above the head.

From here she bends the legs and drops her arms down to the hip. The back should still be straight and the weight should be held over the balls of the feet. The gymnast will be in an on-balance position at this point.

A back flip on the beam does not require a great deal of speed going backwards so the gymnast can afford to be on-balance. Also flips on the beam need to be a little higher than on the floor so that the gymnast can see the beam before the hands make contact.

From this position the gymnast goes very slightly off-balance and begins the flip. The legs straighten and the arms swing over the head and reach for the beam. Arms should make contact with the beam just short of vertical to aid the second flight. The head will go out of alignment slightly to see the beam early.

At this point the gymnast will thrust through the shoulders and make a snap down action through the lower back. These actions together will result in the gymnast making a second flight, that is, hands and feet off the beam at the same time.

Landing positions will differ according to the move to follow. The gymnast could split her legs in the air, land on one leg and hold the other in the air or maybe land the first leg and transfer the weight across to the other leg to land behind the first.

Or it is possible to snap down with two feet together ready for another back flip. If that is the plan, then both feet would land at the same time on the soles, one slightly behind the other.

The gymnast should try to land on-balance in the position described for the beginning of one back flip, the only difference being that the arms would stay above the head and be ready for the next flip. They would not drop to the hips due to the fact that enough momentum has been created by the first flip.

The same landing position would also be correct for the back somersault except the landing would be on the toes instead of flat footed.

The standing back somersault

Start from a standing position with the arms high above the head. Hips must be tucked under, the stomach muscles tight, legs straight and the head in line with the back.

The arms swing forward and downward until they are low behind the hips without losing tension in the middle of the body. Arms begin to retrace their path forward and upward while at the same time knees, ankles and hips flex in preparation for the jump upward. As the arms continue in their movement rising above the horizontal, the knees, ankles and hips begin to extend with explosive power.

The stomach muscles remain contracted and the back is straight with the head still in line with the back. The arms continue to swing powerfully upward until they arrive at a 'stopping' position, usually just past the head. This 'stopping' position will, however, be determined by the shoulder mobility of each particular gymnast and for this reason it is important that the distance between the arms is fairly narrow and the back is very straight.

The arms' stopping position will co-ordinate with the full extension of the legs and hips as the feet leave the beam. The movement of the arms will transfer through the very straight body to the feet and set up the backward rotation.

As this occurs, the knees and hips lift up towards the arms while the head stays forward with the chin just off the chest. As the knees reach the shoulders the arms move in to hold the knees, closing the body into as tight a ball as possible thereby increasing rotation.

The body rotates through a complete 360° backward turn and, as the feet near the beam, one is placed in front of the other to facilitate landing.

As the feet reach the beam, the knees will still be bent and flexed very slightly to absorb the landing. Almost immediately, however, the legs straighten again, the shoulders lift and the hips pull under into a secure standing position. Great body tension is used at this point to pull the weight of the body over the beam and the arms are held down at the side to avoid uneven distribution of weight. The head is held in line with the back straight and the shoulders are down.

Back walkover and back somersault

This is the linking of two elements already described to give a move of extra risk on the beam. The back somi can be preceded by several other elements to give combination tumbles on

Standing back somersault

1

2

Back walkover and back somersault

5

6

7

Front somersault

10

11

12

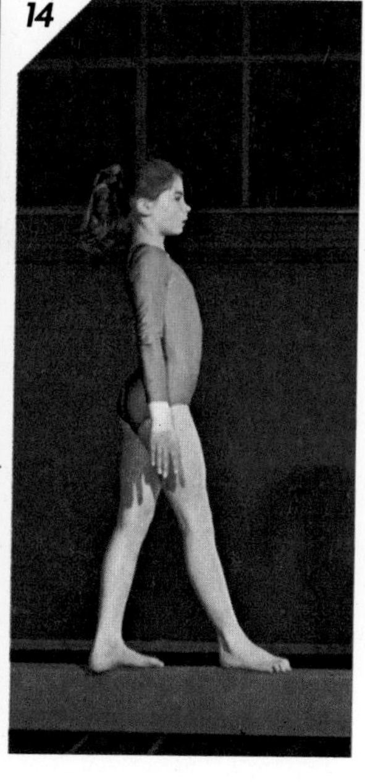

the beam such as roundoff, back flip and cartwheel.

The second half of the backward walkover has to be modified slightly to facilitate a good take-off position for the somersault. As the handstand position with legs in splits, is reached during the backward walkover, the hips and shoulders are moved very slightly behind the hands in order to speed up the last part of the walkover.

As the first foot reaches the beam, the knee flexes slightly and the hands leave the beam. The arms stay either side of the head which is also lifted quickly upward.

The second leg will reach the beam momentarily before the arms are vertically upward. As the second leg touches the beam, the knees and ankles of both legs as well as the hip joint, extend rapidly upwards in co-ordination with the arms moving quickly backwards to stopping position just behind the head.

It is absolutely essential that at this point of take-off, the stomach muscles are fully contracted and the back is kept in a straight position. The head must be kept in a neutral position in line with the body; it must not be thrown backwards with the arms.

This action will create a good take-off and the somersault is completed as previously described.

Front somersault

There are two styles of this move on beam, the first is a one-footed take off, the second is a two-footed take off. The second is a lot more difficult and will not be discussed here.

The take off will be very similar to that of the aerial walkover. Assuming the left leg is the thrusting leg, the gymnast starts in a standing position arms above head. The left leg goes forwards and bends. The arms are driven downwards and backwards whilst the chest is put on the leading thigh. At the same time the right leg straightens quickly and is thrust high into the air. The arms will automatically stop due to the natural range of movement. This stopping action has a transfer of momentum effect to the rest of the body and helps height and rotation of the move. The major rotation effect comes through the right leg whilst the major height factor is due to the left leg thrusting down very quickly. The right leg should move through to a splits position before the left leg leaves the beam.

As soon as both legs are off the beam they bend to a tucked position. The arms pull in behind the thighs to help make the tuck. One leg will stay in front of the other ready for the landing. The gymnast should land on balance and in a slightly bent position. As soon as contact is made the gymnast should stand up and move quickly into the next part of the routine.

It is better for the gymnast to be slightly over-rotated rather than under-rotated. It is much easier to control, and if the gymnast is going to fall off there is the chance that it can be saved by the forward speed.

Gainer back dismount

1

2

3

4

Front aerial dismount with one and a half twists (rudolf)

6

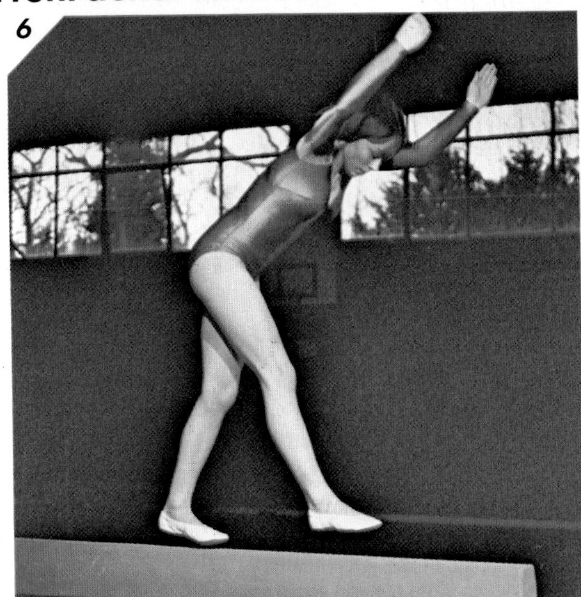

7

8

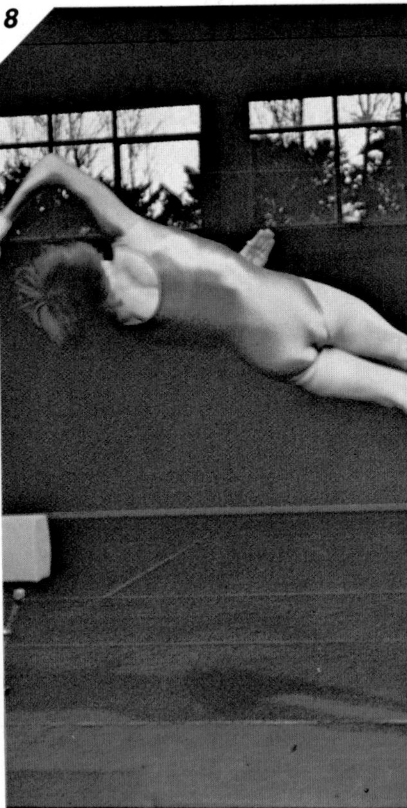

Front aerial dismount with one and a half twists (rudolf)
A general description of this move would be a front somersault in the straight position with a 540° turn through the longitudinal axis. It is a very complex move best suited to gymnasts who twist easily.

To do this movement, the gymnast must be capable of the aerial without using the arms, although arms will be used in initiating the twist. They therefore play little part in making the somersault.

Assuming a left twist is going to take place, the gymnast will place her right foot at the end of the beam. Some gymnasts want to turn left with a left foot lead and, even though it is possible, it is very much more difficult than using the right foot. The chest is put on the thigh of the leading leg which at that point is bent. The back leg will also be bent at that point.

From here the back leg is driven straight and lifted as high above the head as is possible. Most gymnasts get a range somewhere near 180°. At the same time as this, the right leg will straighten as fast as possible. This will be the leg that gives the move height off the beam while the left leg will deal with rotation.

Just before the gymnast leaves the beam, the twist will be initiated. From the beginning of the move to this point, the arms will be above the head in line with the rest of the body. At this

Gainer back dismount, 1–5; Front aerial dismount with one and a half twists, 6–9: Both these dismounts should be performed well above the beam in order to facilitate a good landing.

5

9

point of take-off, the right arm is dropped sideways, cuts across the leading knee and wraps around the body as tightly as possible.

As soon as the gymnast is in the air, the second arm is brought in to the longitudinal axis, either by wrapping around the body as the first arm or behind the head. Around the body will aid the rotation of the somersault, behind the head will aid the twist, but their effects are minimal.

It is very important that the legs come together as quickly as possible because their separation can only slow down the twist. The twist can be initiated from a pike to an extension position. Even though this is not the greatest force being used to make the twist, it will certainly help.

The gymnast must get out of the pike position as quickly as possible, because the most efficient twisting position is a straight line, and any movement out of the straight will result in slowing down the twist.

To drop the twist and make the landing, the gymnast should open her arms sideways and split the legs slightly. The gymnast should bend the legs but try to keep the trunk of the body straight. As soon as the landing has been absorbed, the heels can be drawn together.

Gainer back dismount

The gainer dismount is a backward somersault done whilst moving forwards and it can be performed either off the side of the beam or from the end.

The gymnast generally takes two steps into the move. If she is dismounting from the side, then the left foot will be on the beam with the dismount to the right – and vice versa. Technique changes very little for side or end dismounts.

The gymnast should make sure of good distance when coming off the end of the beam, to allow for clearance.

Assuming a left leg support and a right leg swing, the left will give the move height whilst the right creates rotation. At take-off the left leg will be bent with the foot flat on the beam.

The step in will be long so that the right leg has a long distance to travel to generate speed. The right leg swings past the left in a straight position and then bends as it lifts.

At this point, the left leg will straighten as quickly as possible and the arms will lift above the head. Because the body is travelling forwards, these actions will not be sufficient to land in an upright position. Therefore, the body will be allowed to lean back slightly to rotate the body a little before take-off.

The right leg will be consciously stopped by the gymnast whilst the left is still in contact with the beam. This will transfer the momentum of the leg to the rest of the body.

As soon as the left leg leaves the beam, it immediately joins the right and is pulled in as close to the body as possible. The gymnast should see the floor before landing and so open the legs out to slow rotation to make contact.

The legs will bend to absorb the landing, the body should be straight and a little behind the vertical. The forward movement of this backward rotation will then bring the gymnast to a standing position.

If the gymnast is efficient enough, then the move can be done in the pike position and also the straight position. For the well-orientated gymnast a full twist can be put in the somersault. It is generally done in the 'puck' position which is somewhere between the tuck and pike.

JUDGING AND SCORING

The judges

At the Olympics, World Championships, intercontinental and continental tournaments, the compulsory and voluntary exercises are marked at every apparatus by five men or women: a referee sometimes known as a superior or head judge and four judges seated apart at different points around the apparatus. Although procedures vary considerably between the scoring systems for men and women, both are judged by a panel of five.

The quartet of judges seated around the apparatus write down their scores independently of each other on specially printed paper slips and their assessments, or evaluations as they are frequently called in gymnastics circles, are collected (usually by little girls in leotards) and taken to the referee. He eliminates the highest and lowest of the four marks and works out the average of the other two.

For example, if the marks are 9.60, 9.50, 9.40 and 9.30, the referee eliminates 9.60 and 9.30, adds together the remaining two (18.90) and divides it by two to arrive at 9.45, the score awarded to the gymnast.

While the four judges are writing down their individual marks, the referee also places on the table his own assessment of the exercise. That mark added to the gymnast's score (i.e., the average of the two middle scores) and divided by two, becomes what is known as the basic score. For example, let us suppose the referee assessed the exercise at 9.35: this added to 9.45 and divided by two gives a basic score of 9.40.

The basic score is used as a basis for discussion when there is a certain disparity between the middle scores. When a disparity (fixed by FIG rules on a sliding scale) exists, the referee bases his discussion with the judges on his basic score in an attempt to resolve the matter. The judge or judges concerned may then change his mark to bring about agreement, but if they refuse, as a last resort the referee can declare the basic score to be the gymnast's mark.

In most cases the mark that is flashed on the scoreboard is the result of the four judges' original assessment. There then comes a further safeguard: on seeing the given mark, the gymnast's coach can raise an objection. Complaints about marks are considered by the jury of appeal which sits throughout matches at every apparatus and if they are brought in to examine an appeal by a coach, they consult the referee. Only in rare cases will they consult the original four judges.

If agreement is not reached to the satisfaction of all parties, the director of the competition may be consulted. That official first listens to the referee and considers the basic score. He may then hear the other judges, who must justify their score. If the director in turn cannot satisfy all concerned, the final and irrevocable decision rests with the jury of appeal.

Women's scoring

Before the calculation of the gymnast's score (that is, the average of the middle scores of four judges), the difference between those middle scores must not exceed a stipulated figure. The differences are on a sliding scale as follows: differences for women's scores may not exceed 0.30 for scores between 9.50 and 10.00; 0.50 for scores between 8.50 and 9.45; 1.00 in all other cases. *Example*: If the two middle scores were 9.90 and 9.50, the head judge would not declare the score as 9.70. She would call together the two judges concerned and ask one if she had overlooked some minor fault and the other if perhaps she had been unduly harsh in marking faults. In that way, it would be hoped that one or both the judges would adjust to within the 0.30 limit.

In apparatus finals (that is, the last competition of a major championship when six gymnasts compete at every apparatus) the differences are less. Only 0.20 of a mark may separate middle scores between 9.50 and 10.00, 0.30 for those between 8.50 and 9.45 and 0.50 in all other cases.

Women's compulsory exercises

Women gymnasts work four apparatus: vault (broad horse), asymmetric bars (uneven parallel bars), balance beam, and floor exercises. In the compulsory exercises (also known as set work), they must perform the routine with the elements laid down by FIG (Fédération Internationale de Gymnastique).

If a gymnast omits an element of difficulty, marks are deducted and those penalties cannot be made up, however brilliant the rest of the performance. For an element rated as being of superior difficulty 0.60 of a point is deducted and 0.30 for an element of medium difficulty.

The gymnast starts with 10 marks and deductions are made for faults or omissions of the stipulated elements of difficulty. On asymmetric bars, balance beam and floor exercises, a routine may not be repeated but two vaults over the broad horse are permitted and the better score of the two is counted.

Compulsory exercises must be performed in accordance with the order set by the FIG. The only concession is that a gymnast may start on the right foot in cases where the left is stipulated and a left turn can be made into a right one provided that the required degree of turn is performed.

Women's voluntary exercises

Voluntary or optional exercises are marked out of 10 in the following manner:

Value of Difficulty: 3.00 points

All exercises must contain at least seven elements of difficulty. The 3.00 points are made by three superior difficulties at 0.60 points each (1.80) and four medium difficulties at 0.30 points each (1.20). If the required number of difficulties are not performed during a routine on any of the four apparatus, then 0.60 or 0.30 is deducted and cannot be won back. For example, if a woman gymnast missed out a medium and a superior difficulty thus presenting only three mediums and two superiors, she would in effect be marked from 9.10 points no matter how well she had performed the rest of the routine.

Previous page: Monica Goermann of Canada in a pose on the beam. Beauty of movement, perfect balance and control all contribute to a high score, as well as delighting the audience.

Below and above right: Nadia Comaneci of Rumania flying over the top bar in the Champions All tournament at Wembley in April 1975 and, on the right, after collecting one of her many marks of ten.

Soon after her Wembley success, she took world supremacy away from the Russians to become Olympic champion at Montreal scoring ten marks six times. In the 1977 European Championships she retained the overall title she won at Skien in Norway in 1975, but Nadia failed to win the World Championships in Strasbourg in 1978 because of a weight problem. However, she retained the European title for a third spell at Copenhagen in May, 1979.

Originality and Value of Connections: 1.50 points
Under this heading the way a gymnast puts a routine together is assessed. She will lose marks if the link moves are bad between the superior and medium difficulties and other elements. The judges are looking for good, interesting and original ways of connecting up the recognized elements of the routine. Connecting links are not laid down in the Code of Points.

Value of Composition of Exercises: 0.50 points
Here the judges are looking for variety of moves within a routine, the general construction and the speed of movement.

Execution and Amplitude: 4.00 points
Four points are at stake for errors in performance. Faults looked for vary from minor infringements such as the bending of arms, legs and body, faulty positions of hands and feet, to distinct wobbles, losses of balance, falls from the apparatus and pronounced breaks of rhythm, lack of height in twists and jumps and incorrect technique in skills. For example, half a mark is lost for falling off the apparatus.

General Impression: 1.00 points
Very little is laid down about general impression and yet it accounts for a whole mark. It rests on the judges' overall impression of the routine.

Men's voluntary exercises

A major differing factor in scoring between the sexes is apparent in the men's system for voluntary exercises, for which they are marked from 9.40 points for floor routines, pommel horse, rings, parallel bars and high bar. On the long horse the mark is according to the tariff of the vault.

The fundamental difference is that the missing 0.6 of a mark can be added for ROV (risk, originality and virtuosity), whereas at all other stages of marking for men and women, points are deducted from the starting score. ROV marks are bonus points valued at a maximum of 0.2 under each of the three headings.

For men the breakdown of points is as follows:

Difficulty	3.40 points
Combination	1.60 points
Execution	4.40 points
	9.40 points
ROV	0.60 points
	10.00 points

Difficulty: 3.40 points
The elements of difficulty in men's scoring are in three categories as distinct from two for women. They are: A-parts (basic) 0.2 points; B-parts (medium) 0.4 points; C-parts (difficult) 0.6 points.

The A, B and C parts are all tabulated and illustrated in the Code of Points. There is a somewhat complicated compensation system whereby an excess of certain parts may make up, or partly make up, for a lack of others but the general definition is that 11 parts or elements are required in every routine although the actual number of elements of difficulty varies according to the competition. Irrespective of the required number of elements of difficulty, every routine must contain 11 recognized parts and failure to perform that number results in deductions, under the heading of combination below.

The penalty for falling short in the routine of the minimum required number of elements of difficulty is 0.2 (basic), 0.4 (medium) and 0.6 (difficult).

Execution: 4.40 points
This is the technical execution of the routine with deductions for faults ranging from a bent arm or

a loss of balance to a fall from the apparatus.

Combination: 1.60 points
As with the women's scoring outlined earlier, judges are looking for good connecting and link moves and they will make deductions for anything superfluous or of poor quality.

ROV: 0.60 points
ROV stands for risk, originality and virtuosity, and is the fundamental difference between men's and women's scoring. Men start at 9.40 on floor, side horse, rings, parallel bars and high bar and not at 10.00 as the women do, but marks can be awarded for risk (up to 0.2), originality (up to 0.2) and virtuosity (up to 0.2). It is the exception to the general scoring rule that marks are deducted for faults rather than given for excellence.

Briefly, the judges see the three concepts as follows:

Risk This does not mean risking an accident but is an attempt at a difficult move that puts a big risk on the execution of the exercise. For example, a tricky change of grip on the bar or a twisting somersault above it may greatly increase the chances of falling from the apparatus. In trying to gain marks, the gymnast may lose all. It is a calculated risk.

Originality This speaks for itself; it is either an entirely new move or it may be a novel way of combining various recognized elements.

Virtuosity Slightly more difficult to explain, but it has parallels in art and music. A violinist is a virtuoso when he displays such talent that his playing transcends technical accomplishment. So too with the gymnast who displays skill of a high order.

The scale of points difference in men's scoring is as follows:

9.60 to 10.00 points	0.10 points
9.00 to 9.55 points	0.20 points
8.00 to 8.95 points	0.30 points
6.50 to 7.95 points	0.50 points
4.00 to 6.45 points	0.80 points
1 full point in all other cases	

As detailed in the women's scoring section, if the difference in the scores of the two middle judges exceeds the above scale, the superior judge will call upon one or both of them to reconsider his score.

Men's compulsory exercises
In compulsory exercises the interpretation of the prescribed text together with the form and technique shown are considered by the judges from a starting mark of 9.80 points. The other 0.20 points may be added on for virtuosity.

A compulsory exercise set by FIG will usually have three or four B-parts and a series of A-parts. When the exercise is performed strictly according to the prescribed text, the gymnast has a right to receive 9.80 points. However, perfect execution is rare (quite impossible, most people will say) and there are bound to be deductions for faults of performance.

When an element of difficulty is omitted in a compulsory exercise, the penalty is often greater than in voluntary routines because the omission is likely to upset other elements within the prescribed routine. Conversely, any movements put into a compulsory exercise over and above the prescribed text, are also penalized by a deduction of 0.30 each. This is a basis for the scoring and judging of compulsory exercises as applied to competition one – the team event. In the all-round individual final and apparatus finals the difficulty and combination requirements are greater.

Above: Natalia Shaposhnikova of the Soviet Union on the beam at the World Championships in Strasbourg in 1978, where she was the overall bronze medallist with 77.875. She was also third in the team competition which the Soviet Union won by 4.50 marks over Rumania.
A student from Rostov-on-Don Natalia was the first trainee of former Olympic champion Ludmila Tourischeva to make the international scene.

TOP OF THE PYRAMID
Olympics and World Championships

The competition schedule for world events is formidable, with events spanning six days at the Olympics and seven at the World Championships. The latter are the more exacting because more countries participate, whereas the Olympics are limited by very tight qualifying regulations to a fixed entry.

World team competitions usually start between eight and nine in the morning and carry on all day. Unlucky is the lot of those gymnasts drawn for the early shift; they must arise around six o'clock, have a light breakfast, if indeed they can stomach anything at all, and make their way to the sports hall for a seven-thirty warm-up.

Can anything more ghastly be imagined than having to face the arc lamps and television cameras before the hour of nine in the morning? It is akin to movie stars who must be at the studio by six for make-up – a gymnast once described it to me as being like the morning of an execution.

During the World Championships at

Above: The ground floor for young gymnasts aspiring to international fame. A future Olga Korbut delights in the task of picking up the mark given by one of the four judges who sit at all four of the women's apparatus. She will take the mark sheet to the superior judge at the table so that she can work out the gymnast's marks together with the other three. The scene is the Champions Cup at the Albert Hall, London, 1979.

Strasbourg in 1978 all the team events started at 0830, the all-round competitions at six in the evening and the individual finals at four in the afternoon. At the 1976 Olympics in Montreal the time-table was as follows:–

18 July	0830–1100	Compulsory exercises women
	1230–1415	Compulsory exercises men
	1530–1815	Compulsory exercises women
	1915–2300	Compulsory exercises men
19 July	1400–1645	Free exercises women (voluntaries)
	1900–2200	Free exercises women
20 July	1500–1700	Free exercises men
	1900–2300	Free exercises men
21 July	1600–1815	Individual all-round competition Final: women
	2000–2215	Individual all-round competition Final: men
22 July	1930–2200	Apparatus finals: women
23 July	1930–2300	Apparatus finals: men

World Congress
World events bring together nearly all the gymnastics countries of the world with official delegations and gymnasts arriving at the appointed rendezvous a week or ten days before the competitions. Gymnasts spend the first week practising and acclimatizing themselves while the world officials hold a Congress to discuss administration and technical developments in world gymnastics.

Just as the gymnasts must face the bright lights early in the morning, so the administrators band together after breakfast for meetings that can last all day and sometimes continue into the night and early hours.

The FIG Congress discusses in general assembly revisions to regulations, admissions of non-member countries, resignations, press and propaganda, contracts with television companies, venues for future world events, nominations for honorary membership. The Congress also considers at great length any suggestions for changes in the world rules submitted by member nations.

The second week of their stay is devoted entirely to gymnastics. Although men's and women's events conform to the same pattern, they have entirely separate competitions, even in the team events when the marks for men and women of the same country are not added together.

The three competitions
There are three competitions at the Olympics and World Championships:

Competition 1 – Team Competition (TC)
Competition 2 – Individual All Around Finals (IAAF)
Competition 3 – Individual Event Finals (IEF)

Competition 1 – Team Competition
Six gymnasts make a team with the men working six Olympic apparatus (floor, pommelled horse, still rings, long horse, parallel bars and horizontal bar) and the women working four (broad horse, asymmetric bars, beam and floor).

The lowest individual score at every apparatus is deleted and the top five marks are added together and put towards the team total.

In the Team Competition gymnasts must perform both compulsory and voluntary exercises on every apparatus. The compulsory exercises are laid down in detail by FIG and they are always performed on the first day.

The scoring system needs a little thoughtful examination. Six men working six Olympic apparatus as a team could muster a maximum of 600 points and the women with four disciplines could attain 400 points. Neither score is ever reached because it would mean a competition without a fault.

Optimum marks are worked out as follows: ten points per gymnast are possible at every apparatus, so by multiplying the marks of the top five gymnasts at every piece, giving 50 points, which when again multiplied by six apparatus and four for women results in 300 and 200 points. As all gymnasts must work both compulsory and

COMPETITION 1 Team Competition

SOVIET UNION (Women)		Vault	Bars	Beam	Floor		Team Total
	C	48.35	48.30	48.45	48.90	194.00	
	O	48.90	48.70	48.30	48.85	194.75	388.75
Agapova,	C	9.55	9.60	9.40	9.65	38.20	
Svetlana	O	9.60	9.10	9.30	9.70	37.70	75.90
Arjannikova,	C	9.65	9.50	9.40	9.50	38.05	
Tatiana	O	9.70	9.55	9.50	9.80	38.55	76.60
Mukhina,	C	9.65	9.75	9.70	9.80	38.90	
Elena	O	9.70	9.90	9.80	9.95	39.35	78.25
Filatova,	C	9.70	9.70	9.90	9.80	39.10	
Maria	O	9.80	9.80	9.35	9.50	38.45	77.55
Shaposhnikova,	C	9.70	9.70	9.80	9.90	39.10	
Natalia	O	9.80	9.75	9.90	9.40	38.85	77.95
Kim,	C	9.65	9.55	9.65	9.75	38.60	
Nelli	O	9.90	9.70	9.75	9.90	39.25	77.85

ROMANIA (Women)		Vault	Bars	Beam	Floor		Team Total
	C	47.85	48.50	48.15	47.75	192.25	
	O	48.20	47.75	48.55	47.50	192.00	384.25
Grigoras,	C	9.50	9.55	9.40	9.30	37.75	
Anca	O	9.40	9.40	9.40	9.30	37.50	75.25
Neascu,	C	9.50	9.45	9.60	9.45	38.00	
Marinela	O	9.45	9.40	9.80	9.30	37.95	75.95
Vladarau,	C	9.35	9.65	9.60	9.50	38.10	
Marilena	O	9.55	8.95	9.25	9.50	37.25	75.35
Ungureanu,	C	9.60	9.65	9.50	9.40	38.15	
Teodora	O	9.60	9.50	9.60	9.40	38.10	76.25
Comaneci,	C	9.75	9.75	9.75	9.70	38.95	
Nadia	O	9.80	9.70	9.90	9.60	39.00	77.95
Eberle,	C	9.50	9.90	9.70	9.70	38.80	
Emilia	O	9.80	9.75	9.85	9.70	39.10	77.90

JAPAN (Men)		FX	PH	R	V	PB	HB		Team Total
	C	48.70	47.70	48.70	47.75	48.95	48.35	290.15	
	O	47.70	47.90	48.65	48.80	47.90	48.75	289.70	579.85
Shiraishi,	C	9.55	9.30	9.80	9.30	9.55	9.60	57.10	
Shinzo	O	9.40	9.60	9.50	9.70	9.50	9.75	57.45	114.55
Tsukahara,	C	9.60	9.40	9.70	9.50	9.65	9.30	57.15	
Mitsuo	O	9.50	9.50	9.75	9.70	9.30	9.80	57.55	114.70
Shimizu,	C	9.75	9.50	9.70	9.65	9.80	9.45	57.85	
Junichi	O	9.55	9.30	9.65	9.85	9.65	9.35	57.35	115.20
Kenmotsu,	C	9.65	9.60	9.75	9.80	9.80	9.80	58.40	
Eizo	O	9.45	9.45	9.80	9.65	9.60	9.75	57.70	116.10
Kasamatsu,	C	9.85	9.80	9.75	9.50	9.80	9.80	58.50	
Shigeru	O	9.60	9.80	9.70	9.30	9.40	9.75	57.55	116.05
Kajiyama,	C	9.85	9.40	9.60	9.20	9.90	9.70	57.65	
Hiroji	O	9.60	9.55	9.75	9.90	9.75	9.70	58.25	115.90

SOVIET UNION (Men)		FX	PH	R	V	PB	HB		Team Total
	C	48.15	46.60	48.70	47.80	47.95	48.00	287.20	
	O	48.75	48.30	48.75	48.85	48.35	48.75	291.75	578.95
Azarian,	C	9.50	9.35	9.70	9.45	9.35	9.30	56.65	
Eduard	O	9.50	9.55	9.80	9.70	9.55	9.60	57.70	114.35
Krysin,	C	9.55	9.40	9.40	9.50	9.35	9.55	57.75	
Gennadi	O	9.50	9.60	9.55	9.65	9.55	9.85	57.70	114.45
Tkachev,	C	9.60	9.15	9.70	9.40	9.70	9.60	57.15	
Aleksandre	O	9.80	9.70	9.70	9.80	9.70	9.80	58.50	115.65
Ditiatin,	C	9.60	9.65	9.85	9.60	9.60	9.45	57.75	
Alezsandre	O	9.80	9.65	9.70	9.75	9.60	9.70	58.20	115.95
Markelov,	C	9.60	9.00	9.70	9.60	9.55	9.70	57.15	
Vladimir	O	9.75	9.65	9.70	9.75	9.70	9.45	58.00	115.15
Andrianov,	C	9.80	9.05	9.75	9.65	9.75	9.70	57.70	
Nikolai	O	9.90	9.70	9.85	9.85	9.80	9.80	58.90	116.60

Below: Marcia Frederick of the United States in the World Championships at Strasbourg, in October 1978. She is seen in the asymmetric bars exercise that gave the gold medal with 9.90 in competition 3 (IEF). Marcia came 20th overall with 75.500 in competition 2 (IAAF).

Marcia was the third American to score ten (also on the bars) in the USA championships in 1978. She started gymnastics at the age of nine and has been trained by Don Peters at Connecticut Gym Club.

voluntary routines, a further multiplication by two brings the maximum to 600 and 400 points.

To clarify further the scoring system for Competition 1, let us examine extracts from the results of the World Championships at Strasbourg in October 1978.

First look at the women's result for the Soviet Union: start under **Vault,** where the score for C (compulsory exercises) is 48.35. Running your eye down the column you will find there are two scores for every gymnast – the top one is for compulsory exercises and the second score is for voluntary or optional routines.

The lowest of the six individual scores for compulsory vaulting is 9.55 by Svetlana Agapova. Her mark is deleted and the team score is reached by adding together Arjannikova (9.65), Mukhina (9.65), Filatova (9.70), Shaposhnikova (9.70) and Kim (9.65). That comes to the 48.35 at the top of the column and to it are added (reading at the top from left to right) 48.30 for bars, 48.45 on beam and 48.90 for floor exercises to reach a total of 194.00.

Exactly the same procedure is adopted for O (optional or voluntary exercises) for a total of 194.75 and the two added together come to 388.75, the team total for the Soviet women. Precisely the same method is used for the men.

Competition 2 – Individual All Around Finals (IAAF)

Competition 1 (Team Event) establishes the Olympic and World team champions; Competition 2 determines the individual title holder. Only voluntary exercises are performed and gymnasts carry forward half the scores they were awarded in the Team Competition.

The maximum scores for Competition 2 are 120 points (men) and 80 points (women) which is computed by adding together half the individual gymnast's score in the Team competition (maximum 120 points and 80 points respectively) to the marks awarded in the Individual All Around Finals (competition 2). The highest possible score is 60 points (men), 40 points (women) from competition 1 plus 60 points (men), 40 points (women) from competition 2.

Only 36 gymnasts can take part in competition 2. Until recently all those with highest Team Competition individual scores went through, which usually meant five or six gymnasts from each of the top countries. At the Montreal Olympics, and again at the World championships at Strasbourg in 1978, the regulations were amended so that only three from any country were allowed to go forward. This new ruling allows more countries to participate in the IAAF, thus creating wider interest and involvement.

Now examine the Strasbourg results for competition 2. Take, for example, Nelli Kim, the silver medallist. Her marks across in the table below are 9.90 (vault), 9.90 (bars), 9.90 (beam) and 9.95 (floor). Total – 39.65. Look back at Competition 1 results and you find Kim scored 38.60 (compulsories) and 39.25 (optionals) for a total of 77.85. Divide 77.85 by two, which comes to 38.925, add it to 39.65 and you get 78.575 which is the IAAF (Competition 2) total for Kim.

COMPETITION 2
INDIVIDUAL ALL AROUND FINALS (IAAF)

ALL AROUND - WOMEN

		V	UPB	BB	FX	PRELIM	TOTAL
1	Mukhina, Elena (USSR)	9.90	9.90	9.85	9.95	39.125	78.725
2	Kim, Nelli (USSR)	9.90	9.90	9.90	9.95	38.925	78.575
3	Shaposhnikova, N. (USSR)	9.85	9.85	9.40	9.80	38.975	77.875
4	Comaneci, Nadia (ROM)	9.90	9.25	9.80	9.80	38.975	77.725
5	Eberle, Emilia (ROM)	9.70	9.75	9.25	9.65	38.950	77.300
6	Cerna, Vera (CSSR)	9.70	9.55	9.80	9.70	38.275	77.025
7	Kraker, Steffi (GDR)	9.80	9.80	9.55	9.55	38.250	76.950
8	Johnson, Kathy (USA)	9.80	9.60	9.25	9.90	38.275	76.825
9	Schwandt, Rhonda (USA)	9.85	9.80	9.05	9.80	38.150	76.650
10	Kalmar, Szuzsa (HUN)	9.70	9.65	9.70	9.50	38.050	76.600
11	Hindorff, Silvia (GDR)	9.65	9.20	9.70	9.55	38.300	76.400
12	Ovari, Eva (HUN)	9.40	9.65	9.65	9.50	38.175	76.375
13	Brydlova, Dana (CSSR)	9.55	9.75	9.65	9.45	37.925	76.325
14	Neacsu, Marilena (ROM)	9.50	9.60	9.55	9.65	37.975	76.275
15	Suss, Birgit (GDR)	9.55	9.80	8.90	9.65	38.325	76.225
16	Mareckova, Eva (CSSR)	9.75	9.60	9.40	9.65	37.600	76.000
17	Kelsall, Karen (CAN)	9.55	9.65	9.50	9.50	37.475	75.675
18	Matraszek, Lucja (POL)	9.50	9.60	9.45	9.35	37.700	75.600
19	Kanyo, Eva (HUN)	9.35	9.65	9.50	9.30	37.775	75.575
20	Frederick, Marcia (USA)	9.70	9.90	9.00	9.70	37.200	75.500
21	Michler, Annette (FRG)	9.55	9.65	9.45	9.35	37.375	75.375
22	Schlegel, Elfi (CAN)	9.60	9.25	9.35	9.60	37.475	75.275
23	Kano, Yayoi (JAP)	9.40	9.65	8.90	9.55	37.625	75.125
24	Nozawa, Sakiko (JAP)	9.45	9.65	9.35	9.50	37.100	75.050
24	Kurbjuweit, Petra (FRG)	9.45	9.65	9.30	9.50	37.150	75.050
26	Toifl, Anette (FRG)	9.55	9.65	9.45	9.25	36.975	74.875
27	Georeva, Irena (BUL)	9.45	9.50	9.55	9.45	36.800	74.750
28	Matsumoto, Yoshiko (JAP)	9.60	9.65	8.95	9.35	37.175	74.725
29	Kessler, Romy (SW1)	9.60	9.40	9.35	9.50	36.550	74.400
30	Glouhtcheva, Diliana (BUL)	9.50	9.65	8.90	9.40	36.725	74.175
31	Valentini, Monica (ITA)	9.30	9.40	9.30	9.30	36.750	74.050
32	Topalova, Sylvia (BUL)	9.40	9.70	8.40	9.45	37.050	74.000
33	Hawco, Sherry (CAN)	9.30	9.35	9.45	9.05	36.800	73.950
34	Sosin, Malgorzata (POL)	9.45	9.45	8.90	9.40	36.625	73.825
35	Bolleboom, Ingrid (HOL)	9.35	9.50	8.75	9.30	36.850	73.750
36	Morata, Aurora (SPA)	9.35	9.50	8.20	9.40	36.575	73.025

ALL AROUND - MEN

		FX	PH	R	V	PB	HB	PRELIM	TOTAL
1	Andrianov, Nikolai (USSR)	9.85	9.70	9.90	9.85	9.75	9.85	58.300	117.200
2	Kenmotsu, Eizo (JAP)	9.60	9.75	9.80	9.80	9.80	9.75	58.050	116.550
3	Ditiatin, Alexander (USSR)	9.60	9.75	9.70	9.80	9.75	9.80	57.975	116.375
4	Gienger, Eberhard (FRG)	9.65	9.75	9.65	9.80	9.70	9.80	57.850	116.200
5	Kajiyama, Hiroji (JAP)	9.55	9.70	9.60	9.80	9.70	9.60	57.950	115.900
6	Thomas, Kurt (USA)	9.80	9.75	9.50	9.80	9.65	9.75	57.475	115.725
7	Kasamatsu, Shigeru (JAP)	9.75	8.90	9.70	9.70	9.75	9.80	58.025	115.625
8	Deltchev, Stoyan (BUL)	9.75	9.55	9.40	9.60	9.75	9.50	57.675	115.225
9	Conner, Bart (USA)	9.60	9.80	9.55	9.70	9.65	9.40	57.500	115.200
10	Nikolay, Michael (GDR)	9.40	9.80	9.30	9.80	9.70	9.75	57.425	115.175
11	Tkachev, Alexander (USSR)	9.75	8.70	9.70	9.80	9.75	9.55	57.825	115.075
12	Magyar, Zoltan (HUN)	9.55	9.85	9.30	9.75	9.70	9.65	57.250	115.050
13	Bruckner, Roland (GDR)	9.60	9.70	9.50	9.75	9.50	9.70	57.025	114.775
14	Barthel, Ralph (GDR)	9.60	9.50	9.55	9.70	9.55	9.65	56.900	114.450
15	Kovacs, Peter (HUN)	9.65	9.50	9.55	9.75	9.40	9.70	56.650	114.200
16	Donath, Ferenc (HUN)	9.50	9.65	9.65	9.20	8.95	9.60	57.400	113.950
17	Rohrwick, Volker (FRG)	9.40	9.50	9.50	9.65	9.60	9.60	56.675	113.925
17	Moy, Willie (FRG)	9.70	9.70	9.60	9.75	9.20	9.55	56.425	113.925
19	Bretscher, Robert (SWI)	9.60	9.60	9.50	9.85	9.50	9.55	56.250	113.850
20	Wilson, Mike (USA)	9.80	9.70	9.40	9.75	9.45	9.30	56.400	113.800
21	Boerio, Henry (FRA)	9.30	9.55	9.55	9.60	9.35	9.80	56.325	113.475
22	Boutard, Michel (FRA)	9.55	9.70	9.55	9.30	9.50	9.65	56.075	113.325
23	Szilier, Kurt (ROM)	9.35	9.55	9.40	9.70	9.35	9.55	56.075	112.975
24	Grecu, Danut (ROM)	9.15	9.60	9.70	9.20	9.40	9.50	56.350	112.900
25	Checiches, Ion (ROM)	9.60	9.40	9.50	9.70	9.30	9.50	55.775	112.775
26	Tabak, Jiri (CSSR)	9.65	9.30	9.30	9.70	9.45	9.50	55.850	112.750
27	Jorek, Edgar (FRG)	9.65	9.00	8.85	9.70	9.50	9.45	56.500	112.650
28	Long, Warren (CAN)	9.45	9.30	9.30	9.75	9.00	9.50	55.825	112.125
29	Szajna, Andrzej (POL)	9.60	9.40	8.95	9.80	9.50	9.65	55.100	112.000
30	Schmid, Peter (SWI)	9.20	9.65	9.00	9.60	9.50	9.35	55.150	111.450
31	Migdau, Jan (CSSR)	9.45	9.45	9.25	9.65	8.70	9.60	55.025	111.125
32	Gaille, Philippe (SWI)	9.30	9.10	9.15	9.50	9.50	9.40	55.050	111.000
33	Bertrand, Fernando (SPA)	9.40	9.50	9.35	9.20	9.00	9.40	55.100	110.950
34	Neale, Ian (GBR)	9.40	9.15	8.55	9.60	8.70	9.50	55.700	110.600
35	Choquette, Jean (CAN)	9.30	9.40	8.75	9.10	9.00	9.65	55.350	110.550
36	De La Casa, Juan Jose (SPA)	9.30	9.25	8.85	9.60	8.90	9.30	55.325	110.525

Exactly the same procedure applies to all the other gymnasts' scores.

Competition 3 – Individual Event Finals (IEF)

The Individual Event Finals determine the champion at every apparatus and, in the same way as Competition 2, it is derived from the Team Competition. Eight gymnasts with the highest scores at every apparatus in Competition 1 go forward on that apparatus to the IEF but no more than two from a country are allowed to compete at every discipline.

There are six apparatus finals for men and four for women and the maximum score at every event is 20 points – ten in Competition 3 plus half the apparatus score in Competition 1.

Let us take Nelli Kim again. In Competition 3 she won the gold medal for vaulting. Look back to the Team competition and you find she scored 9.65 for the compulsory vault and 9.90 for the voluntary which added together and divided by two is 9.775. That added to 9.850 she scored for vaulting in Competition 3 brings her final total to 19.625.

The third decimal point comes into Competitions 2 and 3 because of the division of marks from Competition 1: all Competition 1 marks really carry a nought but it is usually omitted from score sheets.

Far left: Nikolai Andrianov of the USSR (centre) after winning the all around with 117.20 marks to become the World Champion at Strasbourg in 1978. He is flanked by Eizo Kenmotsu (Japan), 116.550, and Alexander Detiatin of USSR, 116.375, the silver and bronze medallists.

Andrianov has a remarkable unfinished career that includes overall titles in the 1975 European Championships and World Cup, the Montreal Olympics, the 1977 World Cup and the 1978 World Championships.

COMPETITION 3 INDIVIDUAL EVENT FINALS (IEF)

WOMEN

VAULT	C/O avg.	FINAL	TOTAL
1 Kim, Nelli (USSR)	9.775	9.850	**19.625**
2 Comaneci, Nadia (ROM)	9.775	9.825	**19.600**
3 Kraker, Steffi (GDR)	9.750	9.800	**19.550**
4 Schwandt, Rhonda (USA)	9.675	9.850	**19.525**
5 Eberle, Emilia (ROM)	9.650	9.800	**19.450**
6 Shaposhnikova, Natalia (USSR)	9.750	9.650	**19.400**
7 Kunhardt, Heike (GDR)	9.700	9.500	**19.200**
8 Horacsek, Andrea (HUN)	9.625	9.450	**19.075**
UNEVEN BARS			
1 Frederick, Marcia (USA)	9.850	9.950	**19.800**
2 Mukhina, Elena (USSR)	9.825	9.900	**19.725**
3 Eberle, Emilia (ROM)	9.825	9.800	**19.625**
4 Filatova, Maria (USSR)	9.750	9.850	**19.600**
5 Comaneci, Nadia (ROM)	9.725	9.850	**19.575**
6 Kraker, Steffi (GDR)	9.700	9.800	**19.500**
7 Cerna, Vera (CSSR)	9.600	9.700	**19.300**
8 Suss, Birgit (GDR)	9.625	9.200	**18.825**

BALANCE BEAM			
1 Comaneci, Nadia (ROM)	9.825	9.800	**19.625**
2 Mukhina, Elena (USSR)	9.750	9.850	**19.600**
3 Eberle, Emilia (ROM)	9.775	9.800	**19.575**
4 Ovari, Eva (HUN)	9.700	9.700	**19.400**
5 Cerna, Vera (CSSR)	9.600	9.700	**19.300**
6 Hindorff, Silvia (GDR)	9.625	9.600	**19.225**
7 Kanyo, Eva (HUN)	9.650	9.250	**18.900**
8 Shaposhnikova, Natalia (USSR)	9.850	9.000	**18.850**
FLOOR			
1 Kim, Nelli (USSR)	9.825	9.950	**19.775**
1 Mukhina, Elena (USSR)	9.875	9.900	**19.775**
3 Johnson, Kathy (USA)	9.675	9.850	**19.525**
3 Eberle, Emilia (ROM)	9.700	9.825	**19.525**
5 Hindorff, Silvia (GDR)	9.775	9.700	**19.475**
6 Cerna, Vera (CSSR)	9.700	9.750	**19.450**
7 Suss, Birgit (GDR)	9.675	9.700	**19.375**
8 Comaneci, Nadia (ROM)	9.650	9.600	**19.250**

MEN

FLOOR EXERCISES	C/O avg.	FINAL	TOTAL
1 Thomas, Kurt (USA)	9.750	9.900	**19.650**
2 Kasamatsu, Shigeru (JAP)	9.725	9.850	**19.575**
3 Ditiatin, Alexander (USSR)	9.700	9.700	**19.400**
4 Andrianov, Nikolai (USSR)	9.850	9.500	**19.350**
5 Deltchev, Stoyan (BUL)	9.700	9.500	**19.200**
6 Jorek, Edgar (FRG)	9.725	9.450	**19.175**
7 Bruckner, Roland (GDR)	9.750	9.100	**18.850**
8 Tabak, Jiri (CSSR)	9.725	8.900	**18.625**
POMMEL HORSE			
1 Magyar, Zoltan (HUN)	9.900	9.900	**19.800**
2 Gienger, Eberhard (FRG)	9.725	9.700	**19.425**
3 Deltchev, Stoyan (BUL)	9.700	9.700	**19.400**
4 Ditiatin, Alexander (USSR)	9.650	9.700	**19.350**
4 Donath, Ferenc (HUN)	9.650	9.700	**19.350**
6 Nikolay, Michael (GDR)	9.675	9.650	**19.325**
7 Conner, Bart (USA)	9.650	9.650	**19.300**
8 Kasamatsu, Shigeru (JAP)	9.800	8.950	**18.750**
RINGS			
1 Andrianov, Nikolai (USSR)	9.800	9.900	**19.700**
2 Ditiatin, Alexander (USSR)	9.775	9.900	**19.675**
3 Grecu, Danut (ROM)	9.750	9.900	**19.650**
4 Kasamatsu, Shigeru (JAP)	9.725	9.800	**19.525**
5 Mack, Lutz (GDR)	9.700	9.800	**19.500**
6 Kenmotsu, Eizo (JAP)	9.775	9.700	**19.475**
7 Oprescu, Nicolae (ROM)	9.675	9.650	**19.325**
8 Donath, Ferenc (HUN)	9.725	9.550	**19.275**

VAULT			
1 Shimizu, Junichi (JAP)	9.750	9.850	**19.600**
2 Andrianov, Nikolai (USSR)	9.750	9.825	**19.575**
3 Barthel, Ralph (GDR)	9.725	9.825	**19.550**
4 Ditiatin, Alexander (USSR)	9.675	9.800	**19.475**
5 Mack, Lutz (GDR)	9.700	9.700	**19.400**
6 Jorek, Edgar (FRG)	9.700	9.675	**19.375**
7 Conner, Bart (USA)	9.675	9.525	**19.200**
8 Kenmotsu, Eizo (JAP)	9.725	9.425	**19.150**
PARALLEL BARS			
1 Kenmotsu, Eizo (JAP)	9.700	9.900	**19.600**
2 Andrianov, Nikolai (USSR)	9.775	9.800	**19.575**
2 Kajiyama, Hiroji (JAP)	9.825	9.750	**19.575**
4 Tkachev, Aleksander (USSR)	9.700	9.750	**19.450**
5 Conner, Bart (USA)	9.525	9.850	**19.375**
6 Gienger, Eberhard (FRG)	9.575	9.700	**19.275**
6 Boerio, Henry (FRA)	9.575	9.700	**19.275**
8 Nikolay, Michael (GDR)	9.525	9.700	**19.225**
HORIZONTAL BAR			
1 Kasamatsu, Shigeru (JAP)	9.775	9.900	**19.675**
2 Gienger, Eberhard (FRG)	9.750	9.900	**19.650**
3 Deltchev, Stoyan (BUL)	9.700	9.900	**19.600**
3 Krysin, Gennadi (USSR)	9.700	9.900	**19.600**
5 Tkachev, Alexander (USSR)	9.700	9.800	**19.500**
6 Nikolay, Michael (GDR)	9.650	9.800	**19.450**
7 Ruckrien, Reiner (GDR)	9.575	9.650	**19.225**
8 Kenmotsu, Eizo (JAP)	9.775	9.300	**19.075**

ALTERNATIVE GYMNASTICS

MODERN RHYTHMIC GYMNASTICS

Modern rhythmic gymnastics appears to be mainly of German and Swiss origin, with some Swedish influence, and it is a development of rhythmic gymnastics and dance, which has been based on various movement methods such as those of Bode, Dalcroze, Laban and Medau, but the movement has been adapted from these and it has its own new characteristics.

Group rhythmic gymnastics with apparatus was first introduced in competition in the Olympic Games and World Championships well over thirty years ago, but in those days, competitors were also required to perform on the four pieces of artistic apparatus as well: the beam, bars, vault and floor. However, in the 1956 Olympic Games, the rhythmic section was excluded, and it was after this that it was decided that MRG should become an independent competitive sport. Unfortunately, though, it has still not found a place in the Olympic Games, although there is hope that it will be included in the near future. The World Championships have been held every two years since 1963, and the European Championships and Four-Continent Championships have now been established, the first championships being held recently in 1978.

The movement and the music

The movement in modern rhythmic gymnastics is extremely pleasing to the eye, showing gracefulness, suppleness, co-ordination, control and poise. It consists of floorwork, with the use of hand apparatus, such as the rope, ball, hoop, clubs and ribbon. Body movements to be included in an exercise are: jumps and leaps, turns, steps, balances, bends and waves, which are linked to form an intricate pattern of movement, and choreographed together with a musical accompaniment to form an individual routine, which in competition rules must be between one minute and one and a half minutes long.

Music plays an important part in modern rhythmic gymnastics, for the movement is an interpretation of the music, showing drama, liveliness, gracefulness and mood, and the work and the music should both be composed to suit the character and temperament of the gymnast. The rule for international competition states that music must be played on one instrument only, and it is usual for a gymnast to be accompanied by her own pianist. However, orchestral music is often used to add interest and depth to display individual work and group work.

Apparatus

The apparatus used must conform to special regulations, as laid down by the International Gymnastics Federation. The ball, for instance, is specially weighted. It can be plastic or rubber and must have a minimum weight of 400 grammes. The hoop can be of wood or plastic, with a minimum weight of 500 grammes, and an interior diameter of between 80 and 90 centimetres. The rope, on the other hand, can be of a length suitable to each gymnast, and can be made of hemp, or any pliable synthetic fibre, but without handles. Clubs, the only piece of apparatus which is always worked in pairs, can be of wood or plastic, each one having a minimum weight of 150 grammes and being of a length between 40 and 50 centimetres. The most complex piece of apparatus is perhaps the ribbon at a length of 6 metres, which is double thickness for the first metre, and which is joined to a stick by a swivel attachment. This allows the ribbon to move freely around the stick without becoming tangled. The stick itself should be between 50 and 60 centimetres long, of wood, plastic or fibre-glass.

Each piece of apparatus has its own characteristics, and these are used to emphasize the work and improve the content of the exercise. For instance, the ball is specially used for bouncing and rolling, the hoop for rolling and rotating, the rope for skipping of course, and the clubs for swinging. The ribbon has a definite characteristic of its own, in that it has no solid shape, and cannot move on its own like a rolling ball or hoop. Consequently, it must be kept moving by the gymnast, who works with a continuous perform-

Left and far left: Erica Schiller and Galina Krilenko of the Soviet Union display their skills with the specially weighted ball of modern rhythmic gymnastics.

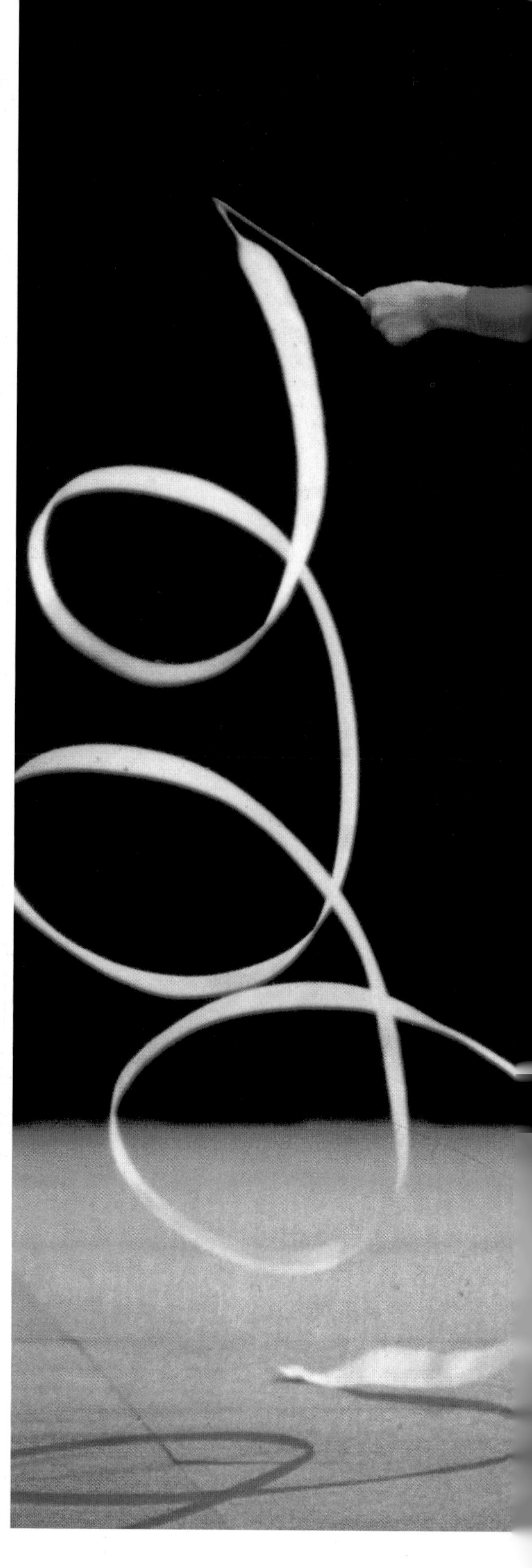

Above: Graceful movement is an important aspect of modern rhythmic gymnastics, as Galina Krilenko demonstrates here in her routine with the hoop.

Right: The ribbon must be kept moving throughout the performance, to create constantly changing patterns in the air. This can be exquisitely beautiful to watch, especially when handled with the artistry of Erica Schiller.

ance to show the flowing technique and patterns of the ribbon. All pieces of apparatus are thrown during the exercise, in different directions and in different ways, and throwing and catching are an important part of the work. Work with both hands is important too, for the gymnast must use her left hand as well as her right hand.

Judging

The judging of the exercises is made according to the International Code of Points book, which lays down the rules and penalties for each piece of apparatus, and states the movements and difficulties which must be included. Each individual exercise is marked out of ten points, with 7.0 points being given for the content, i.e. the elements of difficulty and their placing in the exercise, variation of rhythm, use of floor area and floor patterns, and harmony between the movement and music; the remaining 3.0 points is given for the technical performance of the work, the sureness, elegance, co-ordination, lightness, extension and expression.

Each exercise is marked by four judges, who

are overseen by a master judge. Of the four marks given by the judges, the highest and lowest are discarded, and an average is taken of the middle two. A competition may take place on each individual piece of apparatus, or may be an overall title with a total of marks on several pieces of apparatus.

Group work

Apart from the individual exercises performed by one gymnast, there is a group work section, which is for teams of six gymnasts, who perform together. The group works harmoniously, showing various and intricate floor patterns with changes of place, and exchanges of the apparatus between members of the group. The exercise must include the same body movements and skills with the apparatus as with the individual exercise, but the time limit is between two and a half and three minutes maximum. All members of the group must work together, showing a blend of graceful movement, and difficult elements, combined with a musical and rhythmic interpretation.

For the group work, two sets of judges are used. The 'A' set award marks for the composition of the exercise, i.e. the choreography, content, floor pattern, exchanges, etc., whilst the 'B' set award marks for the technical execution, i.e. the performance, neatness, sureness, extension, correctness of technique with body and apparatus, and for unison in team work. Each set of marks is calculated in the same way as for the individual exercise, with a possible maximum therefore of 20 marks from the two sets of judges.

MRG around the world

In many countries today the sport of modern rhythmic gymnastics is beginning to rise in popularity, although the Eastern Bloc countries still dominate the rest of the world in international competitions. Russia and Bulgaria are supreme, both in individual and group work, and are closely followed by Czechoslovakia, Spain, East and West Germany and Italy. Many of these countries, besides giving the time and facilities to specialized training, incorporate this type of work into the education system, so that many children have the opportunity to enjoy the varied aspects of this sport.

In America modern ryhthmic gymnastics is still young, although there were a number of individual entries at the World Championships in Basle in 1978.

In Great Britain the sport has been active for only four years, but in this time a National Squad has been established and members of the team are beginning to take their place in world class competitions, having entered two World Championships and the European Championships, as well as several other international competitions and tournaments. Much knowledge and experience has been gained from this, but there is still a long way to go.

With colleges beginning to show an interest, it is anticipated that countries such as America and Britain will soon be in a position to give the Eastern Bloc countries some real competition.

SPORTS ACROBATICS

Tumbling and balancing
Another branch of gymnastics also knocking at the Olympian door is Sports Acrobatics – a tumbling and balancing sport more closely allied to the artistry of circus performances than to artistic gymnastics. Because of its sheer dynamism and fast tempo, it is a very exciting competitive sport.

Sports acro can be sub-divided into two main sections. First, it is pure tumbling with the performers executing their routines on a long straight run combining agilities to form a tumbling run out or 'pass' as it is known.

Secondly, there are pairs and group sections working together combining balances, tumbles and moves of the pitched somersault type in a choreographed routine on the 12 metres square floor area. Both sections have their own specific rules. Apart from mats, there is no apparatus. The performers balance on and somersault from their partners.

Although tumbling was included in the 1932 Olympics in San Francisco, the sport of acrobatics in competition form did not develop until 1939 when the USSR held a national championship. But development was slow until 1974 when the International Federation of Sports Acrobatics was formed with eleven member

Left: There has long been a tradition of acrobatics in China, and Tsien Liu and Tsien-Chun Tan are particularly talented mixed pair performers.

Above: Strength is a feature of sports acrobatics for both men and women. Here a Russian gymnast is about to be caught by the two other members of her group.

Above right: Vladimir Machuga and Vassily Pochivalov of the Soviet Union are particularly popular with audiences. Outstanding skill is needed for this extraordinary hand balance.

countries. Each year the number of countries taking up the sport increases and its popularity develops.

At international matches there are seven events: women's tumbling, men's tumbling, women's pairs, men's pairs, mixed pairs, women's threes and men's fours.

Tumbling at international competitions is performed on a sprung track 25 metres long and 1.5 metres wide with a 10 metres approach run. The first sprung floor was developed in the USSR and consisted of snow skis with their curved ends sawn off. They were supported on two strips of wood with a plywood and matting overlay.

The sprung floor enables a performer to obtain more height to give him the time for difficult elements such as the triple somersault and the triple twisting double somis. An added advantage of a sprung floor is safety because it can absorb landings and reduces the possibility of injuries to ankles and wrists.

Tumblers perform two routines. The first is known as the somersault or straight pass and performers are required to show a minimum of three different types of somersaults. The second is called the twisting pass and here different types of twisting somersaults are required.

The pair and group sections also perform two routines. The first is known as the balance exercise and the second is the tempo routine. In the balance, pairs and groups will show a minimum of five balance elements in a choreographed routine to music for a maximum time limit of three minutes. The only exception is in men's fours where a single balance pyramid of exceptional difficulty is performed, for example, a three-man high pyramid with the fourth man executing a one-arm balance on the head of the third man.

Tempo routines which include the men's fours, are also choreographed to music but here the predominance is in tempo moves, like pitched somersaults from shoulders to land either back on the shoulders or on the floor. In this routine the more difficult tumbles are included and the routine is a little faster to tie in with the type of elements performed.

The balance routines require static strength and fine balance whereas the tempo exercises call for dynamic strength and somersaulting awareness.

Judging

Judging of sports acrobatics is very different from artistic gymnastics. It is, in fact, more akin to ice skating.

At major international competitions there are eight judges: a master judge who is also called the arbiter and seven others. They all examine the execution of the exercise and make deductions in accordance with a table of stipulated faults which have been laid down by the International Federation of Sports Acrobatics (IFSA).

The additional duty of the arbiter is to check the difficulty of the exercise against a pre-submitted diagram of scoring elements in the routine. He also checks the duration of individual balance elements and overall time of the exercise whereupon he makes the necessary deductions from the 'tariff' (that is, the maximum points the gymnast's routine is worth).

At the completion of the exercise, the arbiter will display the tariff to the judges and they will use that tariff as the maximum mark and make their deductions from it. The performer's final score is the average of the middle four scores.

In sports acrobatics there is a system of closed/open officiating. After each judge has handed in a slip of paper with his scores to the arbiter, they all display their individual scores to the audience.

At world championships and other major events, sports acrobats perform their two routines in a preliminary competition and the top six carry their scores over to the finals.

There are two sets of finals: those for the overall placings and those for the placings in the individual routines. The finals have a more stringent difficulty requirement.

As mentioned before the fundamental difference between artistic gymnastics and sports acrobatics is the lack of fixed or hand apparatus and the emphasis on team work. But for all that, the basis of sports acrobatics remains the same as for artistic gymnastics and, at an early age, the development of the gymnast is the same. Body preparation in strength, suppleness and muscle control is identical and it is here that the training of the different sections can help each other.

By practising all types of gymnastics in the early years, it is easier for the performers and coaches to decide which they enjoy most and which they are likely to do the best in.

WHO'S WHO

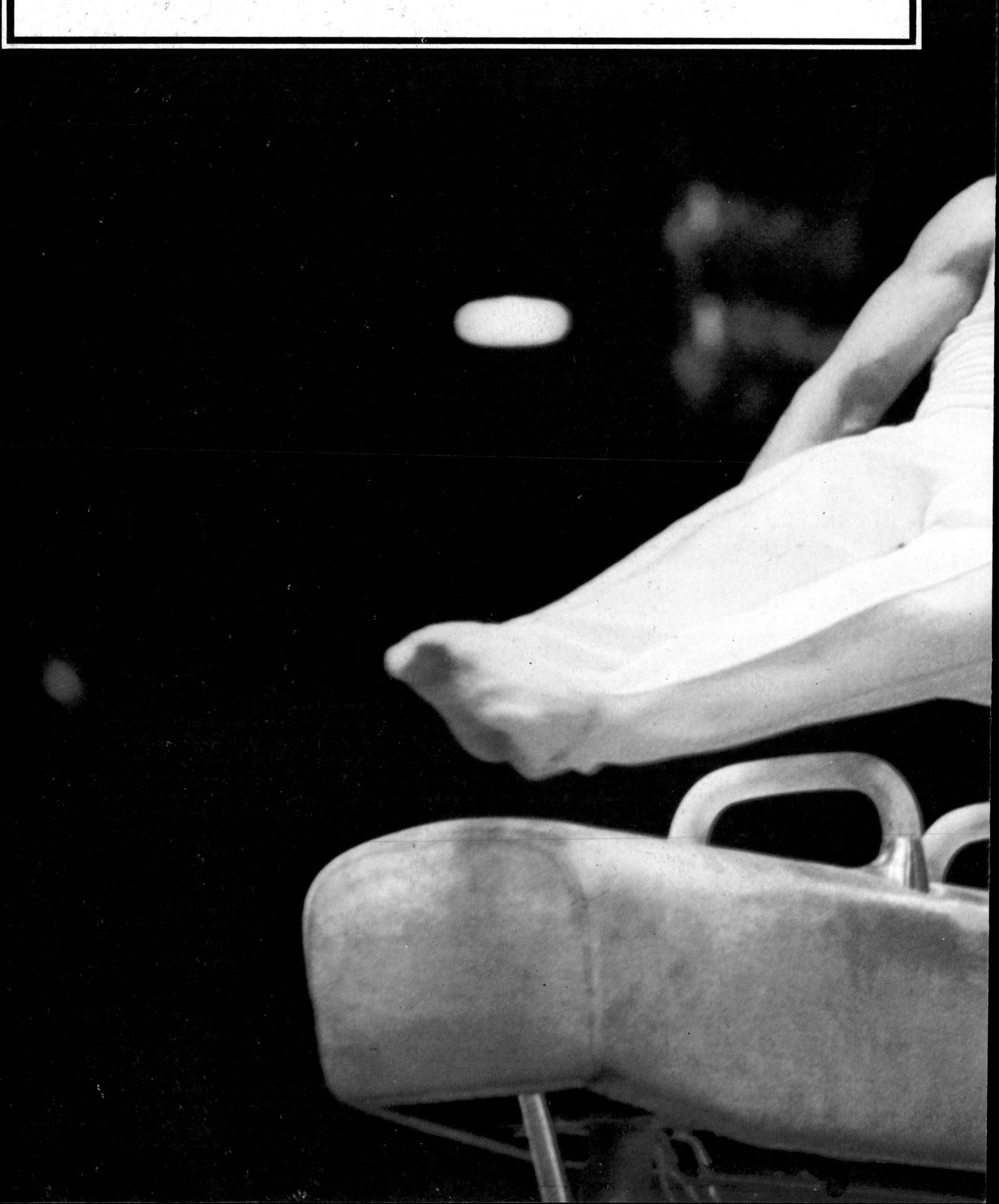